McGraw-Hill Education

500
Math Questions
for the GRE® Test

to know by test day

McGraw-Hill Education

500

Math Questions for the GRE® Test

to know by test day

Sandra Luna McCune, PhD

New York   Chicago   San Francisco   Athens   London   Madrid
Mexico City   Milan   New Delhi   Singapore   Sydney   Toronto

4 5 6 7 8 9   QVS/QVS   20 19 18 17 16

ISBN   978-0-07-182096-7
MHID   0-07-182096-5

e-ISBN   978-0-07-182097-4
e-MHID   0-07-182097-3

Library of Congress Control Number 2013948046

GRE is a registered trademark of Educational Testing Service (ETS). This product is not endorsed or approved by ETS.

McGraw-Hill Education products are available at special quantity discounts to use as premiums and sales promotions or for use in corporate training programs. To contact a representative, please visit the Contact Us pages at www.mhprofessional.com.

This book is printed on acid-free paper.

CONTENTS

INTRODUCTION

Congratulations! You've taken a big step toward GRE® success by purchasing *McGraw-Hill Education: 500 Math Questions for the GRE® Test.* We are here to help you take the next step and score high on your GRE exam so you can get into the graduate school of your choice!

This book gives you 500 GRE-style questions that cover all the most essential course material on the reasoning section. Each question is clearly explained in the answer key. The questions will give you valuable independent practice to supplement your earlier studies.

The math questions in the Quantitative Reasoning section of the computer-based GRE revised General Test are presented in two 35-minute sections, consisting of 20 questions per section. The questions test your knowledge of and skills in arithmetic, elementary algebra, basic geometry, and data analysis and your ability to reason analytically and solve math problems in context. You are allowed to skip questions, move back and forth, and change answers within a section. You also have access to an on-screen basic calculator.

Four question types are presented in the Quantitative Reasoning section: quantitative comparison questions, multiple-choice questions (select one answer choice), multiple-choice questions (select one or more answer choices), and numeric entry questions. Quantitative comparison questions require you to compare two quantities and then decide whether one is greater, whether the two quantities are equal, or whether the relationship cannot be determined from the given information. Multiple-choice questions (select one answer choice) present five answer choices from which you must select the one best answer choice. Multiple-choice questions (select one or more answer choices) present a list of choices from which you must select one or more answer choices, as specified in the question. Numeric entry questions are open-ended questions in which you enter your answer in an answer box.

This book and the others in the series were written by expert teachers who know the subject inside and out and can identify crucial information as well as the kinds of questions that are most likely to appear on the exam.

You might be the kind of student who needs to study extra a few weeks before the exam for a final review. Or you might be the kind of student who puts off preparing until the last minute before the exam. No matter what your preparation style, you will benefit from reviewing these 500 questions, which closely parallel the content, format, and degree of difficulty of the questions on the actual GRE exam. These questions and the explanations in the answer key are the ideal last-minute study tool for those final weeks before the test.

If you practice with all the questions and answers in this book, we are certain you will build the skills and confidence needed to excel on the GRE. Good luck!

—*The Author and Editors of McGraw-Hill Education*

CHAPTER 1

Quantitative Comparison Questions

Compare Quantity A and Quantity B using all the information given. Then select one of the answer choices that follow the question. Unless otherwise stated, you can assume all of the following:

- All numbers used are real numbers.
- All figures lie in a plane and are drawn accurately, but **are not necessarily** drawn to scale.
- Lines shown as straight are straight lines.
- The relative position of points, angles, and regions are in the order shown.
- Coordinate systems, such as number lines and xy-planes, **are** drawn to scale.
- Graphical displays of data, such as bar graphs and frequency distributions, **are** drawn to scale.

1. **Quantity A**

   C $\frac{1}{3}(51)^{24}$ $3.16e^{40}$

   Quantity B

   $17(51)^{23}$ $3.19e^{40}$

   (A) Quantity A is greater.
   (B) Quantity B is greater.
   (C) The two quantities are equal.
   (D) The relationship cannot be determined from the information given.

2. **Quantity A** 12.8

   B Unit price of 16 ounces of product X for $0.80

   Quantity B

   Unit price of 36 ounces of product X for $2.16 $.06$

   (A) Quantity A is greater.
   (B) Quantity B is greater.
   (C) The two quantities are equal.
   (D) The relationship cannot be determined from the information given.

3. **Quantity A**

   The remainder when 145
   is divided by 17

   Quantity B

   The remainder when 145 is divided
   by 11

   (A) Quantity A is greater.
   (B) Quantity B is greater.
   (C) The two quantities are equal.
   (D) The relationship cannot be determined from the information given.

n is a positive integer.

4. **Quantity A**
   $$\frac{n}{2}$$

   Quantity B
   $$\sqrt{n}$$

   (A) Quantity A is greater.
   (B) Quantity B is greater.
   (C) The two quantities are equal.
   (D) The relationship cannot be determined from the information given.

5. **Quantity A**

   The number of positive divisors
   of 144

   Quantity B

   The number of positive divisors
   of 108

   (A) Quantity A is greater.
   (B) Quantity B is greater.
   (C) The two quantities are equal.
   (D) The relationship cannot be determined from the information given.

Suri and Michael bought a previously owned classic car for $1500 and then spend $5000 restoring it to mint condition. Then they sold the car for 250% more than the total amount they spent buying it and restoring it.

6. **Quantity A**

   The price at which Suri and Michael sold the car

   Quantity B

   $16,000

   (A) Quantity A is greater.
   (B) Quantity B is greater.
   (C) The two quantities are equal.
   (D) The relationship cannot be determined from the information given.

A discount store sells pens for $2 and notebooks for $3 to a nonprofit organization, which does not have to pay sales tax on purchases. The nonprofit organization spent $25 for pens and notebooks at the discount store.

7. **Quantity A**

The number of pens the nonprofit bought

Quantity B

The number of notebooks the nonprofit bought

(A) Quantity A is greater.
(B) Quantity B is greater.
(C) The two quantities are equal.
(D) The relationship cannot be determined from the information given.

8. **Quantity A**

$\sqrt{16+9}$ 5

Quantity B

$\sqrt{16}+\sqrt{9}$ 3
    4 ,   3

(A) Quantity A is greater.
(B) Quantity B is greater.
(C) The two quantities are equal.
(D) The relationship cannot be determined from the information given.

9.

Quantity A $1/5$

The fraction of multiples of 2 that are multiples of 5

Quantity B $1/2$

The fraction of multiples of 5 that are multiples of 2

(A) Quantity A is greater.
(B) Quantity B is greater.
(C) The two quantities are equal.
(D) The relationship cannot be determined from the information given.

a and b are positive integers less than 10 such that $2a^3 = 10b^2$.

10. **Quantity A**

a

Quantity B

b

$2a^3 = 10b^2$
$16 = 10b^2$
$\frac{16}{10} = b^2$

(A) Quantity A is greater.
(B) Quantity B is greater.
(C) The two quantities are equal.
(D) The relationship cannot be determined from the information given.

x, y, and z are integers such that $xy > 0$ and $yz < 0$.

11. Quantity A   **Quantity B**

    0 xz

(A) Quantity A is greater.
(B) Quantity B is greater.
(C) The two quantities are equal.
(D) The relationship cannot be determined from the information given.

n is a positive integer.

12. Quantity A   **Quantity B**

    5^n 3^{n+1}

(A) Quantity A is greater.
(B) Quantity B is greater.
(C) The two quantities are equal.
(D) The relationship cannot be determined from the information given.

13. Quantity A   **Quantity B**

    $\gcd(14,56)$ $\gcd(28,72)$

(A) Quantity A is greater.
(B) Quantity B is greater.
(C) The two quantities are equal.
(D) The relationship cannot be determined from the information given.

14. Quantity A   **Quantity B**

    $\dfrac{5^{10} - 5^8}{24}$ 5^8

(A) Quantity A is greater.
(B) Quantity B is greater.
(C) The two quantities are equal.
(D) The relationship cannot be determined from the information given.

15. Quantity A   **Quantity B**

    $\mathrm{lcm}(12,30)$ 120

(A) Quantity A is greater.
(B) Quantity B is greater.
(C) The two quantities are equal.
(D) The relationship cannot be determined from the information given.

m and n are integers such that $-5 < m < 0 < n < 5$.

16. **Quantity A**   **Quantity B**

    $|m|$ $|n|$

    (A) Quantity A is greater.
    (B) Quantity B is greater.
    (C) The two quantities are equal.
    (D) The relationship cannot be determined from the information given.

$$\frac{9}{10} < \frac{a}{b} < \frac{11}{12}$$ $.9 < \frac{a}{b} < .91\overline{6}$

17. **Quantity A**   **Quantity B**

    $\dfrac{a}{b}$ $\dfrac{10}{11}$

    (A) Quantity A is greater.
    (B) Quantity B is greater.
    (C) The two quantities are equal.
    (D) The relationship cannot be determined from the information given.

Three consecutive integers have a sum of -51. $-16, 17, 18$

18. **Quantity A**   **Quantity B**

    The least of the three integers -17

    (A) Quantity A is greater.
    (B) Quantity B is greater.
    (C) The two quantities are equal.
    (D) The relationship cannot be determined from the information given.

$$120\%x = 96$$

19. **Quantity A**   **Quantity B**

    x 80

    (A) Quantity A is greater.
    (B) Quantity B is greater.
    (C) The two quantities are equal.
    (D) The relationship cannot be determined from the information given.

$$x > 0$$

20. **Quantity A**

    x^{10}

    Quantity B

    $(x^{10})^6$

    (A) Quantity A is greater.
    (B) Quantity B is greater.
    (C) The two quantities are equal.
    (D) The relationship cannot be determined from the information given.

21. **Quantity A**

    The greatest prime factor of 68

    Quantity B

    The greatest prime factor of 65

    (A) Quantity A is greater.
    (B) Quantity B is greater.
    (C) The two quantities are equal.
    (D) The relationship cannot be determined from the information given.

A recipe calls for $1\frac{1}{2}$ cups of milk to $1\frac{3}{4}$ cups of flour.

22. **Quantity A**

    The ratio of milk to flour

    Quantity B

    0.85

    (A) Quantity A is greater.
    (B) Quantity B is greater.
    (C) The two quantities are equal.
    (D) The relationship cannot be determined from the information given.

x, y, and z are three positive consecutive even integers such that $x < y < z$.

23. **Quantity A**

    $2(y+z)-6$

    Quantity B

    $2(x+y)+6$

    (A) Quantity A is greater.
    (B) Quantity B is greater.
    (C) The two quantities are equal.
    (D) The relationship cannot be determined from the information given.

24. **Quantity A**

    $(3+\sqrt{5})(3+\sqrt{5})$

    Quantity B

    20

    (A) Quantity A is greater.
    (B) Quantity B is greater.
    (C) The two quantities are equal.
    (D) The relationship cannot be determined from the information given.

25. **Quantity A**

The sum of the whole numbers
from 1 through 50

Quantity B

1280

(A) Quantity A is greater.
(B) Quantity B is greater.
(C) The two quantities are equal.
(D) The relationship cannot be determined from the information given.

26. **Quantity A**

The least positive number that
will leave a remainder of 3 when
divided by 4

Quantity B

The least positive number that will
leave a remainder of 3 when divided
by 5

(A) Quantity A is greater.
(B) Quantity B is greater.
(C) The two quantities are equal.
(D) The relationship cannot be determined from the information given.

Logan has eight US bills that are $5 bills and $10 bills worth $50.

27. **Quantity A**

The number of $10 bills Logan has

Quantity B

The number of $5 bills Logan has

(A) Quantity A is greater.
(B) Quantity B is greater.
(C) The two quantities are equal.
(D) The relationship cannot be determined from the information given.

n is a nonzero integer.

28. **Quantity A**

$n+2$

Quantity B

$$\frac{2n+1}{n}$$

(A) Quantity A is greater.
(B) Quantity B is greater.
(C) The two quantities are equal.
(D) The relationship cannot be determined from the information given.

29. **Quantity A**

$257_{\text{base } 12}$

Quantity B

$2410_{\text{base } 5}$

(A) Quantity A is greater.
(B) Quantity B is greater.
(C) The two quantities are equal.
(D) The relationship cannot be determined from the information given.

Zoe bought a box of cupcakes on her way to work. She gave half of them away to friends at work and ate one on the way home. At home, she gave one to her brother, and she had two left over.

30. Quantity A   **Quantity B**

The number of cupcakes Zoe bought   6

(A) Quantity A is greater.
(B) Quantity B is greater.
(C) The two quantities are equal.
(D) The relationship cannot be determined from the information given.

You are playing a game in which you must place blocks in three stacks so that the second stack has twice as many blocks as the first stack, and the third stack has twice as many blocks as the second.

31. Quantity A   **Quantity B**

The exact number exact of blocks needed   14
   to make the smallest possible stacks

(A) Quantity A is greater.
(B) Quantity B is greater.
(C) The two quantities are equal.
(D) The relationship cannot be determined from the information given.

32. Quantity A   **Quantity B**

55 miles per hour   80 feet per second

(A) Quantity A is greater.
(B) Quantity B is greater.
(C) The two quantities are equal.
(D) The relationship cannot be determined from the information given.

The sum of two numbers is 45 and their difference is 23.

33. Quantity A   **Quantity B**

Three times the lesser number   The greater of the two numbers

(A) Quantity A is greater.
(B) Quantity B is greater.
(C) The two quantities are equal.
(D) The relationship cannot be determined from the information given.

An investor receives interest on two simple interest investments, one at 3%, annually, and the other at 2%, annually. The amount invested at 3% is $20,000. The two investments together earn $900 annually.

34. **Quantity A**

    The amount invested at 2%

    Quantity B

    The amount invested at 3%

    (A) Quantity A is greater.
    (B) Quantity B is greater.
    (C) The two quantities are equal.
    (D) The relationship cannot be determined from the information given.

Willard can paint a room in 6 hours working alone. Jada can do the same job in 4 hours working alone.

35. **Quantity A**

    The number of hours it should take Willard and Jada to paint the room working together

    Quantity B

    $2\frac{1}{2}$ hours

    (A) Quantity A is greater.
    (B) Quantity B is greater.
    (C) The two quantities are equal.
    (D) The relationship cannot be determined from the information given.

36. **Quantity A**

    $$\frac{x^3}{5}$$

    Quantity B

    $$\left(\frac{x}{5}\right)^3$$

    (A) Quantity A is greater.
    (B) Quantity B is greater.
    (C) The two quantities are equal.
    (D) The relationship cannot be determined from the information given.

$$x < -8$$

37. **Quantity A**

    $5x$

    Quantity B

    $2x$

    (A) Quantity A is greater.
    (B) Quantity B is greater.
    (C) The two quantities are equal.
    (D) The relationship cannot be determined from the information given.

A 50-foot rope is cut into two pieces so that one piece is 14 feet longer than the other.

38. Quantity A   **Quantity B**

      Twice the length of the shorter piece   The length of the longer piece

      (A) Quantity A is greater.
      (B) Quantity B is greater.
      (C) The two quantities are equal.
      (D) The relationship cannot be determined from the information given.

All of the 6000 fans at the game are either home team fans or visiting team fans. Twenty percent of the fans at the game are from out of town.

39. Quantity A   **Quantity B**

      The number of home team fans   The number of visiting team fans at
             at the game   the game

      (A) Quantity A is greater.
      (B) Quantity B is greater.
      (C) The two quantities are equal.
      (D) The relationship cannot be determined from the information given.

$$a + b = 13$$

$$\sqrt{4ab} = 12$$

40. Quantity A   **Quantity B**

      The greater of a and b One more than twice the lesser of a and b

      (A) Quantity A is greater.
      (B) Quantity B is greater.
      (C) The two quantities are equal.
      (D) The relationship cannot be determined from the information given.

$$f = \{(-1, 2), (1, 5), (3, -4)\}$$
$$g = \{(-4, 2), (-1, 3), (2, -3)\}$$

41. Quantity A   **Quantity B**

      $f(g(-1))$ $g(f(-1))$

      (A) Quantity A is greater.
      (B) Quantity B is greater.
      (C) The two quantities are equal.
      (D) The relationship cannot be determined from the information given.

x and y are positive integers whose sum is 10 and $37 < 5x + 2y < 41$.

42. Quantity A

x

Quantity B

y

(A) Quantity A is greater.
(B) Quantity B is greater.
(C) The two quantities are equal.
(D) The relationship cannot be determined from the information given.

$2, 7, \ldots, 247$ is an arithmetic sequence.

43. Quantity A

The number of terms in the sequence

Quantity B

50

(A) Quantity A is greater.
(B) Quantity B is greater.
(C) The two quantities are equal.
(D) The relationship cannot be determined from the information given.

A collection of 58 coins consists of nickels, dimes, and quarters. The face value of the coins is $5.

44. Quantity A

The total number of dimes and
    quarters in the collection

Quantity B

The number of nickels in the
    collection

(A) Quantity A is greater.
(B) Quantity B is greater.
(C) The two quantities are equal.
(D) The relationship cannot be determined from the information given.

$w, x, y,$ and z are positive integers such that $x > w$ and $y < z$.

45. Quantity A

$\dfrac{x}{y}$

Quantity B

$\dfrac{w}{z}$

(A) Quantity A is greater.
(B) Quantity B is greater.
(C) The two quantities are equal.
(D) The relationship cannot be determined from the information given.

The selling price of an exercise bike represents a 25% markup from its original cost to the merchant.

46. **Quantity A**   **Quantity B**

The percent the markup is of the selling price   20%

(A) Quantity A is greater.
(B) Quantity B is greater.
(C) The two quantities are equal.
(D) The relationship cannot be determined from the information given.

$$(3^p)^p = 81$$

47. **Quantity A**   **Quantity B**

p 2

(A) Quantity A is greater.
(B) Quantity B is greater.
(C) The two quantities are equal.
(D) The relationship cannot be determined from the information given.

-5 is a solution of $x^2 + x - k = 5$.

48. **Quantity A**   **Quantity B**

k 20

(A) Quantity A is greater.
(B) Quantity B is greater.
(C) The two quantities are equal.
(D) The relationship cannot be determined from the information given.

$$\frac{x}{z} = 5$$

49. **Quantity A**   **Quantity B**

$\dfrac{x+z}{x-z}$ $\dfrac{3}{2}$

(A) Quantity A is greater.
(B) Quantity B is greater.
(C) The two quantities are equal.
(D) The relationship cannot be determined from the information given.

In a group of 180 college graduates, the number who have taken postgraduate courses is $\frac{1}{5}$ the number who have NOT taken postgraduate courses.

50. Quantity A

The number in the group who have taken postgraduate courses

Quantity B

36

(A) Quantity A is greater.
(B) Quantity B is greater.
(C) The two quantities are equal.
(D) The relationship cannot be determined from the information given.

$a_1, a_2, 8, 16, \ldots, 128$ is a geometric sequence.

51. Quantity A

$a_1 + a_2$

Quantity B

The number of terms in the sequence

(A) Quantity A is greater.
(B) Quantity B is greater.
(C) The two quantities are equal.
(D) The relationship cannot be determined from the information given.

In a social club, the number of members is 56. If four additional male members are recruited to the club while the number of female members remains unchanged, the ratio of male members to the number of members in the club would be 5 to 12.

52. Quantity A

The number of female members in the club

Quantity B

21

(A) Quantity A is greater.
(B) Quantity B is greater.
(C) The two quantities are equal.
(D) The relationship cannot be determined from the information given.

53. Quantity A

$x^2 + 1$

Quantity B

$$\frac{x^3 + x^2 + x + 1}{x + 1}$$

(A) Quantity A is greater.
(B) Quantity B is greater.
(C) The two quantities are equal.
(D) The relationship cannot be determined from the information given.

If Sofía gives Zayn $5, they will have the same amount of money. If Zayn gives Sofía $5, she will have twice as much money as he will have.

54. Quantity A

The amount of money Sofía has

Quantity B

$10 more than the amount of money Zayn has

(A) Quantity A is greater.
(B) Quantity B is greater.
(C) The two quantities are equal.
(D) The relationship cannot be determined from the information given.

$$4s + 3t = 27$$
$$t = 2s - 1$$

55. Quantity A

s

Quantity B

t

(A) Quantity A is greater.
(B) Quantity B is greater.
(C) The two quantities are equal.
(D) The relationship cannot be determined from the information given.

If 3 times the lesser of two numbers is added to the greater, the result is 35. If 5 times the lesser is subtracted from the greater, the result is 75.

56. Quantity A

10 percent of the greater number

Quantity B

The absolute value of the lesser number

(A) Quantity A is greater.
(B) Quantity B is greater.
(C) The two quantities are equal.
(D) The relationship cannot be determined from the information given.

$$2x^2 - 5x = -2$$

57. Quantity A

x

Quantity B

1

(A) Quantity A is greater.
(B) Quantity B is greater.
(C) The two quantities are equal.
(D) The relationship cannot be determined from the information given.

58. **Quantity A**

The discriminant of $x^2 + x + 1 = 0$

Quantity B

The discriminant of $x^2 - x + 1 = 0$

(A) Quantity A is greater.
(B) Quantity B is greater.
(C) The two quantities are equal.
(D) The relationship cannot be determined from the information given.

$$\frac{x+2}{2} = \frac{12}{x}, \; x \neq 0$$

59. **Quantity A**

x

Quantity B

5

(A) Quantity A is greater.
(B) Quantity B is greater.
(C) The two quantities are equal.
(D) The relationship cannot be determined from the information given.

$A(2,3)$, $B(5,7)$, $C(-2,5)$, and $D(1,1)$ are points in a coordinate plane.

60. **Quantity A**

The distance between A and B

Quantity B

The distance between C and D

(A) Quantity A is greater.
(B) Quantity B is greater.
(C) The two quantities are equal.
(D) The relationship cannot be determined from the information given.

In a coordinate plane, $(7,7)$ is the midpoint between the point (a,b) and the point $(6,5)$.

61. **Quantity A**

a

Quantity B

b

(A) Quantity A is greater.
(B) Quantity B is greater.
(C) The two quantities are equal.
(D) The relationship cannot be determined from the information given.

$$x < y$$

62. Quantity A

The slope of the line through (x, y) and $(-5, 5)$

Quantity B

0

(A) Quantity A is greater.
(B) Quantity B is greater.
(C) The two quantities are equal.
(D) The relationship cannot be determined from the information given.

The line passing through the points $(2, 3)$ and $(k, 4)$ is perpendicular to the line that has equation $3x + y = 10$.

63. Quantity A

k

Quantity B

$\dfrac{5}{3}$

(A) Quantity A is greater.
(B) Quantity B is greater.
(C) The two quantities are equal.
(D) The relationship cannot be determined from the information given.

$$y = x^2 - x$$
$$y = x - 1$$

64. Quantity A

x

Quantity B

1

(A) Quantity A is greater.
(B) Quantity B is greater.
(C) The two quantities are equal.
(D) The relationship cannot be determined from the information given.

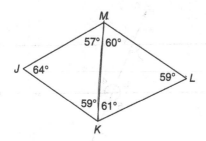

65. Quantity A   **Quantity B**

   KM   *LM*

(A) Quantity A is greater.
(B) Quantity B is greater.
(C) The two quantities are equal.
(D) The relationship cannot be determined from the information given.

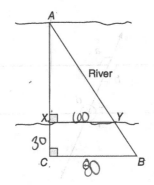

The diagram shows the method that a park ranger is using to estimate the width of a river. *XC* = 30 yards, *BC* = 80 yards, and *XY* = 60 yards.

66. Quantity A   **Quantity B**

   AX   *BC*

(A) Quantity A is greater.
(B) Quantity B is greater.
(C) The two quantities are equal.
(D) The relationship cannot be determined from the information given.

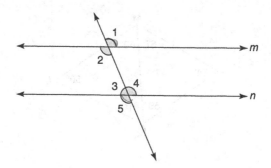

67. **Quantity A**   **Quantity B**

    $m\angle 1$ $m\angle 5$

   (A) Quantity A is greater.
   (B) Quantity B is greater.
   (C) The two quantities are equal.
   (D) The relationship cannot be determined from the information given.

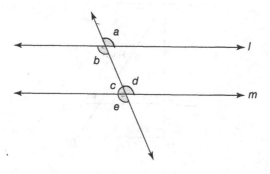

In the preceding figure, $\angle b$ and $\angle c$ are supplementary.

68. **Quantity A**   **Quantity B**

    $m\angle a$ $m\angle d$

   (A) Quantity A is greater.
   (B) Quantity B is greater.
   (C) The two quantities are equal.
   (D) The relationship cannot be determined from the information given.

A side of the larger of two similar triangles is 3 times as long as the corresponding side of the other triangle. The area of the smaller triangle is 25 square inches.

69. Quantity A

The area of the larger triangle

Quantity B

75 square inches

(A) Quantity A is greater.
(B) Quantity B is greater.
(C) The two quantities are equal.
(D) The relationship cannot be determined from the information given.

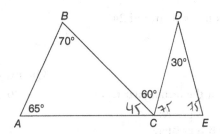

70. Quantity A

$m\angle E$

Quantity B

$m\angle B$

(A) Quantity A is greater.
(B) Quantity B is greater.
(C) The two quantities are equal.
(D) The relationship cannot be determined from the information given.

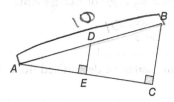

In the preceding figure, $AB = 10$.

71. Quantity A

AD

Quantity B

5

(A) Quantity A is greater.
(B) Quantity B is greater.
(C) The two quantities are equal.
(D) The relationship cannot be determined from the information given.

Given triangle PQR and triangle XYZ such that $\dfrac{PQ}{XY} = \dfrac{QR}{YZ}$ and $\angle Q \cong \angle Y$

72. Quantity A   **Quantity B**

   $m\angle R$ $m\angle Z$

(A) Quantity A is greater.

(B) Quantity B is greater.

(C) The two quantities are equal.

(D) The relationship cannot be determined from the information given.

A rectangular region has an area of 24.

73.

Quantity A 20 **Quantity B**

The perimeter of the rectangular region   30

(A) Quantity A is greater.

(B) Quantity B is greater.

(C) The two quantities are equal.

(D) The relationship cannot be determined from the information given.

In triangle ABC, $m\angle B = 55°$ and $m\angle C = 65°$.

74. Quantity A   **Quantity B**

The measure of an exterior angle of triangle ABC 130°

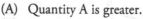

(A) Quantity A is greater.

(B) Quantity B is greater.

(C) The two quantities are equal.

(D) The relationship cannot be determined from the information given.

A box in the shape of a rectangular prism has dimensions 4 by 3 by 12.

75. Quantity A   **Quantity B**

The greatest possible distance between   13
   any two points of the box

(A) Quantity A is greater.

(B) Quantity B is greater.

(C) The two quantities are equal.

(D) The relationship cannot be determined from the information given.

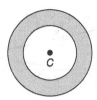

The preceding figure shows two concentric circles with common center C. The diameter of the larger circle is 12, and the diameter of the smaller circle is 8.

76. Quantity A   **Quantity B**

The area of the shaded region   60

(A) Quantity A is greater.
(B) Quantity B is greater.
(C) The two quantities are equal.
(D) The relationship cannot be determined from the information given.

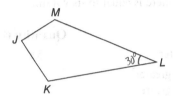

In the preceding quadrilateral, $m\angle L = 30°$.

77. Quantity A   **Quantity B**

$m\angle J + m\angle K + m\angle M$ 350°

(A) Quantity A is greater.
(B) Quantity B is greater.
(C) The two quantities are equal.
(D) The relationship cannot be determined from the information given.

Triangle ABC is isosceles. $AB = 15$ and $BC = 20$.

78. Quantity A   **Quantity B**

The perimeter of triangle ABC 50

(A) Quantity A is greater.
(B) Quantity B is greater.
(C) The two quantities are equal.
(D) The relationship cannot be determined from the information given.

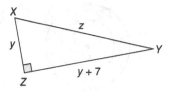

The area of right triangle *XYZ* is 120.

79. Quantity A   **Quantity B**

     z   17

(A) Quantity A is greater.
(B) Quantity B is greater.
(C) The two quantities are equal.
(D) The relationship cannot be determined from the information given.

The surface area of a sphere is equal to its volume.

80. Quantity A   **Quantity B**

The sphere's diameter 3π

(A) Quantity A is greater.
(B) Quantity B is greater.
(C) The two quantities are equal.
(D) The relationship cannot be determined from the information given.

Two jars of the same brand of blueberry jam have a cylindrical shape. One jar is twice the height of the other jar, but its diameter is half as much as the diameter of the other one.

81. Quantity A   **Quantity B**

The capacity of the shorter jar   The capacity of the taller jar

(A) Quantity A is greater.
(B) Quantity B is greater.
(C) The two quantities are equal.
(D) The relationship cannot be determined from the information given.

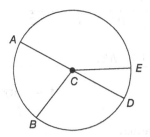

In circle C, $\overline{AD}$ is a diameter, and the measure of central angle BCD is $3x°+10°$, of central angle DCE is $2x°$, and of central angle ACE is $x°+90°$.

82. **Quantity A**

Degree measure of minor arc $\overparen{AB}$

Quantity B

85°

(A) Quantity A is greater.
(B) Quantity B is greater.
(C) The two quantities are equal.
(D) The relationship cannot be determined from the information given.

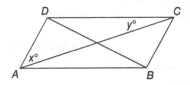

In the preceding figure, $ABCD$ is a parallelogram and $m\angle DAB = 50°$.

83. **Quantity A**

x

Quantity B

y

(A) Quantity A is greater.
(B) Quantity B is greater.
(C) The two quantities are equal.
(D) The relationship cannot be determined from the information given.

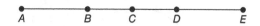

In the preceding figure, $AD = BE$.

84. **Quantity A**   **Quantity B**

    AB DE

    (A) Quantity A is greater.
    (B) Quantity B is greater.
    (C) The two quantities are equal.
    (D) The relationship cannot be determined from the information given.

The lengths of two sides of a triangle are 15 and 6.

85. **Quantity A**   **Quantity B**

    The length of the third side   21

    (A) Quantity A is greater.
    (B) Quantity B is greater.
    (C) The two quantities are equal.
    (D) The relationship cannot be determined from the information given.

86. **Quantity A**   **Quantity B**

    The area of an equilateral triangle   6
    with sides of length 4

    (A) Quantity A is greater.
    (B) Quantity B is greater.
    (C) The two quantities are equal.
    (D) The relationship cannot be determined from the information given.

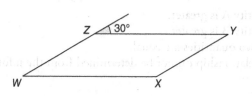

In the preceding figure, $WXYZ$ is a parallelogram. $WX = 10$ and $XY = 8$.

87. **Quantity A**   **Quantity B**

    The area of $WXYZ$ 40

    (A) Quantity A is greater.
    (B) Quantity B is greater.
    (C) The two quantities are equal.
    (D) The relationship cannot be determined from the information given.

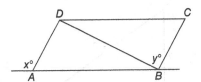

In the preceding figure, *ABCD* is a parallelogram.

88. Quantity A   **Quantity B**

      x   *y*

(A) Quantity A is greater.
(B) Quantity B is greater.
(C) The two quantities are equal.
(D) The relationship cannot be determined from the information given.

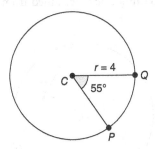

In the preceding figure, *P* and *Q* are points on circle *C*, which has radius 4.

89. Quantity A   **Quantity B**

Length of minor arc $\overarc{PQ}$ π

(A) Quantity A is greater.
(B) Quantity B is greater.
(C) The two quantities are equal.
(D) The relationship cannot be determined from the information given.

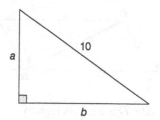

90. **Quantity A**

$$\frac{a}{10}$$

Quantity B

$$\frac{b}{10}$$

(A) Quantity A is greater.
(B) Quantity B is greater.
(C) The two quantities are equal.
(D) The relationship cannot be determined from the information given.

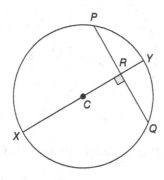

In the preceding figure, $\overline{XY}$ is a diameter of circle C, which has radius 13, and chord $PQ = 24$.

91. **Quantity A**

CR

Quantity B

5

(A) Quantity A is greater.
(B) Quantity B is greater.
(C) The two quantities are equal.
(D) The relationship cannot be determined from the information given.

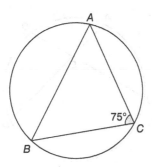

In the preceding figure, triangle *ABC* is inscribed in the circle.

92. Quantity A   **Quantity B**

The degree measure of $\overarc{AB}$, the arc intercepted by $\angle ACB$ 160°

(A) Quantity A is greater.
(B) Quantity B is greater.
(C) The two quantities are equal.
(D) The relationship cannot be determined from the information given.

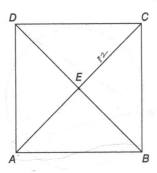

In the preceding figure, *ABCD* is a square and $AC = BD = 12$.

93. Quantity A   **Quantity B**

The length of a side of the square   6

(A) Quantity A is greater.
(B) Quantity B is greater.
(C) The two quantities are equal.
(D) The relationship cannot be determined from the information given.

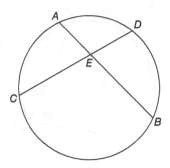

Chords $\overline{AB}$ and $\overline{CD}$ intersect at point E in the circle shown. $AE = 6$, $EB = 10$, and $CE = 9$.

94. Quantity A   **Quantity B**

      ED 7

(A) Quantity A is greater.
(B) Quantity B is greater.
(C) The two quantities are equal.
(D) The relationship cannot be determined from the information given.

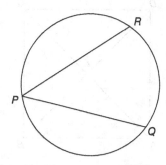

In the figure shown, chords $\overline{PQ}$ and $\overline{PR}$ are congruent, and the degree measure of minor arc $\overset{\frown}{QR}$ is 100°.

95. Quantity A   **Quantity B**

    Degree measure of minor arc PR 130°

(A) Quantity A is greater.
(B) Quantity B is greater.
(C) The two quantities are equal.
(D) The relationship cannot be determined from the information given.

A social club's luncheon menu offers 4 types of salads, 2 types of entreés, 3 types of beverages, and 5 types of desserts. A lunch consists of 1 salad, 1 entrée, 1 beverage, and 1 dessert.

96. **Quantity A**   **Quantity B**

The number of possible lunches that can be selected   14

(A) Quantity A is greater.
(B) Quantity B is greater.
(C) The two quantities are equal.
(D) The relationship cannot be determined from the information given.

97. **Quantity A**   **Quantity B**

The number of different ways five people can line up to buy tickets at a theater

The number of different ways to arrange the letters in the word *logic*

(A) Quantity A is greater.
(B) Quantity B is greater.
(C) The two quantities are equal.
(D) The relationship cannot be determined from the information given.

98. **Quantity A**   **Quantity B**

The number of three-digit numbers that are possible using the digits 1 to 5 if a digit may appear only once in a number

The number of three-digit numbers that are possible using the digits 1 to 5 if a digit may repeat multiple times in a number

(A) Quantity A is greater.
(B) Quantity B is greater.
(C) The two quantities are equal.
(D) The relationship cannot be determined from the information given.

99. **Quantity A**   **Quantity B**

The number of ways to form a committee of two when selecting from five people

The number of ways to form a committee of three when selecting from five people

(A) Quantity A is greater.
(B) Quantity B is greater.
(C) The two quantities are equal.
(D) The relationship cannot be determined from the information given.

A letter is chosen at random from the word *graduate.*

100. Quantity A   **Quantity B**

The probability that the letter is   The probability that the letter is
            a vowel   NOT *a* or *d*

(A) Quantity A is greater.
(B) Quantity B is greater.
(C) The two quantities are equal.
(D) The relationship cannot be determined from the information given.

101. Quantity A   **Quantity B**

The probability of randomly selecting a prime or an $\frac{4}{5}$
even number from the set $\{1, 2, 4, 7, 9\}$

(A) Quantity A is greater.
(B) Quantity B is greater.
(C) The two quantities are equal.
(D) The relationship cannot be determined from the information given.

The probability of Team X beating Team Y is $\frac{2}{3}$. The probability of Team X beating Team Z is $\frac{1}{4}$. Team X plays one game with Team Y and one game with Team Z.

102. Quantity A   **Quantity B**

The probability that Team X wins   The probability that Team X loses
            both games   both games

(A) Quantity A is greater.
(B) Quantity B is greater.
(C) The two quantities are equal.
(D) The relationship cannot be determined from the information given.

A raffle coordinator wants the probability of winning a prize to be 2 percent. Fifteen hundred tickets will be printed.

103. Quantity A   **Quantity B**

The number of tickets that should be marked as winners   25

(A) Quantity A is greater.
(B) Quantity B is greater.
(C) The two quantities are equal.
(D) The relationship cannot be determined from the information given.

Triangle *ABC* is an isosceles triangle.

104. Quantity A

The probability that the altitude drawn from
A to $\overline{BC}$ is congruent to the median drawn from *A* to $\overline{BC}$

Quantity B

$\dfrac{1}{3}$

(A) Quantity A is greater.
(B) Quantity B is greater.
(C) The two quantities are equal.
(D) The relationship cannot be determined from the information given.

A box contains white marbles and black marbles, all identical except for color. If one marble is drawn at random, the probability that it is a white marble is $\dfrac{7}{8}$. Six white marbles are added to the box, but no black marbles are added. Now, if one marble is drawn at random, the probability that it is a white marble is $\dfrac{x}{y}$.

105. Quantity A

$\dfrac{x}{y}$

Quantity B

$\dfrac{14}{15}$

(A) Quantity A is greater.
(B) Quantity B is greater.
(C) The two quantities are equal.
(D) The relationship cannot be determined from the information given.

A committee of four people is to be selected from a group consisting of five women and four men.

106. Quantity A

The probability that two women
and two men are on the committee

Quantity B

The probability that three women
and one man are on the committee

(A) Quantity A is greater.
(B) Quantity B is greater.
(C) The two quantities are equal.
(D) The relationship cannot be determined from the information given.

107. Quantity A

The median of $15, 8, 2, 25, 4$

Quantity B

The median of $15, 8, -20, 200, 4$

(A) Quantity A is greater.
(B) Quantity B is greater.
(C) The two quantities are equal.
(D) The relationship cannot be determined from the information given.

108. **Quantity A**

    Quantity B

    The mean of 15, 8, 2, 25, 4

    The mean of 15, 8, −20, 200, 4

(A) Quantity A is greater.
(B) Quantity B is greater.
(C) The two quantities are equal.
(D) The relationship cannot be determined from the information given.

109. **Quantity A**

    Quantity B

    The standard deviation of 4, 6, 8, 10, 12   The standard deviation of 8, 8, 8, 8, 8

(A) Quantity A is greater.
(B) Quantity B is greater.
(C) The two quantities are equal.
(D) The relationship cannot be determined from the information given.

A normal distribution has a mean of 50. The value 60 is two standard deviations above the mean.

110. **Quantity A**

    Quantity B

    The standard deviation of the distribution

    10

(A) Quantity A is greater.
(B) Quantity B is greater.
(C) The two quantities are equal.
(D) The relationship cannot be determined from the information given.

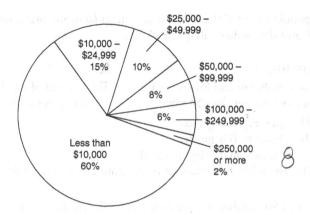

The preceding circle graph shows the distribution of 2000 workers, ages 25 to 34, according to their total savings and investments.

111. Quantity A   **Quantity B**

The number of workers surveyed who have   160
$100,000 or more in total savings and investments

(A) Quantity A is greater.
(B) Quantity B is greater.
(C) The two quantities are equal.
(D) The relationship cannot be determined from the information given.

Ages in Years of 44 US Presidents at Inauguration

Stem	Leaves
4	2 3 6 6 7 7 8 9 9
5	0 0 1 1 1 1 2 2 4 4 4 4 4 5 5 5 5 6 6 6 7 7 7 7 8
6	0 1 1 1 2 4 4 5 8 9

Legend: 5|7 = 57

The preceding stem-and-leaf plot shows the ages in years of 44 US Presidents on inauguration day.

112. Quantity A   **Quantity B**   54.5

The mode of the data   The median of the data

(A) Quantity A is greater.
(B) Quantity B is greater.
(C) The two quantities are equal.
(D) The relationship cannot be determined from the information given.

In a population of 320 employees of a manufacturing plant, the mean salary is $55,000 and the median salary is $48,000.

113. Quantity A   **Quantity B**

The number of employees with   The number of employees with
salaries greater than $48,000   salaries greater than $55,000

(A) Quantity A is greater.
(B) Quantity B is greater.
(C) The two quantities are equal.
(D) The relationship cannot be determined from the information given.

In a set of 50 numbers the mean is 15 and the median is 20.

114. Quantity A   **Quantity B**

The percent of the numbers between 15 and 20   5%

(A) Quantity A is greater.
(B) Quantity B is greater.
(C) The two quantities are equal.
(D) The relationship cannot be determined from the information given.

Set A consists of 20 numbers ranging from 1 to 10. Set B consists of 20 numbers ranging from 11 to 20. The average (arithmetic mean) of the numbers in Set A is 6.8 and the average of the numbers in Set B is 17.2.

115. Quantity A   **Quantity B**

The average of the 40 numbers in   The median of the 40 numbers in
sets A and B combined   sets A and B combined

(A) Quantity A is greater.
(B) Quantity B is greater.
(C) The two quantities are equal.
(D) The relationship cannot be determined from the information given.

116. Quantity A   **Quantity B**

The 90th percentile of the data set   750
0,0,0,0,100,100,100,100,1400

(A) Quantity A is greater.
(B) Quantity B is greater.
(C) The two quantities are equal.
(D) The relationship cannot be determined from the information given.

In a population of 500 teachers, the median salary is $51,500 and the 75th percentile is $59,700.

117. **Quantity A**   **Quantity B**

    The number of teachers with salaries   150
       between $51,500 and $59,700

    (A) Quantity A is greater.
    (B) Quantity B is greater.
    (C) The two quantities are equal.
    (D) The relationship cannot be determined from the information given.

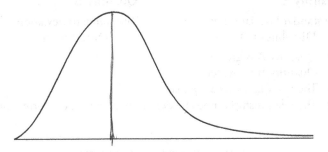

The preceding figure shows the shape of a distribution.

118. **Quantity A**   **Quantity B**

    The mean of the distribution   The median of the distribution

    (A) Quantity A is greater.
    (B) Quantity B is greater.
    (C) The two quantities are equal.
    (D) The relationship cannot be determined from the information given.

A student has scores of 90, 92, 78, and 95 on four of five 100-point exams.

119. **Quantity A**   **Quantity B**

    The score the student must make on   98
       the fifth exam so that the average
    (arithmetic mean) of the five tests is 90

    (A) Quantity A is greater.
    (B) Quantity B is greater.
    (C) The two quantities are equal.
    (D) The relationship cannot be determined from the information given.

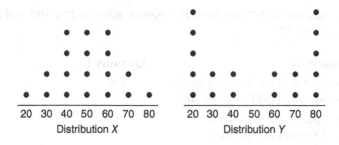

Distribution X   Distribution Y

120. Quantity A

The standard deviation of Distribution X

Quantity B

The standard deviation of Distribution Y

(A) Quantity A is greater.
(B) Quantity B is greater.
(C) The two quantities are equal.
(D) The relationship cannot be determined from the information given.

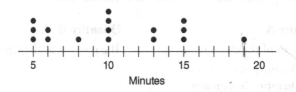

Number of Minutes 16 Customers Waited in Line

Minutes

The preceding dot plot shows the number of minutes 16 customers waited in line at a coffee shop.

121. Quantity A

The interquartile range of the data

Quantity B

The range of the data divided by 2

(A) Quantity A is greater.
(B) Quantity B is greater.
(C) The two quantities are equal.
(D) The relationship cannot be determined from the information given.

Scores for graduates on a university exit exam are normally distributed with a mean of 75 and standard deviation of 10.

122. Quantity A

The probability that a score will be less than 55

Quantity B

The probability that a score will be greater than 95

(A) Quantity A is greater.
(B) Quantity B is greater.
(C) The two quantities are equal.
(D) The relationship cannot be determined from the information given.

IQ scores for adults are normally distributed with mean 100 and standard deviation 15.

123. Quantity A

An IQ score of 115

Quantity B

An IQ score at the 50th percentile

(A) Quantity A is greater.
(B) Quantity B is greater.
(C) The two quantities are equal.
(D) The relationship cannot be determined from the information given.

A normal distribution has a mean of 25 and standard deviation of 2.

124. Quantity A

The percent of the distribution between 21 and 23

Quantity B

The percent of the distribution between 25 and 27

(A) Quantity A is greater.
(B) Quantity B is greater.
(C) The two quantities are equal.
(D) The relationship cannot be determined from the information given.

Scores on standardized Exam X are normally distributed with mean 500 and standard deviation 100. Scores on standardized Exam Y are normally distributed with mean 21 and standard deviation 5.

125. Quantity A

The probability of scoring above 600 on Exam X

Quantity B

The probability of scoring above 31 on Exam Y

(A) Quantity A is greater.
(B) Quantity B is greater.
(C) The two quantities are equal.
(D) The relationship cannot be determined from the information given.

Numeric Entry Questions

Enter your answer in the answer box below the question:

- You may enter a positive or negative integer, decimal, or fraction. Use a hyphen for a negative sign and a period for a decimal point.
- Enter the exact answer unless you are told to round your answer.
- Equivalent forms of the correct answer, such as 1.5 and 1.50 or $\frac{1}{2}$ and $\frac{8}{16}$, are all scored as correct.
- If a question asks specifically for the answer as a fraction, there will be two boxes—a numerator box and a denominator box. Do not use decimal points in fractions.

Unless otherwise stated, you can assume all of the following:

- All numbers used are real numbers.
- All figures lie in a plane and are drawn accurately, but **are not necessarily** drawn to scale.
- Lines shown as straight are straight lines.
- The relative position of points, angles, and regions are in the order shown.
- Coordinate systems, such as number lines and xy-planes, **are** drawn to scale.
- Graphical displays of data, such as bar graphs and frequency distributions, **are** drawn to scale.

126. A grandson and two granddaughters inherit land from their grand-parents. If the grandson inherits $\frac{1}{4}$ of the land, and the older daughter inherits 50 percent more land than does the younger daughter, then what fraction of the land does the younger granddaughter inherit?

127. If $\operatorname{lcm}(n, 50) = 100$, what is the value of the integer n?

128. A flower garden contains only red rose plants and white rose plants. If the total number of rose plants in the garden is 55, and the number of red rose plants is 10 more than twice the number of white rose plants, what is the ratio of white rose plants to red rose plants? Express your answer as a fraction.

$$\boxed{} \atop \boxed{}$$

129. Three hundred thousand dollars in a retirement account is invested in municipal bonds and oil stocks. If the amount invested in oil stocks is 150 percent of the amount invested in municipal bonds, what is the amount invested in oil stocks?

$\boxed{}$

130. An urn contains 15 black marbles, green marbles, and red marbles, all identical except for color. If the number of green marbles is 5, what is the probability of drawing a black or red marble when a single marble is drawn at random from the urn? Express your answer as a fraction.

$$\boxed{} \atop \boxed{}$$

131. Suppose for monthly expenditures, the amount spent on food is $\frac{2}{5}$ of the amount spent on rent, and the amount spent on clothing is $\frac{1}{4}$ of the amount spent on food. The amount spent on rent is how many times the average (arithmetic mean) of the total amounts spent on food and clothing?

$\boxed{}$

132. The sale price of a pair of running shoes was $125. After the sale, the sale price increased by $25. What is the percent increase over the sale price?

$\boxed{}$ %

133. A chemist is making an alloy of tin and copper. The ratio of tin to copper in the alloy is 1 to 4. If the number of grams of copper in the alloy is 36, how many total grams are in the alloy?

$\boxed{}$ grams

134. Parents of a newborn child allocated $20,000 of their savings to an investment that earns 0.75% annual interest, compounded monthly. If there are no other transactions in the investment account, what is the amount of money (to the nearest cent) in the account 1 month after the account is opened?

$\boxed{}$

135. Two friends rented a light-duty moving truck. The rental store charges $19.99 per hour or portion thereof for the truck rental plus $0.55 per mile traveled, with no charge for gasoline. If the total round-trip mileage was 100 miles, and the friends returned the truck after 3 hours 20 minutes, how much did the friends owe for renting the truck?

$ [   ]

136. A driver makes a trip of 266 miles. If the driver's average speed is 63 miles per hour for the first two hours of the trip and 70 miles per hour for the rest of the trip, how long did the second part of the trip take?

[   ] hours

137. What is the least of three consecutive odd integers whose sum is 147?

[   ]

138. If $x = 6m^2 + 4n^2$, and $\gcd(m,n) = 2$, what is the greatest even number that must be a factor of x?

[   ]

139. Of the 3600 full-time and part-time positions at a company, $\dfrac{1}{x}$ $(x > 0)$ are part-time. If the number of part-time positions is reduced by $\dfrac{1}{x}$ and $x^2 = 9$, how many part-time positions are lost?

[   ]

140. In a league of 5 teams, each team plays each of the other teams 2 times during the season. How many total games are played during the season?

[   ]

141. Suppose $y = \dfrac{k}{x}$, where k is a constant. If $y = \dfrac{2}{9}$ when $x = 540$, what is the value of y when $x = 360$?

[   ]

142. A jacket that usually sells for $85.00 is marked down for an end-of-season clearance sale. Including tax, the customer saves a total of $18.36. If the sales tax rate is 8%, how much does a customer pay for the jacket at the marked-down price?

$ [   ]

143. A flower shop has 8 vases on a shelf containing a total of 74 flowers. Some of the bases contain 8 flowers and some contain 10 flowers. How many vases contain 10 flowers?

$$\boxed{}$$

144. During a season, a tennis team won 21 matches. If they lost 30% of their matches, how many matches did they lose?

$$\boxed{}$$

145. What is the percent strength of an alcohol solution that contains 30 liters of a 20 percent alcohol solution and 50 liters of a 60 percent alcohol solution?

$$\boxed{}\ \%$$

146. In the formula $\dfrac{1}{R} = \dfrac{1}{R_1} + \dfrac{1}{R_2}$, if $R = 4$ and $R_1 = 10$, what is the value of R_2? Express your answer as a fraction.

$$\boxed{\dfrac{}{}}$$

147. Twenty years ago, Morgan was $\dfrac{1}{3}$ as old as he will be in 20 years. How old will Morgan be in 5 years?

$$\boxed{}$$

148. The total number of guests at a party is 25. If the ratio of female guests to male guests is 3 to 2, how many male guests are at the party?

$$\boxed{}$$

149. A jogger leaves home at 9:00 a.m., and, without stopping, runs 3 miles to the local running track, runs around the track 8 times, and then runs home along the same route for a total distance of 8 miles. If the jogger arrives home at 10:20 a.m., what is the jogger's average jogging speed?

$$\boxed{}\ \text{miles per hour}$$

150. Three integers, x, y, and z, are in the ratio 1:3:5, respectively. If $z - y = 14$, what is the sum of the three integers?

$$\boxed{}$$

151. Pierre and Mariah each bought fruit at a roadside stand. Pierre paid $35 for 10 mangoes and 5 papayas. At these prices, how much did Mariah pay for one papaya and two mangoes?

$ [_____]

152. If the sum of three consecutive integers is doubled, the result is 71 more than $\frac{5}{2}$ times the greatest of the three integers. What is the value of the greatest integer?

[_____]

153. What number in base 10 is equivalent to $324_{\text{base } 6}$?

[_____]

154. If $m > 1$ divides $(7n+3)$ and also divides $(35n+26)$, what is the value of m?

[_____]

155. If the greatest common divisor of 51 and 288 is 3, what is the least positive common multiple of 51 and 288?

[_____]

156. The integer 72 has how many positive divisors?

[_____]

157. If $(2^x)(4^y) = 64$, then what is x when y is 3?

[_____]

158. A collection of 33 coins amounts to $4.35 in face value. If the collection consists of only dimes and quarters, how many dimes are in the collection?

[_____]

159. Sasha wants a new smartphone. It goes on sale at a local electronics store for 20% less than the original price. Before Sasha can buy the phone, however, the store raises the new price by 20%. If the 20% off sale price was $120, the final price is what percent of the original price?

[_____] %

160. If $\sqrt{3x+3} = \sqrt{3x} + 1$, then what is $3x$?

161. If the sum of two numbers is 35 and their product is 300, what is the value of the greater number?

162. If 2 is added to the numerator of $\dfrac{n}{d}$, the fraction equals $\dfrac{1}{2}$. If 5 is added to the denominator of $\dfrac{n}{d}$, the fraction equals $\dfrac{1}{5}$. What is the value of $\dfrac{n}{d}$?

163. A bookstore has a used book bin in which paperback books sell for $2 each and hardcover books sell for $5 each. Last week, from the used book bin, the number of paperback books that were sold was 42 more than twice the number of hardcover books sold. If last week, the bookstore received a total of $309 from sales of paperback books and hardcover books from the used book bin, how many paperback books from the used book bin did the bookstore sell last week?

164. If a, b, and c are three consecutive integers (in the order given) such that $\dfrac{1}{2}(a+b+c) = a+23$, what is the value of c?

165. Marisha is twice as old as Caleb. The sum of their ages is 30. How old will Marisha be 5 years from now?

166. If $x^2 - 4x = 12$, what is the value of $|x-2|$?

167. The difference of two negative numbers is 4 and their product is 96. What is the value of the larger number?

168. The length of a rectangle is 3 meters more than its width. If the rectangle's area is 154 square meters, what is the rectangle's length?

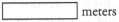 meters

169. If b, c, and h are constants such that $x^2 + bx + c = (x + h)^2$, what is the value of c if $b = 10$?

170. Working together, Laetitia and Ian can paint a room in 1 hour 12 minutes. Working alone, Laetitia can paint the room in 3 hours. How many hours would it take Ian to paint the room working alone?

171. A sales clerk in a computer store makes a 1% commission on all computer and accessory sales that the clerk makes. Last week, the clerk earned $13.72 in commission. What were the clerk's total sales last week?

$ [   ]

172. Solve for x given that $-\left(\dfrac{1}{2}x + 1\right) > 0$. Express your answer using interval notation.

[   ]

173. To make a 20% alcohol solution, x liters of a 60% alcohol solution are added to 30 liters of a 10% alcohol solution. What is x?

[   ]

174. Suppose $\dfrac{4}{3a} + \dfrac{x}{2a} = 1$, where $a \neq 0$. If $\dfrac{x}{a} = \dfrac{2}{3}$, what is the value of x?

175. The sum of the reciprocals of two nonzero numbers is $\dfrac{3}{5}$. If the larger number is 5 times the smaller number, what is the value of the smaller number?

176. An auditorium has only orchestra and balcony seating. Tickets for the first performance of a concert at the auditorium are $80 for orchestra seats and $50 for balcony seats. Ticket receipts were $49,000 for the first performance. If 800 tickets were sold, how many were for balcony seating?

177. A box contains black, red, and white marbles, all identical except for color. If a marble is randomly drawn from the box, what is the probability that the marble is white given that there are twice as many black marbles as white marbles in the box and 50% more red marbles than black marbles? Express your answer as a fraction.

178. What is the value of the greater of two consecutive negative integers whose product is 182?

179. If $x^2 + xy = 100 - y^2 - xy$, what is the value of $(x\sqrt{3} + y\sqrt{3})^2$?

180. If $\sqrt[3]{a} = 2$, what is the value of $a^{-0.6}$?

181. How many days will it take five identical machines working together to do a job if two such machines working together can do the job in 10 days?

 days

$$f = \{(-1,2),(1,5),(3,-4)\}$$
$$g = \{(-4,2),(-1,3),(4,-4)\}$$

182. Suppose the functions f and g are defined as shown. What is the value of $f(g(-1))$?

183. At what value of x does the function $y = \dfrac{(x-2)^2(x+3)}{(x-2)^3(x+3)}$ have a vertical asymptote?

184. If $a_4 = 17$ and $a_{10} = 47$, what is the value of a_{20} given $a_n = a_1 + (n-1)d$?

185. Two vehicles leave the same location at exactly the same time, the first traveling due west and the second traveling due east. The average speed of the first vehicle is 10 miles per hour faster than the average speed of the second vehicle. When the two vehicles are 390 miles apart, the second vehicle has gone a distance of 180 miles. In how many hours will the two vehicles be 390 miles apart?

$$\boxed{}\ \text{hours}$$

186. A team of biologists introduces a herd of deer onto an uninhabited island. The function $P(t) = P_0 \cdot 2^{0.25t}$ models the expected growth of the deer population on the island, where P_0 is the initial population and t is the elapsed time in years. If the expected deer population in 12 years is 200, what is the expected deer population in 20 years?

$$\boxed{}\ \text{deer}$$

187. The point $(5,-1)$ lies on the circle whose equation is $(x-2)^2 + (y+1)^2 = r^2$. What is the value of r?

$$\boxed{}$$

188. In the x-y coordinate plane, if (u,v) and $(u+3, v+k)$ are two points on the line $y = 2x+5$, what is the value of k?

$$\boxed{}$$

189. In the x-y coordinate plane, what is the distance between $P(-5,5)$ and $Q(3,20)$?

$$\boxed{}$$

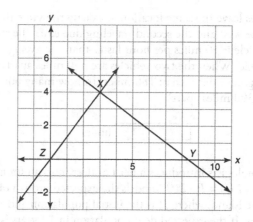

190. In the figure shown, if (slope $\overrightarrow{XZ}$)(slope $\overrightarrow{XY}$) $= -1$, what is the measure of angle *ZXY*?

 °

191. In triangle *ABC*, sides $\overline{AB}$ and $\overline{AC}$ are congruent, and the measure of angle *C* is 65°. What is the measure of angle *A*?

[   ] °

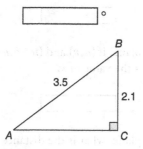

192. What is the perimeter of triangle *ABC* with measures as shown?

[   ]

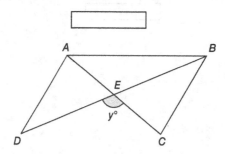

193. In the preceding figure, $m\angle BCE = 88°$ and $m\angle EBC = 38°$. What is *y*?

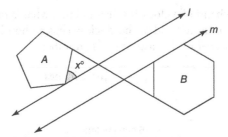

194. In the preceding figure, A and B are regular polygons and lines l and m are parallel. What is x?

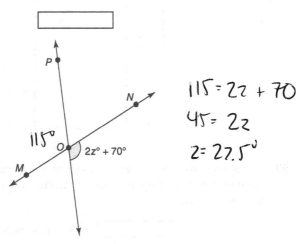

$115 = 2z + 70$

$45 = 2z$

$z = 27.5°$

195. In the preceding figure, $m\angle POM = 115°$. What is z?

$22.5°$

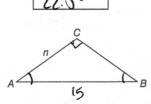

196. In triangle ABC, $\angle A \cong \angle B$ and $AB = 15$. What is the smallest possible whole number value for n?

8

197. How many centimeters will a cylindrical barrel roll in 10 revolutions along a smooth surface given that the diameter of the barrel is 56 centimeters? Use $\pi \approx 3.14$ and round your answer to the nearest whole number.

 centimeters

198. If the minute hand of a clock is 6 inches long, what is the area of the circle created as the minute hand of the clock sweeps an hour? Use $\pi \approx 3.14$ and round your answer to the nearest whole number.

[   ] square inches

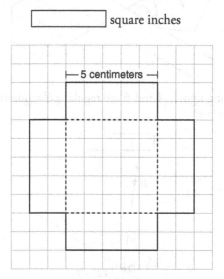

199. The figure shown on the grid consists of five rectangles. If the four sides of the figure are folded up and taped to make an open box, what is the volume of the box?

[   ] cubic centimeters

200. A quilted shawl is made up of 9×9 inch squares. The shawl has 4 rows and 6 columns of squares. What is its perimeter?

[   ] inches

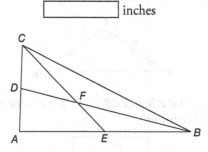

201. In the preceding figure, $\overline{DB}$ and $\overline{CE}$ are medians. If $DF = 15$, what is the length of $\overline{FB}$?

[   ]

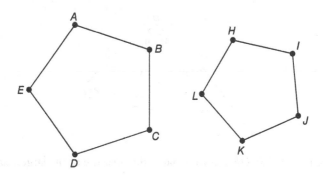

202. In the preceding figure, *ABCDE* ≈ *HIJKL* and the ratio of corresponding sides is $\frac{4}{3}$. What is the ratio of the area of *ABCDE* to the area of *HIJKL*? Express your answer as a fraction.

203. A bicycle's front wheel is traveling at 5 miles per hour. If the front wheel has a diameter of 25 inches, how fast is it turning in revolutions per minute? Use $\pi \approx 3.14$ and round your answer to the nearest whole number.

 revolutions per minute

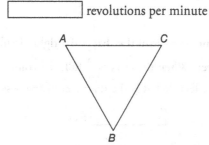

204. In triangle *ABC*, $m\angle A = m\angle B = m\angle C = 60°$ and *AB* = 12. What is the area of triangle *ABC*? Round your answer to the nearest whole number.

205. How many sides does a regular convex polygon have if the measure of each of its exterior angles is 45°?

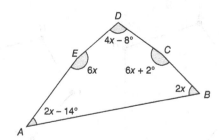

206. In pentagon *ABCDE* shown, what is the measure of the largest angle?

[ ] °

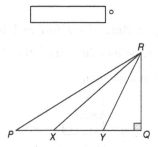

207. In triangle *PQR* shown, triangles *RPY* and *RYQ* have areas 90 and 45 respectively. If $PY = XQ = 10$, what is the length of $\overline{XY}$?

[ ]

208. A tank for holding water is in the shape of a right circular cylinder with height, *h*, of 8 feet. When the tank is $\frac{3}{4}$ full, the volume of water in the tank is 96π cubic feet. What is the diameter of the base of the tank?

[ ] feet

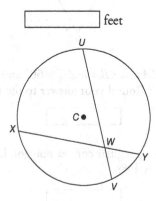

209. In the preceding diagram of circle *C*, chord $\overline{XY}$ intersects chord $\overline{UV}$ at *W*. $XW = z + 12$, $UW = z + 3$, $WV = z$, and $WY = 3$. What is the length of $\overline{XY}$?

[ ]

210. The area of rectangle *ABCD* is 12. What is its perimeter if *BD* = *AC* = 5?

☐

211. If the area of a square having sides of length 10 is equal to the area of a parallelogram having base 20, what is the parallelogram's height, *h*, to that base?

☐

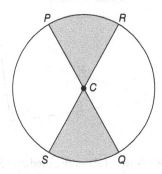

212. If ∠*PCS* = 120°, what fraction of circle *C* shown is shaded?

☐

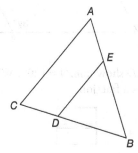

213. In the figure shown, $\overline{AC} \parallel \overline{ED}$ and $\overline{BD} \cong \overline{DE}$. If *m*∠*A* = 58°, what is the measure of ∠*C*?

☐ °

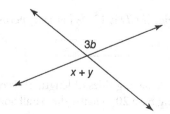

214. In the preceding figure, $\frac{1}{3}y = b - 24°$. What is x?

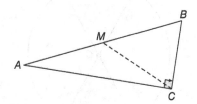

215. In right triangle *ABC* shown, $\overline{CM}$ is the median to the hypotenuse. If *AC* is 24, and *BC* is 10, what is the measure of $\overline{CM}$?

216. In parallelogram *ABCD* shown, $m\angle 1 = 120°$. What is the ratio of *x* to *y*? Express your answer as a fraction.

217. What is the perimeter of square *ABCD* if $BD = 15\sqrt{2}$?

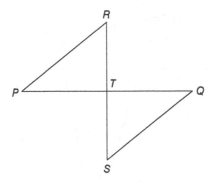

218. In the preceding figure, $\angle R \cong \angle S$ and T is the midpoint of $\overline{PQ}$. If $PR = 10$, what is the length of $\overline{QS}$?

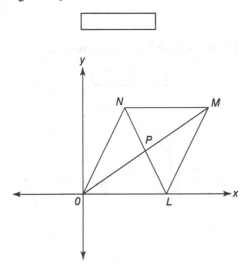

219. In parallelogram $LMNO$, $P(x_0, y_0)$ is the point of intersection of the diagonals and point M has coordinates $(9,10)$. What is x_0?

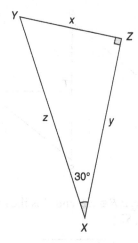

220. In triangle *XYZ*, $x = 4\sqrt{3}$. What is the value of *y*?

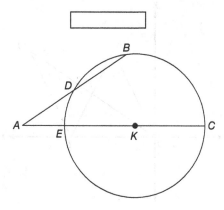

221. In the preceding diagram of circle *K*, $\overline{AB}$ intersects circle *K* at *D* and *B*, and $\overline{AKC}$ intersects circle *K* at *E* and *C*. If $AB = 24$, $BD = 12$, and $AE = 8$, what is the length of the radius of circle *K*?

222. At an appliance store's going-out-of-business sale, 152 customers bought either a washer or a dryer or both. Twenty-two customers bought both a washer and a dryer. If 58 customers bought only a dryer, how many customers bought only a washer?

223. In a survey asking about juice preferences (apple, orange, grape, none) of 25 students in a classroom, 15 like orange juice and 10 like apple juice, 1 student does not like any kind of juice, and 3 students like grape juice, but not orange or apple juice. How many students like both orange and apple juice?

224. The number of elements in the union of sets A and B is 200, and the number of elements in the intersection of sets A and B is 50. If set A has 10 more elements than set B, what is the number of elements in set B?

225. Penelope is selecting a vegan sandwich consisting of one bread type and one bean-based sandwich filling. If she has a choice of 4 types of bread and 5 kinds of fillings, how many different sandwiches are possible?

226. A class consists of 20 students. A committee consisting of five members is selected. How many distinct committees are possible?

227. A shoe store has 30 styles of shoes. If each style is available in 6 lengths, 3 widths, and 5 colors, how many different shoes are kept in stock?

228. There are 30 separate candidates for three vice-president positions at a university. Assuming all 30 candidates are equally qualified to be selected for any one of the three VP positions, how many different ways can the three positions be filled?

229. How many three-digit codes are possible using only the four digits 1 to 4 if repetition of digits is allowed?

230. A three-digit number is formed by using only the six digits 4 through 9, with no repetition. How many such three-digit numbers are greater than 700?

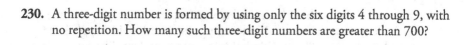

231. There are two more girls than boys in a family. If the probability of randomly selecting a girl from among the children in the family is $\frac{2}{3}$, how many boys are in the family?

232. When star basketball player Katniss goes to the foul line for a free-throw shot, she has a 0.8 probability of scoring. Assuming that the outcomes of the free-throw shots are independent, what is the probability that Katniss will make exactly one of her next two free-throw shot attempts?

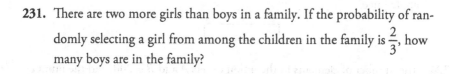

233. On the number line shown, a point between points A and B is randomly selected. If $AP = 14$ and $PB = 6$, what is the probability that the point selected is within 2 units of the point P? Express your answer as a fraction.

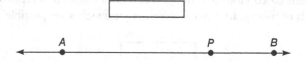

234. The preceding graph shows the allocations in an investment portfolio. According to the graph, if $10,000 is invested in commodities, how much more money is invested in US stocks than in foreign stocks?

$ 30,000

Questions 235 to 237 are based on the following data.

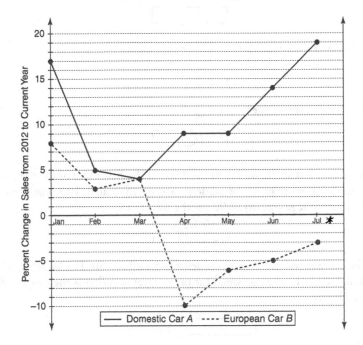

235. What is the range for the European Car *B* data?

[18] %

236. In July, what is the seven-month average percent change in sales from 2012 to the current year for Domestic Car *A*?

[   ] %

237. What is the maximum monthly difference in percent change in sales from 2012 to the current year between the two cars?

[   ] %

Questions 238 to 240 are based on the following frequency distribution showing the ages of students in a high school glee club.

Age in Years	Frequency	
18	2	36
17	11	187
16	12	192

238. What is the mean age?

> 16.6

239. What is the median age?

> 17

240. What is the mode age?

> 16

241. A student has scores of 77, 91, and 94 on the first three of four 100-point tests. What score must the student earn on the fourth 100-point test to have an average (mean) of 90 for the four tests?

> 98

242. The average weight of three students is 55 kilograms. If a fourth student is included, the average weight is 60 kilograms. What is the weight of the fourth student?

> _____ kilograms

$$2a + 3b + 5c = 42$$
$$4a + 3b + c = 30$$

243. Using the preceding information, determine the average of a, b, and c.

> _____

Starting Weights in Pounds of 36 Female Students Participating in a Weight Loss Program

Stem	Leaves
12	3 8 8 9
13	2 3 3 4 4 8 9
14	0 2 2 4 5 5 5 6 8 8 9
15	0 1 3 3 5 6 7 8 9 9
16	1 2 5 9
Legend: 12|3 = 123	

244. What is the 95th percentile for the data shown in the preceding stem-and-leaf plot?

> _____

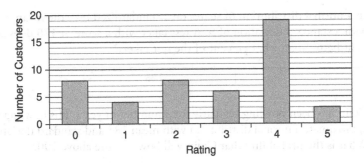

245. What is the interquartile range for the data shown in the preceding bar graph?

246. What is the variance of a data set whose standard deviation is 3.5?

247. In a normal distribution of the heights of fourth-grade boys the mean is 54 inches and the standard deviation is 2.5 inches. What height is one standard deviation above the mean?

inches

For questions 248 to 250 use the following information.

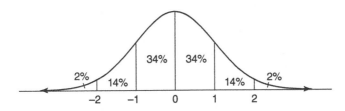

The preceding figure shows approximate percentages for six regions of the standard normal distribution, with mean 0 and standard deviation 1.

248. In a normal distribution of the years of service for teaching staff at a large school district, the mean is 15 years and the standard deviation is 4.5 years. What percent of the teachers have years of service between 6 years and 24 years?

 %

249. In a normal distribution of scores on a standardized test, the mean is 152 with a standard deviation of 9. A test taker with a score of 170 does as well as or better than what percent of the test takers?

$$\boxed{}\ \%$$

250. Colin has been bowling regularly for a number of years. His bowling scores approximate a normal distribution with mean 183 and standard deviation 7. What is the probability that Colin will bowl a score above 190?

$$\boxed{}$$

Multiple-Choice Questions with One Correct Answer

Select the best *one* of the given answer choices. Unless otherwise stated, you can assume all of the following:

- All numbers used are real numbers.
- All figures lie in a plane and are drawn accurately, but **are not necessarily** drawn to scale.
- Lines shown as straight are straight lines.
- The relative position of points, angles, and regions are in the order shown.
- Coordinate systems, such as number lines and *xy*-planes, **are** drawn to scale.
- Graphical displays of data, such as bar graphs and frequency distributions, **are** drawn to scale.

251. Suppose n is an integer such that $2 < n^2 < 100$. If the units digit of n^2 is 6 and the units digit of $(n-1)^2$ is 5, what is the units digit of $(n+1)^2$?

(A) 2
(B) 4
(C) 6
(D) 8
(E) 9

252. If the square root of the product of two positive integers is 15, which of the following CANNOT be the sum of the two integers?

(A) 34
(B) 42
(C) 50
(D) 78
(E) 226

253. What is the least positive integer that is *not* a factor of 20! and is *not* a prime?

(A) 19
(B) 23
(C) 36
(D) 46
(E) 58

254. Three daughters and two sons inherit land from their parents. The older son inherits $\frac{1}{4}$ of the land and the oldest daughter inherits $\frac{1}{3}$. The three remaining children equally share the remaining land. What fraction of the land does the younger son inherit?

(A) $\frac{1}{12}$

(B) $\frac{5}{36}$

(C) $\frac{5}{21}$

(D) $\frac{7}{36}$

(E) $\frac{7}{21}$

255. The football coach at a certain midsize university earns $\frac{1}{4}$ more in salary than does the university's basketball coach. The basketball coach's salary represents what percent of the football coach's salary?

(A) 125%
(B) 120%
(C) 90%
(D) 80%
(E) 75%

256. A biology textbook has scale drawings of crickets. The scale shows that 1 centimeter in the drawing represents 2.5 centimeters of actual length. What is the length (in centimeters) of the scale drawing of a cricket if the cricket is actually 9.0 centimeters long?

(A) 3.6
(B) 4.0
(C) 4.5
(D) 18.0
(E) 22.5

257. The ratio of zinc to copper in a certain alloy is 2 to 5. If 120 grams of copper are used, how many grams of zinc are needed to make this alloy?

(A) 20
(B) 48
(C) 180
(D) 200
(E) 300

258. Liam has been saving money to buy a trendy but expensive toy. It goes on sale at a local toy store for 15% less than the original price. Before Liam can buy the toy, however, the toy store raises the new price by 20%. If the 15% off sale price was $119, the final price is what percent of the original price?

(A) 95%
(B) 98%
(C) 102%
(D) 105%
(E) 120%

259. A 50-foot rope is cut into two pieces so that the longer piece is 50% longer than the shorter piece. How many feet long is the longer piece?

(A) $16\dfrac{2}{3}$
(B) 20
(C) 25
(D) 30
(E) $33\dfrac{1}{3}$

260. A college student recently worked four weeks in a new summer job. In the fourth week, the student worked 20% more hours than in the third week. In the third week, the student worked 25% more hours than in the second week. In the second week, the student worked 40% more hours than in the first week. If the student worked 42 hours in the fourth week on the job, how many hours did the student work in the first week on the job?

(A) 15
(B) 20
(C) 25
(D) 30
(E) 35

261. Which of the following expressions is equivalent to $\sqrt{400}$?

    (A) $\sqrt{200} + \sqrt{200}$

    (B) $100\sqrt{4}$

    (C) $(\sqrt{20})^2$

    (D) $4\sqrt{100}$

    (E) 200

262. A grocery store's electricity cost in January is $1420. After installing a new energy-efficient heating and cooling system, the manager estimates that the electricity cost will decrease by 2.5% per month over the next six months. Based on this estimate, which of the following expressions represents the grocery store's electricity cost in March of the same year?

    (A) $(\$1420)(0.975) + (\$1420)(0.950)$

    (B) $(\$1420 - (\$1420)(0.025)(0.025)$

    (C) $(\$1420 - (\$1420)(0.025)(0.025)(0.025)$

    (D) $(\$1420)(0.975)(0.975)$

    (E) $(\$1420)(0.975)(0.950)$

263. If $m = a^4 b^2 c^5 d$ is the prime factorization of m, what is the number of positive divisors of m?

    (A) 12

    (B) 40

    (C) 80

    (D) 90

    (E) 180

264. Of the 4800 residents of an apartment complex, $\frac{1}{4}$ are college students. Suppose the number of college students is reduced by $\frac{1}{3}$. If no other changes occur, what portion of the total remaining residents are college students?

    (A) $\frac{1}{12}$

    (B) $\frac{2}{11}$

    (C) $\frac{1}{8}$

    (D) $\frac{1}{6}$

    (E) $\frac{1}{5}$

265. Suppose that the value of an investment triples every 10 years, then by what factor does the value increase over a 30-year period?

(A) 3
(B) 6
(C) 9
(D) 27
(E) 30

266. Fifty percent of a couple's retirement account is invested in stocks, 25 percent in a mutual fund, 20 percent in Treasury bonds, and the remaining $20,000 in certificates of deposit. In the couple's retirement account, what is the total amount invested?

(A) $200,000
(B) $300,000
(C) $400,000
(D) $1,000,000
(E) $4,000,000

267. The sale price of a video game console was $300. After the sale, the price increased to $375. What is the percent increase over the sale price?

(A) 0.2%
(B) 0.25%
(C) 20%
(D) 25%
(E) 30%

268. Given that x is a positive integer such that 19 divided by x has a remainder of 3, what is the sum of all the possible values of x?

(A) 12
(B) 20
(C) 24
(D) 28
(E) 32

269. What is the units digit of 3^{102}?

(A) 1
(B) 3
(C) 6
(D) 7
(E) 9

270. The tokens in a game are distributed among five locations in the ratio 5:3:2:4:1. To win the game, a player must collect at least $\frac{1}{8}$ of the tokens in each of three or more of the five locations. In order to win, what is the minimum percent of the total tokens that must be collected by a player?

(A) 3%
(B) 4%
(C) 5%
(D) 6%
(E) 7%

271. The government allocated $800 million for disaster relief in a hurricane-damaged region. This amount of money is about equal to spending $1 per second for how many years?

(A) 5
(B) 25
(C) 50
(D) 100
(E) 150

272. Two hundred people will attend a university fund-raiser if tickets cost $30 per person. For each $15 increase in ticket price, 25 fewer people will attend. What ticket price will yield the maximum amount of money for the university?

(A) $30
(B) $45
(C) $60
(D) $75
(E) $90

273. A mixture weighs 7.8 grams. It consists of ingredients X, Y, and Z in the ratio 2:5:6, respectively, by weight. How many fewer grams of ingredient X than ingredient Z are in the mixture?

(A) 0.8
(B) 1.2
(C) 1.8
(D) 2.4
(E) 3.0

274. A vehicle leaves City A at 9 a.m., moving at an average speed of 50 miles per hour, and without making any stops arrives at City B at 2 p.m. At approximately what time would the vehicle have arrived if the driver had driven an average speed of 65 miles per hour?

   (A) 12:24 p.m.
   (B) 12:51 p.m.
   (C) 1:24 p.m.
   (D) 1:51 p.m.
   (E) 2:24 p.m.

275. Katrina inherited a gold and diamond pendant from her grandmother in 2010. In 2011, the value of the pendant decreased by 10%. In 2012, its value increased by 20%, and then decreased by 10% in 2013. How does the 2013 value of the pendant compare to its value in 2010?

   (A) 2.8% decrease in value
   (B) 1.4% decrease in value
   (C) No change
   (D) 1.4% increase in value
   (E) 2.8% increase in value

Ages of Students at Community College X

Age (in years)	Number of students
Under 20	950
20	1450
21	1040
Over 21	560

4,000 total

276. The preceding chart shows the age distribution of students attending Community College X. What percent of the students are 21 or over?

   (A) 9%
   (B) 25%
   (C) 40%
   (D) 60%
   (E) 67%

277. A solution of water and sugar is 20% sugar by weight. After several weeks, some of the water evaporates so that the solution is 60% sugar by weight. What is the ratio of the final weight of water to the initial weight of water in the mixture?

(A) 1:6
(B) 1:3
(C) 1:4
(D) 4:1
(E) 6:1

278. What is the value of $\left(\sqrt{5+\sqrt{17}} - \sqrt{5-\sqrt{17}}\right)^2$?

(A) -6
(B) 0
(C) 2
(D) $10-4\sqrt{2}$
(E) $10-2\sqrt{2}$

279. If n is a non-negative integer not divisible by 2 or 3, then which of the following could be the remainder when n is divided by 6?

(A) 0
(B) 2
(C) 3
(D) 4
(E) 5

280. If $562_{\text{base }7} = 187_{\text{base }12}$, what is the face value of the digit b?

(A) 0
(B) 2
(C) 4
(D) 5
(E) 6

281. What is n if 12 is the greatest common divisor of n and 84, and 756 is the least common multiple of n and 84?

(A) 52
(B) 108
(C) 168
(D) 324
(E) 378

282. Effie is a delivery person for a specialty frozen food company. Besides her base weekly pay of $350, she makes a 6% commission on all items she sells to customers. Last week Effie's weekly pay plus commissions totaled $920. What was the total of Effie's sales for last week?

(A) $604.20
(B) $1105.80
(C) $9000.00
(D) $9500.00
(E) $15,333.33

283. Mario is twice as old as Shirin. In five years, the sum of their ages will be 52. How old will Mario be 10 years from now?

(A) 24
(B) 28
(C) 33
(D) 38
(E) 43

$$(m+n)^2 - 2 + 2(m+n) + \frac{m+n}{3}$$

284. When $m + n = -6$, what is the value of the preceding expression?

(A) −52
(B) −28
(C) 20
(D) 28
(E) 44

285. Which of the following expressions is equivalent to $\left(\dfrac{x^{-5}}{x^{-9}}\right)^{\frac{1}{2}}$?

(A) x^{-2}
(B) x^{-7}
(C) x^2
(D) x^4
(E) x^7

$$z = \frac{1.2\,y}{x^2}, \; x \neq 0$$

286. Which of the following shows the preceding equation correctly solved for x?

(A) $x = \dfrac{1.2\,y}{z}$

(B) $x = \pm\dfrac{1.2\,y}{z}$

(C) $x = \sqrt{\dfrac{1.2\,y}{z}}$

(D) $x = \pm\sqrt{\dfrac{1.2\,y}{z}}$

(E) $x = \pm\sqrt{1.2\,yz}$

287. If $x = \left(1 + (2 + 3^{-1})^{-1}\right)^{-1}$, then $10x =$

(A) $\dfrac{100}{3}$ 33.33

(B) $\dfrac{100}{7}$

(C) $\dfrac{60}{7}$

(D) 7

(E) 3

288. A candy store owner mixes candy that normally sells for $2.50 per pound and candy that normally sells for $3.75 per pound to make a 90-pound mixture to sell at $3.00 per pound. To make sure that $3.00 per pound is a fair price, how many pounds of the $2.50 candy should the owner use?

(A) 54

(B) 50

(C) 42

(D) 36

(E) 30

289. If $y = 5 - (2x - 3)^2$, then y is less than or equal to 5 when

(A) x is zero

(B) x is 3

(C) x is 5

(D) x is $\dfrac{3}{2}$

(E) x is any real number

290. The operation $\otimes$ is defined on the set of real numbers by $a \otimes b = 2a + ab$, where a and b are real numbers and the operations on the right side of the equal sign denote the standard operations for the real number system. What is $(3 \otimes 2) \otimes 5$?

(A) 30
(B) 60
(C) 74
(D) 84
(E) 96

291. Which of the following expressions is equivalent to $12^x + 15^x$?

(A) 27^{2x}
(B) 27^x
(C) $3^x \cdot 9^x$
(D) $3(4^x + 5^x)$
(E) $3^x(4^x + 5^x)$

292. Which of the following expressions is equivalent to $(c^2 + 9)^{-\frac{1}{2}}$?

(A) $\dfrac{1}{c+3}$

(B) $-\dfrac{c^2+9}{2}$

(C) $\dfrac{1}{\sqrt{c^2+9}}$

(D) $-\sqrt{c^2+9}$

(E) $-\dfrac{1}{c+3}$

293. If $\sqrt{3x+3} = \sqrt{3x} + 1$, then what is the value of $3x$?

(A) 0
(B) $\dfrac{1}{3}$
(C) $\pm\dfrac{1}{3}$
(D) 1
(E) ± 1

294. Which of the following number lines illustrates the solution set of $-7 < 2x + 1 < 5$?

(A)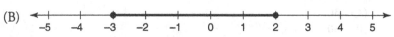

(B)

(C)

(D)

(E)

$$
\begin{array}{|l|}
\hline
ax^2 + bx + c = 0 \\
a \neq 0 \\
b^2 - 4ac = 17 \\
\hline
\end{array}
$$

295. From the information given, which of the following statements is true about the equation $ax^2 + bx + c = 0$?

(A) It has no real roots.
(B) It has exactly one real, rational root.
(C) It has exactly one real, irrational root.
(D) It has exactly two real, rational roots.
(E) It has exactly two real, irrational roots.

296. A 30-ounce mixture contains cornmeal, wheat germ, and flaxseed by weight in the ratio 5:3:2, respectively. What is the number of ounces of flaxseed in the mixture?

(A) 2
(B) 3
(C) 6
(D) 9
(E) 15

297. If $\dfrac{x}{y} = 20$ and $\dfrac{y}{z} = 10$, with $y \cdot z \neq 0$, what is the value of $\dfrac{x}{y+z}$?

(A) $\dfrac{11}{200}$

(B) $\dfrac{11}{20}$

(C) $\dfrac{20}{11}$

(D) $\dfrac{200}{11}$

(E) $\dfrac{100}{3}$

$$3(x+1)(x-1)+\frac{x(4x-6)}{2}$$

298. Which of the following expressions is equivalent to the preceding expression?

(A) $5x^2 + 3x - 6$
(B) $3x^2 + 3x - 6$
(C) $-x^2 + 3x + 3$
(D) $5x^2 - 3x + 3$
(E) $5x^2 - 3x - 3$

299. If 5 is one solution of the equation $x^2 - 2x + k = 12$, where k is a constant, what is the other solution?

(A) -5
(B) -3
(C) 3
(D) 5
(E) 15

$$\begin{aligned}
4x+5y &= -2 \\
-4x+3y+5z &= 13 \\
2x+5y-z &= 5
\end{aligned}$$

300. For the preceding system of equations, what is the value of y?

(A) -3
(B) -1
(C) 1
(D) 2
(E) 3

$$2t(t-2)=1$$

301. Which of the following shows the preceding equation correctly solved for t?

(A) $t=1\pm\sqrt{3}$

(B) $t=1\pm\sqrt{6}$

(C) $t=\dfrac{-2\pm\sqrt{6}}{2}$

(D) $t=\dfrac{2\pm\sqrt{6}}{2}$

(E) $t=\dfrac{1}{2}$ or 3

302. Which of the following sets of ordered pairs is NOT a function?

(A) $\{(-1,3),(1,2),(1,5),(3,8)\}$
(B) $\{(4,4)\}$
(C) $\{(-3,6),(-2,2),(0,0)(2,2),(3,6)\}$
(D) $\{(3,3),(3^2,3),(3^3,3^3),(3^4,3^4)\}$
(E) $\{(1,5),(2,5),(3,5),(4,5)\}$

303. If $f(x)=x^2+x+1$ and $g(x)=\sqrt{x}$, then what is the value of $\dfrac{f(1)}{g(4)}$?

(A) $\dfrac{3}{2}$

(B) $\dfrac{3}{16}$

(C) 3

(D) $\pm\dfrac{3}{2}$

(E) ±3

x	f (x)	g (x)
1	5	3
2	4	1
3	3	4
4	2	2
5	1	5

304. The preceding table shows selected values of the functions f and g. What is the value of $g(f(4))$?

(A) 1
(B) 2
(C) 3
(D) 4
(E) 5

$$\left(\sqrt{\sqrt{\sqrt{x}}}\right)^6$$

305. Assuming $x \geq 0$, which of the following expressions is equivalent to the preceding expression?

(A) x^3

(B) x^2

(C) x

(D) $x^{\frac{3}{4}}$

(E) $x^{\frac{1}{24}}$

$$\frac{m}{m^2 - n^2} - \frac{n}{m^2 + mn}$$

306. Which of the following expressions is equivalent to the preceding expression?

(A) $\dfrac{m^2 - mn - n^2}{m(m + n)}$

(B) $\dfrac{m^2 - mn + n^2}{m(m + n)(m - n)}$

(C) $\dfrac{m^2 - mn - n^2}{m(m + n)(m - n)}$

(D) $\dfrac{m - n}{m(m + n)}$

(E) $\dfrac{m - n}{n(m + n)}$

307. Which of the following intervals is the solution of $|2x - 1| > 7$?

(A) $(-3, 4)$

(B) $(-4, 4)$

(C) $(-\infty, -3) \cup (4, \infty)$

(D) $(-\infty, -3] \cup [4, \infty)$

(E) $(-\infty, -4) \cup (4, \infty)$

308. Given $f(t) = \left(\dfrac{1+\dfrac{1}{t}}{1-\dfrac{1}{t}}\right)^2$, where $t \neq 0, 1$, and $g(t) = \dfrac{1}{t}$, where $t \neq 0$, then

$f(g(t))$ equals which of the following expressions?

(A) $\dfrac{t^2 - 1}{t^2 + 1}$

(B) $\left(\dfrac{t+1}{t-1}\right)^2$

(C) $\left(\dfrac{t-1}{t+1}\right)^2$

(D) $-\left(\dfrac{1+t}{1-t}\right)^2$

(E) $\dfrac{t^2 + 1}{t^2 - 1}$

309. Two vehicles leave the same location at exactly the same time, one traveling due north at r miles per hour and the other traveling due south at $(r+10)$ miles per hour. In how many hours will the two vehicles be d miles apart?

(A) $\dfrac{d}{2r+10}$

(B) $\dfrac{d}{r^2+10}$

(C) $\dfrac{r(r+10)}{d}$

(D) $\dfrac{d}{r} + \dfrac{d}{r+10}$

(E) $\dfrac{0.5d}{r} + \dfrac{0.5d}{r+10}$

310. A chemist is making a 50 percent alcohol solution. How many milliliters of distilled water must the chemist add to 600 milliliters of an 80 percent alcohol solution to obtain a 50 percent solution?

(A) 180
(B) 300
(C) 360
(D) 480
(E) 600

311. Two identical devices working together can complete a task in 6 hours. How many hours will it take one such device working alone to do the same task?

(A) 2
(B) 3
(C) 6
(D) 9
(E) 12

312. What is the equation of the line through the point $(3,1)$ that is parallel to the line whose equation is $6x+5y=10$?

(A) $6x+5y=21$
(B) $-6x+5y=-13$
(C) $6x+5y=23$
(D) $5x-6y=9$
(E) $5x+6y=9$

313. If the line through the points $(-8,k)$ and $(2,1)$ is parallel to the line through the points $(11,-1)$ and $(7,k+1)$, what is the value of k?

(A) -4
(B) $-\dfrac{1}{4}$
(C) $-\dfrac{2}{7}$
(D) 2
(E) 4

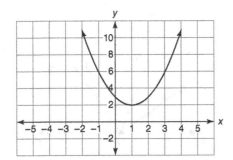

314. The preceding figure shows the graph of a parabola. Which of the following could be the parabola's equation?

(A) $y=x^2+2x-3$
(B) $y=x^2-2x-3$
(C) $y=x^2-2x+3$
(D) $y=-x^2+2x-3$
(E) $y=-x^2+2x+3$

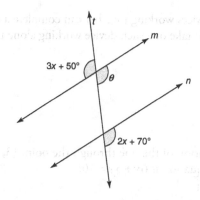

315. In the preceding figure, lines *m* and *n* are parallel and cut by the transversal *t*. What is the measure of angle θ?

(A) 20°

(B) 40°

(C) 60°

(D) 110°

(E) 120°

316. In triangle *ABC*, sides $\overline{AB}$ and $\overline{AC}$ are congruent. If the measure of angle *C* is 36°, what is the measure of angle *A*?

(A) 28°

(B) 36°

(C) 72°

(D) 104°

(E) 108°

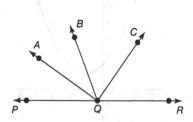

317. In the preceding figure, ∠*AQP* ≅ ∠*AQB* and ∠*BQC* ≅ ∠*CQR*. What is the measure of ∠*AQC*?

(A) 100°

(B) 90°

(C) 80°

(D) 75°

(E) 70°

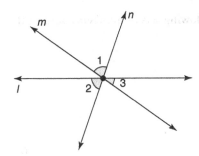

318. In the preceding figure, lines *l*, *m*, and *n* intersect in a point, the measure of ∠1 is 65°, and the measure of ∠2 is 85°. What is the measure of ∠3?

(A) 20°
(B) 25°
(C) 30°
(D) 35°
(E) 40°

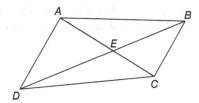

319. How many triangles are in the preceding figure?

(A) 4
(B) 7
(C) 8
(D) 9
(E) 10

320. Points *R*, *P*, and *S* lie above line segment $\overline{MN}$ in the relative order given. Line segment $\overline{PQ}$ is perpendicular to line segment $\overline{MN}$ at the point *Q*. Hence, Point *R* lies to the left of $\overline{PQ}$ and point *S* lies to its right. The segment $\overline{PQ}$ bisects ∠*RPS* and $\overline{RP} \cong \overline{PS}$. If ∠*PQS* = 35°, what is the measure of ∠*RQM*?

(A) 35°
(B) 45°
(C) 55°
(D) 65°
(E) 75°

321. Which of the following sets of numbers could be the lengths of the sides of a triangle?

(A) 8, 14, 18   324
(B) 6, 16, 24   576
(C) 6, 15, 7   225
(D) 2, 3, 5   25.
(E) 12, 8, 3   144

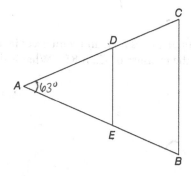

322. In the preceding figure, $\overline{AC} \cong \overline{AB}$, $\angle ABC \cong \angle ADE$, and $\angle ACB \cong \angle AED$. If the measure of $\angle ADE$ is 63°, what is the measure of $\angle A$?

(A) 27°
(B) 37°
(C) 44°
(D) 54°
(E) 63°

323. The measures of the interior angles of a triangle are in the ratio 2:3:5. What is the measure of the smallest angle?

(A) 9°
(B) 18°
(C) 36°
(D) 54°
(E) 90°

324. Suppose that you are constructing a triangle having two sides of lengths 3 and 7. If you use only whole number lengths, how many triangles are possible?

(A) 1
(B) 2
(C) 3
(D) 4
(E) 5

325. In triangle ABC, the measure of $\angle A$ is 25 degrees more than the measure of $\angle B$, and the measure of $\angle C$ is 9 degrees less than twice the measure of $\angle B$. What is the measure of the largest angle?

(A) 36°
(B) 41°
(C) 66°
(D) 73°
(E) 82°

$A = 25 + b$ $a + b + c = 180$
$C = 2b - 9$ $b = 180 - a - c$

326. Two consecutive angles of a parallelogram have measures $x - 30°$ and $2x + 60°$. What is the measure of the smaller angle?

(A) 20°
(B) 40°
(C) 50°
(D) 70°
(E) 160°

327. If the perimeter of triangle ABC is 60 centimeters, what is the perimeter in centimeters of the triangle formed by connecting the midpoints of the sides of triangle ABC?

(A) 10
(B) 15
(C) 20
(D) 25
(E) 30

$A + B + C = 60$

20

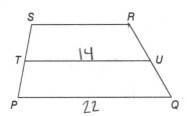

328. In trapezoid $PQRS$ shown, $\overline{TU}$ is the median. If $PQ = 22$ and $TU = 14$, what is the measure of $\overline{SR}$?

(A) 6
(B) 7
(C) 11
(D) 12
(E) 18

329. If a rhombus has a side of length 16 inches and the measure of one interior angle is 150°, what is the area of the rhombus in square inches?

(A) 256
(B) 144
(C) 128
(D) 96
(E) 64

330. How many 4-inch by 4-inch tiles are needed to cover a wall 8 feet by 6 feet?

(A) 6912
(B) 1728
(C) 864
(D) 432
(E) 216

331. A square and a rectangle have equal areas. If the rectangle has dimensions 16 centimeters by 25 centimeters, what is the perimeter in centimeters of the square?

(A) 20
(B) 40
(C) 60
(D) 80
(E) 100

332. Which of the following sets of numbers could NOT be the lengths of the sides of a right triangle?

(A) 5, 13, 12

(B) $2, 2\sqrt{3}, 4$

(C) 4, 7.5, 8.5
(D) 7, 10, 13

(E) $1, \dfrac{3}{4}, 1\dfrac{1}{4}$

333. A bike rider leaves camp and travels 7 miles due north, then goes 3 miles due east, and then 3 miles due south and stops to rest. At this point, what is the rider's true distance (in miles) from camp?

(A) 13
(B) 10
(C) 7
(D) 5
(E) 4

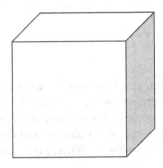

334. The crate shown is a rectangular prism. If 81 cubes measuring 4 inches on each edge will fill the crate to capacity, what is its volume in cubic inches?

(A) 64
(B) 81
(C) 324
(D) 1296
(E) 5184

335. What is the area in square inches of an equilateral triangle that has altitude of length 12 inches?

(A) $4\sqrt{3}$

(B) $8\sqrt{3}$

(C) $24\sqrt{3}$

(D) $48\sqrt{3}$

(E) $96\sqrt{3}$

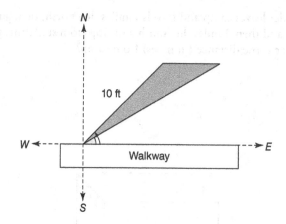

336. A homeowner wants to put decorative bricks around the triangular flower bed shown in the preceding figure. One side of the flower bed is 10 feet long and makes a 45° angle with a walkway that runs east to west. A second side runs parallel to the east-west walkway, and the third side makes a 30° angle with the east-west walkway. What is the perimeter in feet of the flower bed?

(A) $10(2+\sqrt{2}+\sqrt{6})$
(B) $10(2+\sqrt{2}+\sqrt{3})$
(C) $10(2+\sqrt{8})$
(D) $5(2+\sqrt{2}+\sqrt{6})$
(E) $5(2+\sqrt{2}+\sqrt{3})$

337. In a circle whose radius is 13 centimeters, a chord is 12 centimeters from the center of the circle. What is the length in centimeters of the chord?

(A) 12
(B) 10
(C) 8
(D) 6
(E) 5

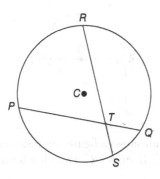

338. In the preceding diagram of circle C, chord $\overline{PQ}$ intersects chord $\overline{RS}$ at T. If $PQ = 4x + 6$, $TQ = 5$, $RS = 6x + 8$, and $TS = 3$, what is the value of x?

(A) 3

$4X + 6 - 5$

(B) 5

(C) 10

(D) 21

(E) 35

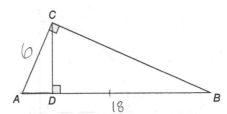

339. In right triangle ABC, $\overline{CD}$ is the altitude drawn to the hypotenuse $\overline{AB}$. If $AB = 18$ and $AC = 6$, what is the length of $\overline{AD}$?

(A) 1.5

(B) 2

(C) 3

(D) 12

(E) 16

340. A solid cube of metal has sides 18 cm long. A jeweler melts the cube down and uses all the molten metal to make three smaller cubes, all exactly the same size. What is the length in centimeters of an edge of one of these smaller cubes?

(A) $6\sqrt[3]{3}$

(B) $6\sqrt[3]{9}$

(C) $3\sqrt[3]{3}$

(D) $3\sqrt[3]{9}$

(E) 6

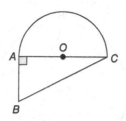

341. The preceding diagram shows a figure composed of right triangle ABC adjacent to semicircle AC. If $AB = OC = x$, what is the perimeter of the figure?

(A) $x + x\sqrt{5} + \pi x$

(B) $x + x\sqrt{5} + 2\pi x$

(C) $x + x\sqrt{3} + \pi x$

(D) $3x + x\sqrt{5} + \pi x$

(E) $x + x\sqrt{5} + \dfrac{\pi x^2}{2}$

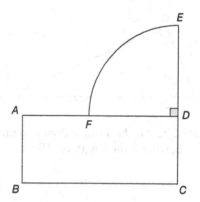

342. The figure $ABCDEF$ is composed of arc $\overset{\frown}{EF}$, with center at D, and rectangle $ABCD$. If $ED = 4$ units, $AD = 7$ units, and $DC = 3$ units, what is the approximate area in square units of figure $ABCDEF$?

(A) 24

(B) 27

(C) 34

(D) 41

(E) 64

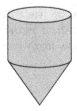

343. The grain storage bin shown has a right cylindrical top and a right conical base. The bin's overall height is 25 feet. If the bin's cylindrical top has radius 7 feet and its conical base has altitude 12 feet, what is the approximate capacity in cubic feet of the storage bin?

(A) 748
(B) 1100
(C) 1188
(D) 2617
(E) 10468

344. For a craft project, a rectangular piece of cardboard with dimensions 20 centimeters by 18 centimeters is to be made into a gift box by cutting congruent squares out of each corner and then folding up and taping together the remaining flaps. If each congruent square that is cut out of the corners has sides of length s, which of the following expressions represents the volume of the box?

(A) $4s^3 - 76s^2 + 360s$
(B) $4s^3 + 76s^2 + 360s$
(C) $s^3 - 38s^2 + 360s$
(D) $s^2 - 38s + 360$
(E) $4s^2 - 76s + 360$

345. A triangle in the x-y plane has vertices $A(2,3)$, $B(-1,-1)$, and $C(3,-4)$. What is the perimeter of the triangle?

(A) $10 + 5\sqrt{2}$
(B) $10 + \sqrt{2}$
(C) $5 + \sqrt{5} + 5\sqrt{2}$
(D) $5 + \sqrt{41} + 5\sqrt{2}$
(E) $\sqrt{5} + \sqrt{41} + 5\sqrt{2}$

346. In a survey of 200 students, 65 students said they like science and 40 students said they like math. If all the students who said they like math also said they like science, how many students said they like at least one of these subjects?

(A) 25
(B) 40
(C) 65
(D) 95
(E) 105

347. The number of elements in the union of sets A and B is 160, and the number of elements in the intersection of sets A and B is 20. If the number of elements in set A is 50, what is the number of elements in set B?

(A) 30
(B) 60
(C) 90
(D) 110
(E) 130

348. How many different meal combinations consisting of one sandwich, one drink, and one type of chips are possible from a selection of 8 kinds of sandwiches, 5 drinks, and 7 types of chips?

(A) 280
(B) 140
(C) 40
(D) 35
(E) 20

349. In a video game, a player is faced with the task of moving from point A to point B to point C, and then returning from point C to point A through point B, without retracing any path. There are 5 paths from point A to point B, and 8 paths from point B to point C. In how many different ways can the player accomplish the task?

(A) 2240
(B) 1600
(C) 1120
(D) 68
(E) 24

350. Four people are to be seated in four identical chairs placed in a circle. How many different arrangements of the four people (relative to one another) in the four chairs are possible?

(A) 256

(B) 128

(C) 48

(D) 24

(E) 6

351. How many different ways can three prizes be distributed to 10 competitors if each person can receive at most one prize?

(A) 30

(B) 120

(C) 360

(D) 720

(E) 1000

352. An urn contains 7 black marbles, 6 green marbles, and 10 red marbles, all identical except for color. What is the probability of drawing a black or red marble when a single marble is drawn at random from the urn?

(A) $\dfrac{7}{23}$

(B) $\dfrac{10}{23}$

(C) $\dfrac{13}{23}$

(D) $\dfrac{16}{23}$

(E) $\dfrac{17}{23}$

353. A quiz consists of 5 multiple-choice questions, each of which has 4 possible answer choices (A, B, C, and D), one of which is correct. Suppose that an unprepared student does not read the questions but simply makes a random guess for each question. What is the probability that the student will guess correctly on at least one question?

(A) $\dfrac{1}{1024}$

(B) $\dfrac{20}{1024}$

(C) $\dfrac{243}{1024}$

(D) $\dfrac{781}{1024}$

(E) $\dfrac{1023}{1024}$

354. Suppose you randomly draw two marbles, successively without replacement, from a box containing 8 red marbles and 6 blue marbles. What is the probability of drawing a blue marble on the second draw, given that you drew a red marble on the first draw? (Assume the marbles are identical except for color.)

(A) $\dfrac{12}{49}$

(B) $\dfrac{3}{7}$

(C) $\dfrac{3}{13}$

(D) $\dfrac{6}{13}$

(E) $\dfrac{24}{91}$

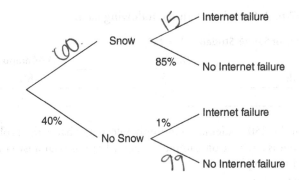

355. The preceding probability diagram represents the incidence of Internet failure during weather in which snow might occur. What is the probability that it snows and an Internet failure occurs?

(A) 0.4%
(B) 9%
(C) 39.6%
(D) 60%
(E) 75%

60×15

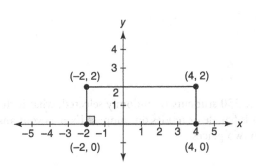

356. The preceding diagram shows a rectangle with vertices $(-2,0)$, $(-2,2)$, $(4,2)$, and $(4,0)$. What is the probability that the x-coordinate of a randomly selected point in the rectangle is negative?

(A) 1

(B) $\dfrac{1}{3}$

(C) $\dfrac{1}{6}$

(D) $\dfrac{1}{12}$

(E) 0

Questions 357 to 359 are based on the following data.

Residence Status of Senior Students ($N = 250$)

	On-Campus	Off-Campus
Female	52	86
Male	38	74

357. If one of the 250 students is randomly selected, what is the probability that the student is a female on-campus resident? Express your answer as a decimal rounded to two places.

(A) 0.21
(B) 0.33
(C) 0.38
(D) 0.42
(E) 0.58

358. If one of the 250 students is randomly selected, what is the probability that the student resides on campus, given that the student selected is a male student? Express your answer as a decimal rounded to two places.

(A) 0.15
(B) 0.34
(C) 0.42
(D) 0.51
(E) 0.66

359. If one of the 250 students is randomly selected, what is the probability that the student is female or resides on campus? Express your answer as a decimal rounded to two places.

(A) 0.36
(B) 0.47
(C) 0.55
(D) 0.62
(E) 0.70

360. To estimate the number of turtles in a lake, a team of biologists captures and tags 20 turtles and then releases the turtles unharmed back into the lake. Two weeks later, the team returns to the lake and captures 30 turtles, 6 of which have tags indicating that they are recaptured turtles. Based on this capture-recapture method, what is the best estimate of the number of turtles in the lake?

(A) 200
(B) 100
(C) 75
(D) 50
(E) 25

361. In a cooking contest five judges score each contestant. To calculate the contestant's final score, the highest number and lowest number are discarded and then the arithmetic average of the remaining numbers is taken. If the five judges score a contestant as 6.3, 7.1, 6.4, 6.5, and 6.2, then what is the contestant's final score?

(A) 6.7
(B) 6.6
(C) 6.5
(D) 6.4
(E) 6.3

Sunday	Monday	Tuesday	Wednesday	Thursday	Friday	Saturday
–7°F	0°F	15°F	–20°F	–5°F	2°F	13°F

362. The preceding information shows midnight temperature readings during winter in a cold region of the United States. What is the range of these data?

(A) –35°F
(B) –20°F
(C) –33°F
(D) 20°F
(E) 35°F

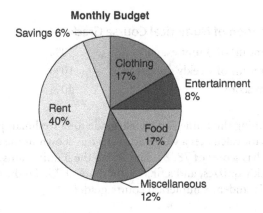

Monthly Budget

363. The preceding circle graph displays a budget for a monthly income of $3,500 (after taxes). According to the graph, how much more money is budgeted for rent than for food and clothing combined?

(A) $60
(B) $210
(C) $595
(D) $1,190
(E) $1,400

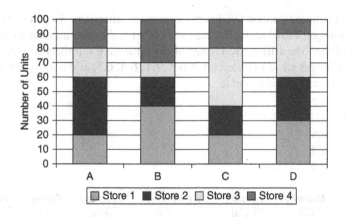

364. The stacked bar graph shows the number of units of products A, B, C, and D sold by each of four stores (Store 1, Store 2, Store 3, and Store 4). According to the graph, the number of units sold by Store 1 is what percent greater than the number of units sold by Store 4?

(A) 10%
(B) 20%
(C) 27.3%
(D) 30%
(E) 37.5%

Determination of Numerical Course Grade

78 Average (mean) of 3 unit exams	50%	39
92 Average (mean) of weekly quizzes	10%	9.2
75 Final exam score	40%	

365. In determining the numerical course grade for a freshman psychology class, the instructor calculates a weighted average as shown in the preceding table. A student has scores of 78, 81, and 75 on the 3 unit exams, an average of 92 on weekly quizzes, and a final exam score of 75. To the nearest tenth, what is this student's numerical course grade?

(A) 76.2
(B) 78.2
(C) 80.2
(D) 82.2
(E) 84.2

Questions 366 and 367 are based on the following data.

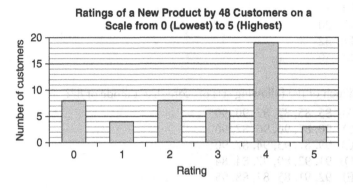

**Ratings of a New Product by 48 Customers on a
Scale from 0 (Lowest) to 5 (Highest)**

366. For the data shown in the bar graph, what is the median rating of the new
product?

    (A) 2.0
    (B) 2.5
    (C) 3.0
    (D) 3.5
    (E) 4.0

367. For the data shown in the bar graph, what is the 25th percentile?

    (A) 1.0
    (B) 1.5
    (C) 2.0
    (D) 2.5
    (E) 3.0

Questions 368 and 369 are based on the following information.

In a population of 320 employees of a manufacturing plant, the mean salary is
$55,000, the median salary is $48,000, and the 60th percentile is $57,500.

368. How many employees have salaries that are equal to or less than $57,500?

    (A) 40
    (B) 60
    (C) 128
    (D) 160
    (E) 192

369. How many employees have salaries between $48,000 and $57,500?

(A) 10
(B) 16
(C) 20
(D) 32
(E) 40

370. Which of the following sets of scores has a mode of 87?

(A) 85, 85, 87, 87, 90, 90
(B) 90, 87, 96, 96, 87, 96
(C) 99, 87, 93, 94, 87, 90
(D) 91, 92, 89, 97, 84, 84
(E) 92, 91, 85, 87, 88, 95

	Exam 1	Exam 2	Exam 3	Exam 4	Exam 5
Student's grade	75	87	92	70	90
Class mean	65	88	86	60	85
Class standard deviation	5	2	4	10	5

371. The preceding table shows a student's scores on five exams in a college biology class along with the means and standard deviations of the scores for all the students in the class of 50 students. On which of the exams did the student perform best relative to the performance of the student's classmates?

(A) Exam 1
(B) Exam 2
(C) Exam 3
(D) Exam 4
(E) Exam 5

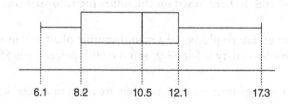

372. What is the interquartile range of the preceding box plot?

(A) 11.2
(B) 9.1
(C) 6.8
(D) 6.0
(E) 3.9

For Questions 373 to 375, use the following information.

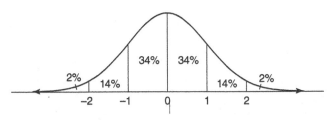

The figure shows approximate percentages for six regions of the standard normal distribution, which has mean 0 and standard deviation 1.

373. IQ scores for adults are normally distributed with mean 100 and standard deviation 15. What percent of adults have IQ scores greater than 130?

(A) 2%
(B) 34%
(C) 50%
(D) 68%
(E) 98%

374. Suppose that scores on a standardized college admissions exam are normally distributed with mean 500 and standard deviation 100. Find the probability that a randomly selected test taker's score on the exam will be at least 400.

(A) 0.14
(B) 0.16
(C) 0.50
(D) 0.84
(E) 0.98

375. A local deli chain makes a signature sandwich. Suppose the measures of fat grams in the signature sandwiches are normally distributed with mean 16 grams and standard deviation 1.5 grams. Find the probability that a randomly selected signature sandwich will have no more than 19 fat grams.

(A) 0.02
(B) 0.16
(C) 0.34
(D) 0.84
(E) 0.98

Multiple-Choice Questions with One or More Correct Answers

Select *all* the answer choices that apply. The correct answer may be just one of the choices or may be as many as all of the choices, depending on the question directions. No credit is given unless you select *exactly* the number of correct choices specified in the question.

Unless otherwise stated, you can assume *all* of the following:

- All numbers used are real numbers.
- All figures lie in a plane and are drawn accurately, but **are not necessarily** drawn to scale.
- Lines shown as straight are straight lines.
- The relative position of points, angles, and regions are in the order shown.
- Coordinate systems, such as number lines and xy-planes, **are** drawn to scale.
- Graphical displays of data, such as bar graphs and frequency distributions, **are** drawn to scale.

376. Which of the following expressions has $\frac{2}{3}$ as a numerical value? Indicate *all* such expressions.

.667

(A) $2\frac{1}{2} \div 3\frac{3}{4}$

(B) $\frac{1}{2} \times 1\frac{1}{3}$

(C) $2\frac{1}{3} \div 3\frac{1}{2}$

(D) $\frac{5}{24} + \frac{3}{8}$

(E) $\frac{20}{21} - \frac{2}{7}$

(F) $2.5 \div 3.75$

377. If the square root of the product of two positive integers is 14, which can be the sum of the two integers? Indicate *all* such sums.

(A) 35
(B) 53
(C) 84
(D) 100
(E) 197

378. Suppose n is a positive integer such that the smallest whole number that is greater than or equal to $\dfrac{n}{33}$ is 1 or 2. Which are possible values for the integer n? Indicate *all* such integers.

(A) 15
(B) 24
(C) 50
(D) 66
(E) 70

379. Which of the following expressions is equivalent to 125%? Indicate *all* such expressions.

(A) $1\dfrac{1}{4}\%$
(B) 1.25
(C) 0.125
(D) $\dfrac{5}{4}$
(E) 12.5%

380. The operation $*$ is defined on the set of real numbers by $a*b$ = the larger of the numbers a and b. If $a*0.5 = 0.5$, which CANNOT be a value for a? Indicate *all* such values.

(A) 0.4
(B) $\dfrac{1}{2}$
(C) $\dfrac{5}{11}$
(D) $\sqrt{2}$
(E) $\sqrt{3}$
(F) $\dfrac{1}{\sqrt{2}}$

381. If x is a number in the interval shown, which can be a value of x? Indicate *all* such values.

(A) $-\sqrt[5]{33}$

(B) $-\dfrac{17}{4}$

(C) $-\pi$

(D) $\sqrt[3]{8}$

(E) $\sqrt{5}$

(F) $\dfrac{\pi}{2}$

(G) $\dfrac{13}{3}$

382. If $A = \{$products of 2 and an odd number$\}$ and $B = \{$even multiples of 3$\}$, which of the following numbers is in the intersection of A and B? Indicate *all* such numbers.

(A) 6

(B) 12

(C) 18

(D) 24

(E) 30

383. If a is a positive divisor of both 30 and 42, then a is also a positive divisor of which integer? Indicate *all* such integers.

(A) −41

(B) −12

(C) 12

(D) 37

(E) 102

384. Kobe has four US bills that are five-dollar and one-dollar bills. Which amount could be the worth of Kobe's four bills? Indicate *all* such amounts.

(A) $8

(B) $13

(C) $16

(D) $20

385. Along a straight sidewalk, a building contractor erected n flags 50 feet apart so that the distance from the first flag to the last flag is 200 feet. Which whole number could be n? Indicate *all* such whole numbers.

(A) 4
(B) 5
(C) 6
(D) 7
(E) 8

386. When a positive integer m is divided by 17, the remainder is 3. Which integer could be m? Indicate *all* such integers.

(A) 73
(B) 240
(C) 258
(D) 274
(E) 292

387. Which of the following statements must be true? Indicate *all* such statements.

(A) On a number line $-x$ is to the left of x.
(B) If $x \neq 0$, then $-x$ is a negative number.
(C) $-x$ and x are never equal.
(D) The negative of $-x$ is x.

388. Which of the following number sentences is false? Indicate *all* such sentences.

(A) $|6| - |-6| = 0$

(B) $2|-5| = |-2||-5|$

(C) $\dfrac{|-10|}{|5|} = -|2|$

(D) $|-4||2| - \dfrac{|-16|}{|-2|} = 0$

(E) $|10||-10| = -100$

389. To include a penalty for guessing, the scoring formula for a 60-question, multiple-choice test is $s = r - \frac{1}{4}w$, where s is the score on the test, r is the number of correct responses, and w is the number of incorrect responses. If a student answers all 60 questions, which of the following scores could be the student's score? Indicate *all* such scores.

(A) −20

(B) −15

(C) −5

(D) 10

(E) 32

(F) 65

390. Which of the following ratios is equivalent to the ratio 7:6? Indicate *all* such ratios.

(A) 45:30

(B) $1\frac{1}{8}:\frac{3}{8}$

(C) $1\frac{3}{4}:1\frac{1}{2}$

(D) 9.6:7.2

391. Hiroshi has three boxes of markers. Box 1 contains only black markers, Box 2 contains only red markers, and Box 3 contains only blue markers. The covers on the box have labels. However, when the covers were put on the boxes, each box ended up with an incorrect label accidentally. Hiroshi opens the box marked "red markers" and finds that the box contains black markers. Which of the following statements must be true? Indicate *all* such statements.

(A) Box 1 is labeled "red markers."

(B) Box 1 is labeled "blue markers."

(C) Box 2 is labeled "black markers."

(D) Box 2 is labeled "blue markers."

(E) Box 3 is labeled "blue markers."

(F) Box 3 is labeled "black markers."

392. Shail and Jackwyn work at a restaurant that is open seven days a week. Shail's schedule is to work three days in a row, and then have one day off. Jackwyn's schedule is to work five days in a row, and then have two days off. In September, neither Shail nor Jackwyn worked on September 1, but both worked on September 2. What other date in September were both Shail and Jackwyn off on the same day? Indicate *all* such dates.

(A) September 13
(B) September 17
(C) September 21
(D) September 29

393. Which of the following numbers is rational? Indicate *all* such numbers.

(A) $-\sqrt{36}$

(B) $-\sqrt{120}$

(C) $-\sqrt{\dfrac{4}{9}}$

(D) $\sqrt{\dfrac{1}{2}}$

(E) $\sqrt{0.49}$

(F) $\sqrt{40}$

(G) $\sqrt{400}$

394. If x is a positive integer, what is the units digit of 27^x? Indicate *all* such digits.

(A) 1
(B) 2
(C) 3
(D) 7
(E) 9

395. Which of the following expressions is equivalent to $3\sqrt{18}$? Indicate *all* such expressions.

(A) $27\sqrt{2}$

(B) $\sqrt{54}$

(C) $\sqrt{162}$

(D) $9\sqrt{2}$

(E) $3\sqrt{6}$

396. Which of the following expressions is equivalent to $3\sqrt{8}+6\sqrt{2}$? Indicate *all* such expressions.

(A) $12\sqrt{2}$

(B) $\sqrt{288}$

(C) $2\sqrt{72}$

(D) $9\sqrt{10}$

(E) $18\sqrt{10}$

397. Which of the following products yields an irrational number? Indicate *all* such products.

(A) $(4\sqrt{3})(5\sqrt{12})$

(B) $\left(\dfrac{1}{2}\sqrt{10}\right)(8\sqrt{5})$

(C) $(3\sqrt{32})(2\sqrt{2})$

(D) $\left(\dfrac{2}{3}\sqrt{3}\right)^{2}$

(E) $(4\sqrt{3})(9\sqrt{6})$

(F) $\left(\dfrac{1}{2}\sqrt{8}\right)\left(\dfrac{1}{6}\sqrt{18}\right)$

398. Which of the following quotients yields a rational number? Indicate *all* such quotients.

(A) $\dfrac{\sqrt{11}}{\sqrt{121}}$

(B) $\dfrac{\sqrt{18}}{\sqrt{25}}$

(C) $\dfrac{\sqrt{50}}{\sqrt{2}}$

(D) $\dfrac{\sqrt{18}}{\sqrt{3}}$

(E) $\dfrac{\sqrt{5}}{\sqrt{16}}$

(F) $\dfrac{\sqrt{9}}{\sqrt{64}}$

399. Two integers are in the ratio 4:3. Which of the following is a possible sum of the two integers? Indicate *all* such sums.

(A) 14
(B) 35
(C) 70
(D) 120
(E) 140

400. The difference of two integers is 30. Which of the following is a possible ratio of the larger to the smaller integer? Indicate *all* such ratios.

(A) 5:2
(B) 7:3
(C) 8:5
(D) 9:4
(E) 11:1

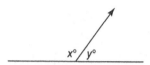

401. In the preceding figure, *x* and *y* are integers. Which of the following is a possible ratio of *x* to *y*? Indicate *all* such ratios.

(A) 2:1
(B) 5:4
(C) 9:2
(D) 9:4
(E) 10:5

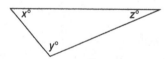

402. In the preceding figure, *x*, *y*, and *z* are integers. Which of the following is a possible ratio of *x* to *y* to *z*? Indicate *all* such ratios.

(A) 1:1:1
(B) 2:2:3
(C) 4:5:6
(D) 4:5:10
(E) 5:2:2

403. Which of the following pairs of ratios could form a true proportion? Indicate *all* such pairs.

(A) $\dfrac{19}{15}, \dfrac{38}{25}$

(B) $\dfrac{1.6}{2.5}, \dfrac{64}{100}$

(C) $\dfrac{4}{3}, \dfrac{10}{5}$

(D) $\dfrac{14}{18}, \dfrac{18}{14}$

(E) $\dfrac{3.6}{3}, \dfrac{18}{15}$

404. Which of the following expressions is equivalent to $12\dfrac{1}{2}\%$ of 400? Indicate *all* such expressions.

(A) 125% of 40

(B) $33\dfrac{1}{3}\%$ of 150

(C) 2.5% of 2000

(D) $\dfrac{1}{8}\%$ of 4000

(E) $\dfrac{1}{2}\%$ of 10,000

(F) 0.1% of 500

405. Triangle *ABC* is similar to triangle *DEF*. Triangle *ABC* has sides 4, 6, and 8. Which could be the corresponding sides of triangle *DEF*? Indicate *all* that apply.

(A) 1, 1.5, and 2
(B) 1.5, 2.25, and 3
(C) 6, 9, and 12
(D) 8, 12, and 16
(E) 10, 15, and 20

406. The ratio of the perimeters of two similar polygons is 5:9. Which could be the areas of the two polygons? Indicate *all* that apply.

(A) 20 and 45
(B) 55 and 99
(C) 25 and 81
(D) 100 and 324
(E) 200 and 360

407. Which of the following expressions is equivalent to $\dfrac{6}{4+\sqrt{7}}$? Indicate *all* such expressions.

(A) $\dfrac{2(4-\sqrt{7})}{3}$

(B) $\dfrac{6(4+\sqrt{7})}{23}$

(C) $\dfrac{4-\sqrt{7}}{3}$

(D) $\dfrac{6(4-\sqrt{7})}{23}$

408. Which of the following 12-digit numbers yields a remainder of 0 when divided by 8? Indicate *all* such numbers.

(A) 403,127,531,808
(B) 100,190,999,064
(C) 325,121,750,548
(D) 113,200,211,132
(E) 431,333,209,112
(F) 786,920,325,120

409. For which of the following expressions is $x - y$ a factor? Indicate *all* such expressions.

(A) $y^3 - x^3$
(B) $(x^2 - y^2)^5$
(C) $x^3 - 3x^2 y + 3xy^2 - y^3$
(D) $x^2 + y^2$
(E) $x^4 - 2x^2 y^2 + y^4$

$$|2x-1|>5$$

410. Which of the following numbers satisfies the absolute value inequality shown? Indicate *all* such numbers.

(A) $-\pi$

(B) $-\dfrac{3}{2}$

(C) $-\sqrt{10}$

(D) $\dfrac{\sqrt{2}}{2}$

(E) 2π

$$\begin{cases} y = 3x - 5 \\ y = x^2 - x - 5 \end{cases}$$

411. Which of the following values of x is in the solution set of the system of equations shown? Indicate *all* such numbers.

(A) −5
(B) −2
(C) 0
(D) 2
(E) 4
(F) 5

412. If $16x^2 = 81$ and $x > 0$, then what is the value of $\sqrt{x}$? Indicate *all* such values.

(A) $-\dfrac{9}{2}$

(B) $-\dfrac{3}{2}$

(C) $\sqrt{\dfrac{3}{2}}$

(D) $\dfrac{3}{2}$

(E) $\dfrac{9}{4}$

413. What is the difference between m and n if $m^2 = 36$ and $n^2 = 16$? Indicate *all* such differences.

(A) −20
(B) −10
(C) −2
(D) 2
(E) 10
(F) 20

414. If $x = \sqrt{\dfrac{(-4)^2}{7^2}}$, what is the value of x? Indicate *all* such values.

(A) $-\dfrac{4}{7}$

(B) $-\dfrac{16}{49}$

(C) $\dfrac{16}{49}$

(D) $\dfrac{4}{7}$

415. Suppose $x + y = 2$. If $y = x^2$, what is the value of x? Indicate *all* such values.

(A) -2
(B) -1
(C) 0
(D) 1
(E) 2
(F) 4

416. Suppose $3.5x + 1.5y + 1 = -0.5y - 2.5x$. If $y^2 = 4$, what is the value of x? Indicate *all* such values.

(A) -2

(B) $-\dfrac{5}{6}$

(C) $-\dfrac{1}{2}$

(D) $\dfrac{1}{2}$

(E) $\dfrac{5}{6}$

(F) 2

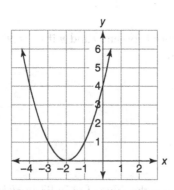

417. Which is an equation of the preceding graph? Indicate *all* such equations.

(A) $y = -x^2 + 4x + 4$
(B) $y = -(x + 2)^2$
(C) $y = (x - 2)^2$
(D) $y = x^2 - 4x + 4$
(E) $y = (x + 2)^2$
(F) $y = x^2 + 4x + 4$

418. If x is an integer such that $|x+1| < 2$, which of the following is a possible value of $2x^2 - 5x + 3$? Indicate *all* such values.

(A) 0

(B) 1

(C) 3

(D) 10

(E) 21

(F) 36

419. Ciara earns $5 each time she signs up a new client for an online service. If she signs up more than 100 new clients in one month, she is given an additional $2 for every new client over that number. Assuming that she always signs up at least 100 clients, which of the following amounts could be Ciara's monthly earnings from this activity? Indicate *all* such amounts.

(A) $400

(B) $500

(C) $640

(D) $800

(E) $850

420. If $2x + 3 < 7.5$, then which of the following is a possible value for x? Indicate *all* such values.

(A) 2.1

(B) 2.2

(C) 2.3

(D) 2.4

(E) 2.5

421. Which of the following equations is equivalent to the numerical relationship expressed in the statement, "Fifteen less than four times a number x equals twice the number x increased by nine and one-half." Indicate *all* such equations.

(A) $15 - 4x = 2x + 9\dfrac{1}{2}$

(B) $15 - 4x = 9.5 + 2x$

(C) $4x - 15 = 2x + 9.5$

(D) $\dfrac{1}{4}x - 15 = 2x + 9\dfrac{1}{2}$

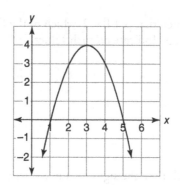

422. Which is an equation of the preceding graph? Indicate *all* such equations.

(A) $y = -x^2 + 6x - 5$

(B) $y = -x^2 + 6x + 5$

(C) $y = x^2 - 6x - 5$

(D) $y = x^2 - 6x + 5$

(E) $y = -(x-3)^2 + 4$

(F) $y = -(x-3)^2 - 4$

423. If $ax^2 + bx + c = 3(x+1)(x-1) + \dfrac{x(4x-6)}{2}$, which of the following sums CANNOT equal $a + b + c$? Indicate *all* such sums.

(A) -1

(B) 0

(C) 1

(D) 2

(E) 5

424. Last week, Javier worked seven hours more than three times the number of hours that Devlin worked. If Javier worked j hours and Devlin worked d hours, where j and d are integers, which of the following is a possible value for j? Indicate *all* such values.

(A) 10

(B) 15

(C) 18

(D) 22

(E) 40

425. Which of the following number sentences must be true? Indicate *all* such sentences.

(A) $9^4 \cdot 9^3 = 9^7$
(B) $2^2 \cdot 3^3 = 6^5$
(C) $5^4 \cdot 5^2 = 5^8$
(D) $10^4 \cdot 10 = 10^5$
(E) $2^2 \cdot 3^3 = 6^6$
(F) $(2^3)^4 = 2^{12}$

426. If $-3x(x-3) = 6$, which is a value of x? Indicate *all* such values.

(A) -2
(B) -1
(C) 1
(D) 2
(E) 9

427. Which of the following number sentences must be false? Indicate *all* such sentences.

(A) $\dfrac{6^8}{3^4} = 2^4$

(B) $\dfrac{5^6}{5^2} = 5^4$

(C) $\dfrac{12^4}{4^4} = 3^4$

(D) $\dfrac{4^5}{2^3} = 2^2$

(E) $\dfrac{9^2}{3^4} = 1$

(F) $\dfrac{4^3}{2^3} = 2^3$

428. Which of the following number sentences must be true? Indicate *all* such sentences.

(A) $(-6)^0 + 2^{-4} = 1\dfrac{1}{16}$

(B) $6(3^{-3}) = -\dfrac{2}{9}$

(C) $10^{-2} = -100$

(D) $4^5 \cdot 4^{-3} = \dfrac{1}{16}$

(E) $(2^3)^{-2} = 2$
(F) $(2^{-2})^{-2} = 16$

429. The length of a fence is represented by $2x - 30$. Which CANNOT be a value of x? Indicate *all* such values.

(A) 5
(B) 10
(C) 15
(D) 20
(E) 25

430. The length of a rectangle is $x + 3$ and its width is $x - 9$. Which expression represents the rectangle's area in terms of x? Indicate *all* such expressions.

(A) $x^2 - 27$
(B) $(x - 3)^2 - 36$
(C) $(x - 3)^2 - 18$
(D) $x^2 - 6x - 27$
(E) $x^2 + 6x - 27$

431. Which quadratic equation has roots of 4 and –4? Indicate *all* such equations.

(A) $x^2 - 4 = 0$
(B) $x^2 = 8$
(C) $x^2 - 16 = 0$
(D) $x^2 - 8x + 16 = 0$
(F) $2x^2 = 32$

432. Which two of the following values are roots of the equation $x^2 + 6x = -4$? Indicate *two* values.

(A) –10
(B) –4
(C) $-3 - \sqrt{5}$
(D) $-3 + \sqrt{5}$
(E) $-3 - \sqrt{20}$
(F) $-3 + \sqrt{20}$

433. For which of the following equations is the graph a circle? Indicate *all* such equations.

(A) $3x^2 = 27 + 3y^2$
(B) $2x^2 + 2y^2 = 50$
(C) $3x^2 = 27 - 3y^2$
(D) $2x^2 + 3y^2 = 16$

434. Which of the following points is on the circle whose equation is $x^2 + y^2 = 17^2$? Indicate *all* such points.

(A) (7,10)
(B) (1,16)
(C) (−8,15)
(D) (−8,−15)
(E) (−7,−10)

435. Which set of the following ordered pairs is a function? Indicate *all* such sets.

(A) {(6,1),(6,2),(6,3),(6,5),(6,6)}
(B) {(2,1),(3,5),(4,7),(6,5),(8,8)}
(C) {(1,2),(2,3),(3,1),(3,2)}
(D) {(5,2),(6,2),(7,3),(8,1),(10,6)}

436. Let $S = \{(-2,4),(0,6),(3,7),(7,5),(8,2),(x,1)\}$. If S is a function, then x CANNOT be which value? Indicate *all* such values.

(A) −2
(B) 0
(C) 3
(D) 4
(E) 5
(F) 7
(G) 8

437. Which of the following equations does NOT define a function? Indicate *all* such equations.

(A) $y = 2x + 3$
(B) $x = 2y + 3$
(C) $y = 2$
(D) $x = 3$
(E) $y^2 = 2x + 3$
(F) $x^2 = 2y + 3$

438. Which value of x is NOT in the domain of the function defined by $y = \dfrac{(x-3)(x+5)}{(x+2)(x-1)}$? Indicate *all* such values.

(A) −5
(B) −2
(C) 1
(D) 3

439. For which value of x will $y = \dfrac{(x-3)(x+5)}{(x+2)(x-1)}$ equal zero? Indicate *all* such values.

(A) -5

(B) -2

(C) 1

(D) 3

440. Which of the following statements must always true? Indicate *all* such statements.

(A) Every rhombus is a square.

(B) Every rectangle is a parallelogram.

(C) Every square is a rectangle.

(D) Every parallelogram is a rectangle.

(E) Every square is a rhombus.

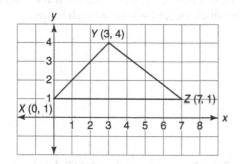

441. For triangle XYZ shown in the preceding x-y plane, which of the following quantities is irrational? Indicate *all* such quantities.

(A) The perimeter of triangle XYZ

(B) The x-coordinate of the midpoint of $\overline{XZ}$

(C) The length of $\overline{YZ}$

(D) The length of the altitude to $\overline{XZ}$

(E) The area of triangle XYZ

(F) The length of $\overline{YX}$

442. Which of the following sets of numbers can be the lengths of the sides of a triangle? Indicate *all* such sets.

(A) $\{5,8,14\}$

(B) $\{4,4,8\}$

(C) $\{1,2,\sqrt{2}\}$

(D) $\left\{\frac{3}{5},1,1\frac{2}{5}\right\}$

(E) $\{6.5,7.5,10.5\}$

(F) $\{2,5,\sqrt{40}\}$

(G) $\left\{1\frac{1}{3},2\frac{5}{6},3\frac{2}{3}\right\}$

443. The lengths of two sides of a triangle are 10 and 14. Which can be the perimeter of the triangle? Indicate *all* such perimeters.

(A) $24+\sqrt{20}$

(B) 36.5

(C) 47.9

(D) 48

(E) $24+10\sqrt{3}$

(F) 54

444. The lengths of two sides of a triangle are 8 and 15. Which expression best describes the length of the third side, x? Indicate *all* such expressions.

(A) $8<x<15$

(B) $8<x<23$

(C) $7<x<23$

(D) $15<x<23$

(E) $7<x<15$

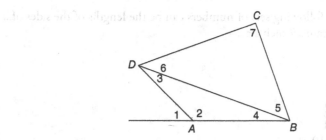

445. Based on the figure shown, which of the following statements must be true? Indicate *all* such statements.

    (A) $m\angle 1 > m\angle 2$
    (B) $m\angle 1 > m\angle 3$
    (C) $m\angle 4 < m\angle 1$
    (D) $m\angle 2 > m\angle 6$
    (E) $m\angle 5 < m\angle 7$

446. In the figures shown, which can be proved congruent by using only the marked congruent parts? Indicate *all* such figures.

(A)

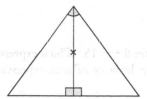

(D)

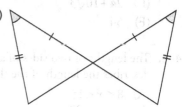

(B)

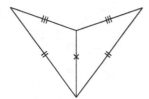

(E)

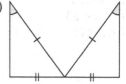

(C)

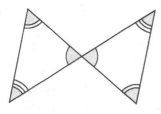

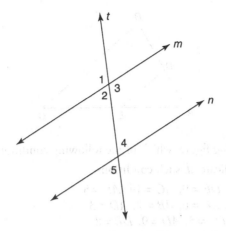

447. In the preceding figure, lines *m* and *n* are cut by a transversal *t*. For which of the following conditions would it follow that lines *m* and *n* are parallel? Indicate *all* such conditions.

(A) $\angle 2 \cong \angle 4$

(B) $\angle 3$ and $\angle 4$ are supplementary

(C) $\angle 1 \cong \angle 2$

(D) $\angle 3$ and $\angle 4$ are right angles

(E) $\angle 1$ and $\angle 5$ are supplementary

448. Which of the following conditions for a quadrilateral would be sufficient to prove the quadrilateral is a parallelogram? Indicate *all* such conditions.

(A) It is equilateral.

(B) Its diagonals are congruent and perpendicular.

(C) It has two parallel sides.

(D) Its diagonals bisect each other.

(E) Each pair of consecutive angles is supplementary.

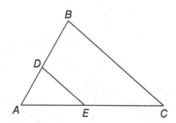

449. In the preceding figure, which of the following conditions will make $\overline{DE} \parallel \overline{BC}$? Indicate *all* such conditions.

(A) $AB = 21$, $DE = 9$, $AC = 14$, $AE = 5$
(B) $AC = 14$, $AE = 6$, $AB = 7$, $AD = 3$
(C) $AE = 6$, $EC = 5$, $AD = 9$, $DB = 8$
(D) $AC = 12$, $EC = 3$, $AB = 8$, $AD = 6$
(E) $AD = 2$, $DB = 8$, $AE = 3$, $EC = 12$

450. In isosceles triangle ABC, $\overline{AB} \cong \overline{AC}$, and D is a point between B and C on $\overline{BC}$. Which of the following statements must be true? Indicate *all* such statements.

(A) $AD > AB$
(B) $AC > AD$
(C) $m\angle B = m\angle C$
(D) $m\angle B > m\angle ADB$
(E) $m\angle C > m\angle ADC$

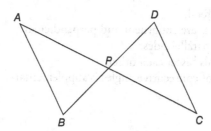

451. In the figure shown, if $\overline{AC}$ and $\overline{BD}$ bisect each other at P, which of the following statements must be true? Indicate *all* such statements.

(A) $\triangle APB \cong \triangle CPD$
(B) $\angle A \cong \angle D$
(C) $AB = CD$
(D) $m\angle B = m\angle C$
(E) $\overline{AB} \parallel \overline{CD}$

452. Which of the following can be the measures of the three angles of a triangle? Indicate *all* such measures.

(A) 55°, 45°, 90°
(B) 20°, 100°, 60°
(C) 30°, 40°, 110°
(D) 60°, 45°, 90°
(E) 35°, 125°, 10°

453. If two interior angles of a pentagon are 100° and 120°, which could be the measures of the other three interior angles of the pentagon? Indicate *all* such measures.

(A) 155°, 75°, 90°
(B) 200°, 60°, 60°
(C) 230°, 140°, 170°
(D) 100°, 40°, 180°
(E) 135°, 125°, 70°

454. Which of the following could be the measure of each of the interior angles of a regular polygon? Indicate *all* such measures.

(A) 75°
(B) 90°
(C) 100°
(D) 128°
(E) 240°

455. The measure of each of the exterior angles of a regular polygon is $k \cdot 15°$, where $k = 2, 3, 4, 6, 8$. Which could be the number of sides of the regular polygon? Indicate *all* that apply.

(A) 3
(B) 4
(C) 5
(D) 6
(E) 8
(F) 12

456. Which of the following statements about parallelogram $ABCD$, with diagonals $\overline{AC}$ and $\overline{DB}$, must always be true? Indicate *all* such statements.

(A) $\triangle CBA \cong \triangle ADC$
(B) $\angle A \cong \angle B$
(C) $\overline{AC} \perp \overline{DB}$
(D) $m\angle CAB = m\angle ACD$
(E) $\overline{AC} \cong \overline{DB}$
(F) $\overline{AC}$ and $\overline{DB}$ bisect each other.

457. Which of the following statements about rectangle *ABCD* must always true? Indicate *all* such statements.

(A) All of its angles are right angles.
(B) Its diagonals are congruent.
(C) Its diagonals are perpendicular to each other.
(D) Opposite sides are parallel.
(E) Its diagonals bisect its angles.

458. If the altitude to the hypotenuse of a right triangle measures 8, which can be the measures of the segments of the hypotenuse formed by the altitude? Indicate *all* such measures.

(A) 2 and 32
(B) 3 and 24
(C) 4 and 16
(D) 6 and 12
(E) 8 and 8

459. The altitude to the hypotenuse of a right triangle *ABC* divides the hypotenuse into segments of lengths 16 and 2. Which of the following statements must be true? Indicate *all* such statements.

(A) The altitude measures 32.
(B) One leg of right triangle *ABC* measures 4.
(C) The altitude measures 16.
(D) The area of triangle *ABC* is $36\sqrt{2}$.
(E) One leg of right triangle *ABC* measures 6.

460. Which of the following sets of lengths can be the sides of a right triangle? Indicate *all* such sets.

(A) {7,8,12}
(B) {4,8,4√3}
(C) {12,16,20}
(D) {4,√20,6}
(E) {1,√3,2}
(F) {25,24,7}

461. Which of the following statements about a circle must always be true? Indicate *all* such statements.

(A) Every diameter is a chord.
(B) Every chord is a diameter.
(C) All radii are congruent.
(D) Every chord contains exactly two points of the circle.
(E) A radius that bisects a chord is perpendicular to the chord.

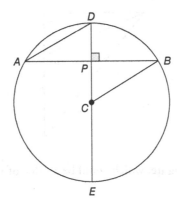

462. In the preceding figure, C is the center of the circle and $\overline{DE} \perp \overline{AB}$. For which of the following problems is there sufficient information to solve for the unknown quantity? Indicate *all* such problems.

(A) $CE = 15$, $AB = 24$, $AD = ?$
(B) $AD = 9$, $CB = ?$
(C) $AP = 5$, $AB = ?$
(D) $CB = 13$, $CP = 5$, $AB = ?$
(E) $CE = 16$, $CP = 8$, $m\angle A = ?$

463. Which pair of the following points determines horizontal lines? Indicate *all* such pairs.

(A) $(0,6)$ and $(3,0)$
(B) $(5,7)$ and $(-4,7)$
(C) $(0,-5)$ and $(4,-5)$
(D) $(0,0)$ and $(0,8)$
(E) (a,b) and (c,b)

464. Which pair of the following points determines vertical lines? Indicate *all* such pairs.

(A) $(0,6)$ and $(0,-5)$
(B) $(6,8)$ and $(-4,6)$
(C) $(3,-5)$ and $(4,-5)$
(D) $(2,4)$ and $(2,8)$
(E) (a,b) and $(-a,c)$

465. For the preceding figure, which could be a value of x? Indicate *all* such values.

(A) 10
(B) 15
(C) 20
(D) 25
(E) 30

466. A bike rider leaves camp and travels 4 miles to a river, then rides 5 miles. At this point, the rider is x miles from camp. Which of the following is a possible value for x? Indicate *all* such values.

(A) 1
(B) 4
(C) 5
(D) 9
(E) 14

467. Two sides of a triangle have measures 10 and 15. Which could be the area of the triangle? Indicate *all* that apply.

(A) 90
(B) 85
(C) 75
(D) 60
(E) 50

468. In triangle ABC, the measure of angle A is three times the measure of angle B. The sum of the measures of the two angles is 120°. Which of the following statements must be true? Indicate *all* such statements.

(A) Triangle ABC is obtuse.
(B) Triangle ABC is acute.
(C) Triangle ABC is a right triangle.
(D) Angles A and B are complementary.
(E) BC is twice the length of AC.

469. Which of the following number of ways of selecting r objects from a set of n distinct objects, without regard to order, are equal? Select *two* that are equal.

(A) Selecting 1 object from a set of 6 objects.
(B) Selecting 6 objects from a set of 6 objects.
(C) Selecting 1 object from a set of 5 objects.
(D) Selecting 5 objects from a set of 5 objects.

470. Which of the given probabilities equals $\dfrac{3}{8}$? Select *all* that apply.

(A) The probability of randomly selecting a multiple of 3 from the set $\{4,6,9,11,13,18,20,22\}$
(B) The probability of randomly selecting the letter t from the letters in the word *statistic*.
(C) The probability of randomly drawing a red marble from a bag containing three red marbles, two black marbles, and six white marbles, all identical except for color.
(D) The probability of getting exactly two heads on three tosses of a fair coin.
(E) The probability of randomly selecting a prime or an even number from the set $\{2,9,11,15,18,21,27,35\}$.

471. Students in a finance course take four 100-point exams. Students A, B, C, D, and E have taken three of the four exams. For which student is it possible to obtain an average exam score of 85. Indicate *all* such students.

(A) Student A, who has scores of 79, 80, and 81 on three of the four exams.
(B) Student B, who has scores of 65, 80, and 100 on three of the four exams.
(C) Student C, who has scores of 75, 80, and 80 on three of the four exams.
(D) Student D, who has scores of 90, 80, and 76 on three of the four exams.
(E) Student E, who has scores of 60, 99, and 75 on three of the four exams.

472. For which of the given data will the mean, median, and mode all be equal? Indicate *all* that apply.

(A) 5, 1, 2, 1, 1
(B) 8, 5, 1, 9, 2, 5
(C) $-6, -9, -2, -10, -3, -6$
(D) 5, 1, 2, 7, 3
(E) 50, 50, 50, 50, 50

473. Which of the given data have standard deviations of 0? Indicate *all* that apply.
    (A) 50, 50, 50, 50, 50
    (B) 48, 48, 50, 52, 52
    (C) −100,0,50,100,150
    (D) 0,0,50,100,100
    (E) −50,−50,−50,−50,−50

474. Which of the given data have more than one mode? Indicate *all* that apply.
    (A) 4, 5, 4, 5, 4, 6
    (B) 1, 3, 5, 7, 1, 2, 5
    (C) −6,−9,−2,−10,−3,−6
    (D) 5, 1, 2, 7, 5, 5, 5, 2, 2
    (E) 2,5,−2,1,11,4,8,−5

For Questions 475 to 480, use the following information.

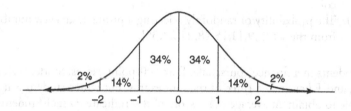

The figure shows approximate percentages for six regions of the standard normal distribution, with mean 0 and standard deviation 1.

475. Scores on an assessment are normally distributed with a mean of 138 and standard deviation 5. Which of the following scores will occur less than 2% of the time? Indicate *all* such scores.
    (A) 120
    (B) 125
    (C) 130
    (D) 140
    (E) 145
    (F) 150

476. IQ scores for adults are normally distributed with mean 100 and standard deviation 15. Which of the following scores is within one standard deviation of the mean? Indicate *all* such scores.

(A) 80
(B) 86
(C) 99
(D) 105
(E) 120
(F) 145

477. The weights of newborn baby boys born at a metropolitan hospital are normally distributed with mean 118 ounces and standard deviation 9.5 ounces. Which of the following weights (in ounces) would fall below the first quartile? Indicate *all* such weights.

(A) 115
(B) 109
(C) 101
(D) 95
(E) 90

478. A plumbing company has determined that the length of time, in minutes, for installing a bathtub is normally distributed with mean 160 minutes and standard deviation 25 minutes. Which of the following times (in minutes) would fall above the 98th percentile? Indicate *all* such times.

(A) 145
(B) 175
(C) 200
(D) 215
(E) 225

479. A standardized test was administered to 10,000 students. Suppose the scores are approximately normally distributed with a mean of 430 and standard deviation of 108. If Josh scored at the 90th percentile, which of the following statements could be false? Indicate *all* such statements.

(A) Josh answered 90% of the questions on the test correctly.
(B) Josh answered 90 questions on the test correctly.
(C) Of the students who took the test, about 9000 had the same score as Josh.
(D) Of the students who took the test, about 1000 scored higher than Josh.
(E) Of the students who took the test, about 90% scored lower than Josh.

480. For a set of normally distributed data, the 50th percentile is 45. Which of the following statements must be true? Indicate *all* such statements.

(A) 50% of the scores equal 45.
(B) Half of the scores are greater than 45.
(C) The median is 45.
(D) The mode is greater than the median.
(E) The mean is 45.

Questions 481 and 482 are based on information in the following pictograph.

Weekly T-Shirt Sales (Key: $ = \$20$; ⌇ = \$10$)

Week 1	$$$
Week 2	$$$$$$⌇
Week 3	$$$$$
Week 4	$$$$$$$$
Week 5	$$$$$⌇
Week 6	$$$$$

481. In which week are sales over \$120? Indicate *all* such weeks.

(A) Week 1
(B) Week 2
(C) Week 3
(D) Week 4
(E) Week 5
(F) Week 6

482. In which week are sales under \$100? Indicate *all* such weeks.

(A) Week 1
(B) Week 2
(C) Week 3
(D) Week 4
(E) Week 5
(F) Week 6

Questions 483 and 484 are based on the data in the following table.

Life expectancy at birth in the United States, 2000–2009, all races

Year	Both sexes	Male	Female
2000	76.8	74.1	79.3
2001	76.9	74.2	79.4
2002	76.9	74.3	79.5
2003	77.1	74.5	79.6
2004	77.5	74.9	79.9
2005	77.4	74.9	79.9
2006	77.7	75.1	80.2
2007	77.9	75.4	80.4
2008	78.1	75.6	80.6
2009	78.5	76.0	80.9

Source: US National Center for Health Statistics, 2011

483. Based on the information in the graph, which of the following statements must be true? Indicate *all* such statements.
   (A) Between 2000 and 2009, life expectancy at birth increased 1.9 years for males.
   (B) Between 2000 and 2009, life expectancy at birth increased 1.6 years for females.
   (C) Between 2000 and 2009, life expectancy at birth has increased every year for both sexes.
   (D) From 2000 to 2009, the gap in life expectancy at birth between males and females has widened.
   (E) In general, women have higher life expectancy at birth than do men.

484. Between which two consecutive years did the gap in life expectancy at birth between males and females decrease by 0.1? Indicate *all* such years.
   (A) 2000 and 2001
   (B) 2001 and 2002
   (C) 2002 and 2003
   (D) 2003 and 2004
   (E) 2004 and 2005
   (F) 2005 and 2006
   (G) 2006 and 2007
   (H) 2007 and 2008
   (I) 2008 and 2009

Questions 485 and 486 are based on the data in the following bar graphs.

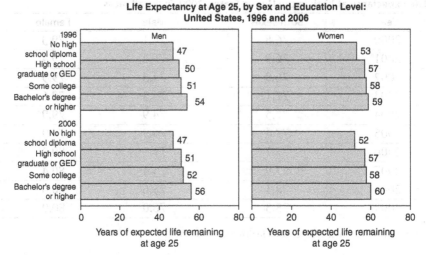

Source: US National Center for Health Statistics, 2011

485. Based on the information in the graphs, which of the following statements must be true? Indicate *all* such statements.

(A) For men, life expectancy at age 25 goes up as educational level decreases.

(B) For women, life expectancy at age 25 goes up as educational level increases.

(C) At age 25, men with bachelor's degrees or higher have greater life expectancy than women with bachelor's degrees or higher.

(D) In 1996, at age 25 women with no high school diploma could expect to live, on average, 6 years less than those with a bachelor's degree or higher.

(E) In 2006, at age 25 men with a bachelor's degree or higher could expect to live, on average, 7 years longer than those with no high school diploma.

(F) From 1996 to 2006, the gap in life expectancy at age 25 between those with a bachelor's degree or higher and those with no diploma widened by the same amount for both men and women.

486. From 1996 to 2006, at which of the following educational levels did life expectancy at age 25 increase for both men and women? Indicate all such educational levels.

(A) No high school diploma
(B) High school graduate or GED
(C) Some college
(D) Bachelor's degree or higher

Questions 487 to 489 are based on the data in the following table.

Comparison of Second Quarter (2Q), Ending June 2013, to 2Q, 2012, for Four Companies

Company	Net revenue, in billions of dollars		Net income, in millions of dollars		Number of full-time employees	
	2Q, 2013	2Q, 2012	2Q, 2013	2Q, 2012	2Q, 2013	2Q, 2012
A	$1.50	$1.40	$160	$130	12,300	11,700
B	$1.25	$1.20	$105	$100	11,400	10,200
C	$1.70	$1.60	$155	$140	15,300	16,700
D	$1.20	$1.10	$130	$120	13,200	11,900

487. From 2Q, 2012, to 2Q, 2013, which company increased net revenue by less than 7%? Indicate *all* such companies.

(A) Company A
(B) Company B
(C) Company C
(D) Company D

488. From 2Q, 2012, to 2Q, 2013, which company saw profit (net income) rise more than 10%? Indicate *all* such companies.

(A) Company A
(B) Company B
(C) Company C
(D) Company D

489. From 2Q, 2012, to 2Q, 2013, for which company did the number of full-time employees increase by at least 1000? Indicate *all* such companies.

(A) Company A
(B) Company B
(C) Company C
(D) Company D

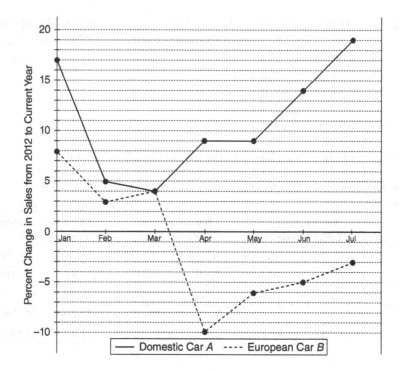

490. According to the graph shown, in which month was the monthly difference in percent change in sales from 2012 to the current year between the two cars greater than 15%? Indicate *all* such months.

(A) January
(B) February
(C) March
(D) April
(E) May
(F) June
(G) July

491. A survey of 500 middle-school students revealed the students surveyed receive a median weekly allowance of $8.55, and 25 percent of the students receive no allowance at all. Which of the following statements is a definite conclusion from the information provided? Indicate *all* such statements.

(A) Two hundred fifty of the students receive an allowance of $8.55 or less.
(B) The mean allowance for the 500 students is $8.55.
(C) The mean allowance for the 500 students is less than $8.55.
(D) The mean allowance for the 500 students is greater than $8.55.
(E) One hundred twenty-five students receive no allowance at all.

492. Josiah has exam grades of 75, 88, 67, 56, and 93 in his biology class and exam grades of 75, 78, 83, 83, 81, and 77 in his history class. Which of the following statements about Josiah's exam grades in the two classes is correct? Indicate *all* that apply.

(A) The grades in the biology class have greater variability.

(B) The grades in the history class have greater variability.

(C) The mean in the biology class is higher than the mean in the history class.

(D) The means in the two classes are equal.

(E) The median in the biology class is less than the median in the history class.

(F) The medians in the two classes are equal.

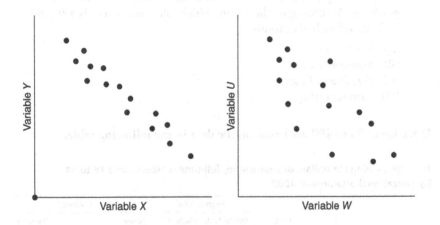

493. Which statement is an appropriate interpretation of the data shown in the preceding scatterplots? Indicate *all* that apply.

(A) The association between variables X and Y is stronger than the association between variables W and U.

(B) The association between variables X and Y is linear.

(C) The association between variables W and U is quadratic.

(D) The association between variables X and Y is negative.

(E) The association between variables X and Y is positive.

(F) The association between variables W and U is positive.

45%
US Stocks

30%
Foreign Stocks

20%
Bonds
and Cash

5%
Commodities

494. The preceding graph shows the allocations of $200,000 in an investment portfolio. According to the graph, which allocation exceeds $40,000? Indicate *all* such allocations.

(A) US Stocks
(B) Foreign Stocks
(C) Bonds and Cash
(D) Commodities

Questions 495 to 498 are based on the data in the following table.

Average earnings in dollars of year-round, full-time workers, ages 18 to 64, by educational attainment: 2009

Sex and age	All workers	Less than 9th grade	High school			College		
			9th to 12th grade (no diploma)	High school graduate[1]	Some college, no degree	Associate degree	Bachelor's degree or more
Male, total	62,445	26,604	33,194	43,140	52,580	55,631	92,815
18 to 24 years old	29,599	20,041	19,556	27,822	29,564	33,915	42,299
25 to 34 years old	49,105	25,067	27,074	38,037	44,020	48,313	67,555
35 to 44 years old	66,788	26,685	39,949	43,518	55,686	58,689	98,045
45 to 54 years old	71,661	28,067	36,239	48,224	61,072	62,000	109,163
55 to 64 years old	71,222	29,648	36,837	47,164	60,230	58,176	99,572
Female, total	44,857	19,588	23,478	32,227	36,553	42,307	62,198
18 to 24 years old	24,117	(B)	16,921	22,620	21,127	26,922	32,103
25 to 34 years old	40,475	18,278	21,996	27,993	32,229	36,202	52,102
35 to 44 years old	47,260	19,963	24,218	32,947	38,057	42,092	65,881
45 to 54 years old	48,929	19,591	23,987	34,145	42,068	47,716	69,698
55 to 64 years old	48,232	20,469	26,729	34,900	41,707	45,938	67,663

(B) Base figure too small to meet statistical standards for reliability of derived figure.
[1]Includes equivalency.
Source: US Census Bureau, 2010

495. Based on the information in the table, which of the following statements must be true? Indicate *all* such statements.

(A) For male workers, average earnings go up as educational attainment increases.

(B) For female workers, average earnings go up as educational attainment increases.

(C) For male workers, average earnings go up as age increases.

(D) For female workers, average earnings go up as age increases.

(E) Generally, workers who have some college, even without having earned a degree, have average earnings greater than that of workers with no college experience.

496. For all workers, in which of the following age groups is average earnings of female workers less than 72% of the average earnings of male workers? Indicate *all* such age groups.

(A) 18 to 24 years old

(B) 25 to 34 years old

(C) 35 to 44 years old

(D) 45 to 54 years old

(E) 55 to 64 years old

497. For male workers, in which of the following age groups is average earnings of workers with at least a bachelor's degree more than $50,000 greater than the average earnings of workers who are high school graduates only? Indicate *all* such age groups.

(A) 18 to 24 years old

(B) 25 to 34 years old

(C) 35 to 44 years old

(D) 45 to 54 years old

(E) 55 to 64 years old

498. For female workers, in which of the following age groups is average earnings of workers with at least a bachelor's degree more than $30,000 greater than the average earnings of workers who are high school graduates only? Indicate *all* such age groups.

(A) 18 to 24 years old

(B) 25 to 34 years old

(C) 35 to 44 years old

(D) 45 to 54 years old

(E) 55 to 64 years old

Questions 499 to 500 are based on the data in the following stacked bar graph.

Responses by gender of 750 middle-school children to the question "Are you in favor of school uniforms for your school?"

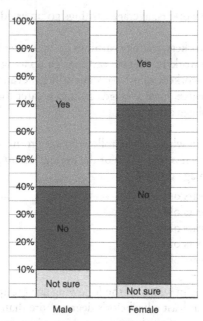

499. Based on the information in the graph, which of the following statements must be true? Indicate *all* such statements.

   (A) Sixty percent of male students are in favor of school uniforms.
   (B) The number of male students opposed to school uniforms is the same as the number of female students in favor of school uniforms.
   (C) Ninety percent of the students surveyed are in favor of school uniforms.
   (D) The percent of female students opposed to school uniforms is 35% more than the percent of male students opposed to school uniforms.
   (E) The number of female students opposed to school uniforms is greater than the number of male students opposed to school uniforms.

500. Of the 750 students surveyed, 350 were boys and 400 girls. In which of the following segments does the number of students exceed 200? Indicate *all* such segments.

   (A) Male, Not sure
   (B) Male, No
   (C) Male, Yes
   (D) Female, Not sure
   (E) Female, No
   (F) Female, Yes

Chapter 1: Quantitative Comparison Questions

Tip: For quantitative comparison questions, when both Quantity A and Quantity B are strictly numerical (containing no variable), (D) is NOT the correct answer.

1. (C) Eliminate (D) because only numbers are involved. Factor $(51)^{23}$ from Quantity A and then simplify. Quantity A equals $\frac{1}{3}(51)^{24} = \frac{1}{3}(51)(51)^{23} = 17(51)^{23}$. The two quantities are equal.

2. (B) Eliminate (D) because only numbers are involved. Calculate the unit price for each. Quantity A has unit price $\frac{\$0.80}{16 \text{ oz}} = \$0.05$. Quantity B has unit price $\frac{\$2.16}{36 \text{ oz}} = \$0.06$. Quantity B is greater.

3. (A) Use the calculator to perform the division. To obtain the remainder, multiply the divisor by the whole number part of the answer, and then subtract the result from the dividend. Quantity A: $(145 \div 17 = 8.52..., 17 \times 8 = 136)$ implies remainder $= 145 - 136 = 9$. Quantity B: $(145 \div 11 = 13.18..., 11 \times 13 = 143)$ implies remainder $= 145 - 143 = 2$. Quantity A is greater.

4. (D) Substitute values for n. If $n = 4$, Quantity A is $\frac{n}{2} = \frac{4}{2} = 2$, and Quantity B is $\sqrt{n} = \sqrt{4} = 2$. In this case, the two quantities are equal. If $n = 9$, Quantity A is $\frac{n}{2} = \frac{9}{2} = 4.5$, and Quantity B is $\sqrt{n} = \sqrt{9} = 3$. In this case, Quantity A is greater. Because you found different results (one when the quantities were equal and one when Quantity A was greater), the relationship cannot be determined from the information given.

5. (A) Eliminate (D) because only numbers are involved. Factor each number completely into distinct primes using exponential notation. Then for each number, using only its exponents, add 1 to each exponent and multiply the results. This gives you the number of positive divisors for the number. The number $144 = 2^4 \cdot 3^2$. Thus, 144 has $(4+1)(2+1) = 5 \cdot 3 = 15$ positive divisors (Quantity A). The number $108 = 2^2 \cdot 3^3$. Thus, 108 has $(2+1)(3+1) = 3 \cdot 4 = 12$ positive divisors (Quantity B). Quantity A is greater.

6. (A) Suri and Michael spent $\$1500 + \$5000 = \$6500$ buying and restoring the car. They sold the car for $250\%(6500) = 2.5(6500) = \$16,250$ (Quantity A). Quantity A is greater.

7. (D) Let $x =$ the number of pens bought and $y =$ the number of notebooks bought. Then $\$2x + \$3y = \$25$. This is a single equation with two unknowns. Without additional information (such as the value of $x + y$), exact values for x and y cannot be determined. Thus, the relationship cannot be determined from the information given.

8. (B) Eliminate (D) because only numbers are involved. Quantity A equals $\sqrt{16+9} = \sqrt{25} = 5$. *Tip:* The square root symbol is a grouping symbol, so add before determining the square root. Quantity B equals $\sqrt{16} + \sqrt{9} = 4+3 = 7$. *Tip:* Perform square roots before addition when there is no grouping indicated. Quantity B is greater.

9. (B) Multiples of 2 are 2, 4, 6, 8, 10, ... Multiples of 5 are 5, 10, 15, 20, 25, ... The common multiples of 2 and 5 are multiples of 10. Every fifth multiple of 2 is a multiple of 10, so Quantity A is $\frac{1}{5}$. Every even multiple of 5 is a multiple of 10, so Quantity B is $\frac{1}{2}$. Quantity B is greater.

10. (C) $2a^3 = 10b^2$ implies $a^3 = 5b^2$. $a,b \in \{1,2,3,4,5,6,7,8,9\}$. From the possible values for a and b, only $a=b=5$ satisfies $a^3 = 5b^2$. The two quantities are equal. Select (C).

11. (A) $xy > 0$ and $yz < 0$ implies $yz < 0 < xy$. If $y > 0$, then $yz < 0 < xy$ implies $z < 0 < x$. Thus, x and z have opposite signs, so $xz < 0$. In this case, Quantity A is greater. If $y < 0$, then $yz < 0 < xy$ implies $z > 0 > x$. Thus, x and z have opposite signs, so $xz < 0$. In this case, Quantity A is greater. Therefore, in either case, Quantity A is greater.

12. (D) Substitute values for n, which is a positive integer. If $n = 1$, Quantity A is $5^n = 5^1 = 5$, and Quantity B is $3^{n+1} = 3^{1+1} = 3^2 = 9$. In this case, Quantity B is greater. If $n = 4$, Quantity A is $5^n = 5^4 = 625$, and Quantity B is $3^{n+1} = 3^{4+1} = 3^5 = 243$. In this case, Quantity A is greater. Because you found different results (one when Quantity B was greater and one when Quantity A was greater), the relationship cannot be determined from the information given.

13. (A) Eliminate (D) because only numbers are involved. The greatest common divisor (gcd) of two numbers (also called the greatest common factor, or gcf) is the largest factor they have in common. The greatest common divisor of 14 ($= 2 \cdot 7$) and 56 ($= 2^3 \cdot 7$) is $2 \cdot 7 = 14$ (Quantity A). The greatest common divisor of 28 ($= 2^2 \cdot 7$) and 72 ($= 2^3 \cdot 3^2$) is $2^2 = 4$ (Quantity B). Quantity A is greater.

14. (C) Eliminate (D) because only numbers are involved. Quantity A is $\dfrac{5^{10} - 5^8}{24} = \dfrac{5^8(5^2 - 1)}{24} = \dfrac{5^8(25-1)}{24} = \dfrac{5^8(24)}{24} = 5^8$. The two quantities are equal. Select (C).

15. (B) The lcm(12,30) is the least common multiple of 12 and 30; that is, the least product that is a multiple of both 12 and 30. A quick way to find the lcm of two integers is to multiply them and then divide the product by their greatest common divisor (gcd). Thus, Quantity A is $\text{lcm}(12,30) = \dfrac{12 \cdot 30}{\text{gcf}(12,30)} = \dfrac{360}{6} = 60$. Quantity B is greater. Select (B).

16. (D) $m = -4,-3,-2,-1$ and $n = 1, 2, 3, 4$. If $m = -4$ and $n = 1$, then Quantity A is $|m| = |-4| = 4$ and Quantity B is $|n| = |1| = 1$. In this case, Quantity A is greater. If $m = -1$ and $n = 4$, then Quantity A is $|m| = |-1| = 1$ and Quantity B is $|n| = |4| = 4$. In this case, Quantity B is greater. Because you found different results (one when Quantity A was greater and one when Quantity B was greater), the relationship cannot be determined from the information given.

17. (D) The common denominator for 10, 11, and 12 is 660. So, $\dfrac{10}{11}=\dfrac{600}{660}$ and $\dfrac{9}{10}<\dfrac{a}{b}<\dfrac{11}{12}$ implies $\dfrac{594}{660}<\dfrac{a}{b}<\dfrac{605}{660}$. Thus, you can pick any fraction between $\dfrac{594}{660}$ and $\dfrac{605}{660}$ as the value for Quantity A, which is $\dfrac{a}{b}$. If Quantity A $=\dfrac{595}{660}<\dfrac{600}{660}=\dfrac{10}{11}$, then Quantity B is greater. If Quantity A $=\dfrac{601}{660}>\dfrac{600}{660}=\dfrac{10}{11}$, then Quantity A is greater. Because you found different results (one when Quantity A was greater and one when Quantity B was greater), the relationship cannot be determined from the information given.

18. (B) The middle integer of three consecutive integers is their sum divided by 3. Thus, the middle integer is $\dfrac{-51}{3}=-17$. Hence, the three consecutive integers are $-18,-17$, and -16. Quantity A is the least of the three integers, -18. Quantity B is greater.

19. (C) $120\%x=96$ implies $x=\dfrac{96}{120\%}=\dfrac{96}{1.2}=80$ (Quantity A). The two quantities are equal.

20. (D) Substitute values for x. If $x=2$, Quantity A is $x^{10}=2^{10}$ and Quantity B is $(x^{10})^6=(2^{10})^6=2^{60}$. In this case, Quantity B is greater. If $x=\dfrac{1}{2}$, Quantity A is $\left(\dfrac{1}{2}\right)^{10}=\dfrac{1}{2^{10}}$ and Quantity B is $\left(\left(\dfrac{1}{2}\right)^{10}\right)^6=\left(\dfrac{1}{2}\right)^{60}=\dfrac{1}{2^{60}}$. In this case, Quantity B is greater. Because you found different results (one when Quantity A was greater and one when Quantity B was greater), the relationship cannot be determined from the information given.

21. (A) Eliminate (D) because only numbers are involved. The number 68 is $2^2\cdot17$, so its greatest prime factor is 17 (Quantity A). The number 65 is $5\cdot13$, so its greatest prime factor is 13 (Quantity B). Quantity A is greater. Select (A).

22. (A) Quantity A, the ratio of milk to flour, equals $\dfrac{1\frac{1}{2}}{1\frac{3}{4}}=\dfrac{1.5}{1.75}\approx0.857$. Quantity A is greater. Select (A). *Tip:* Knowing the decimal equivalents of common fractions such as $\dfrac{1}{2}=0.5$ and $\dfrac{3}{4}=0.75$ is helpful.

23. (B) Express x, y, and z as x, $x+2$, and $x+4$, respectively. Quantity A is $2(y+z)-6=2((x+2)+(x+4))-6=2(2x+6)-6=4x+12-6=4x+6$. Quantity B is $2(x+y)+6=2(x+(x+2))+6=2(2x+2)+6=4x+4+6=4x+10$. Quantity B is greater.

24. (A) Eliminate (D) because only numbers are involved. Quantity A is $(3+\sqrt5)(3+\sqrt5)=9+3\sqrt5+3\sqrt5+(\sqrt5)^2=9+6\sqrt5+5=14+6\sqrt5>20$ (because $6\sqrt5>6$). Quantity A is greater.

25. (B) Eliminate (D) because only numbers are involved. The sum of the whole numbers from 1 to n is $\frac{n(n+1)}{2}$. Thus, Quantity A is $\frac{50 \cdot 51}{2} = 1275$. Quantity B is greater.

Tip: Another way to work this problem is to list the sum of the numbers from 1 to 50 in two ways, one in increasing order and one in decreasing order, and then add the pairs of numbers as shown here.

$$1 + 2 + 3 + 4 + 5 + \cdots + 46 + 47 + 48 + 49 + 50$$
$$50 + 49 + 48 + 47 + 46 + \cdots + 5 + 4 + 3 + 2 + 1$$
$$51 + 51 + 51 + 51 + 51 + \cdots + 51 + 51 + 51 + 51 + 51$$

There are 50 pairs, each with a sum of 51. The double sum is $50(51) = 2550$, so the single sum is $2550 \div 2 = 1275$.

26. (C) Because $3 = 4 \cdot 0 + 3$, the least positive number that will leave a remainder of 3 when divided by 4 is 3 (Quantity A). Because $3 = 5 \cdot 0 + 3$, the least positive number that will leave a remainder of 3 when divided by 5 is 3 (Quantity B). The two quantities are equal.

27. (B) Let $x =$ the number of \$5 bills and $y =$ the number of \$10 bills. You have two equations: (1) $x + y = 8$, $y = 8 - x$; and (2) $\$5x + \$10y = \$50$. Substitute (1) $y = 8 - x$ into (2) and solve for x (omitting units for convenience).

$$5x + 10y = 50$$
$$5x + 10(8 - x) = 50$$
$$5x + 80 - 10x = 50$$
$$30 = 5x$$
$$x = 6 \text{ (Quantity B)}; \quad y = 8 - x = 8 - 6 = 2 \text{ (Quantity A)}$$

Quantity B is greater.

28. (D) Substitute values for n. If $n = 1$, Quantity A is $n + 2 = 1 + 2 = 3$, and Quantity B is $\frac{2n+1}{n} = \frac{2(1)+1}{1} = 3$. In this case, the two quantities are equal. If $n = 2$, Quantity A is $n + 2 = 2 + 2 = 4$, and Quantity B is $\frac{2n+1}{n} = \frac{2(2)+1}{2} = 2.5$. In this case, Quantity A is greater. Because you found different results (one when the quantities were equal and one when Quantity A was greater), the relationship cannot be determined from the information given.

29. (C) Eliminate (D) because only numbers are involved. Quantity A is $257_{\text{base }12} = 2 \cdot 12^2 + 5 \cdot 12 + 7 = 288 + 60 + 7 = 355$. Quantity B is $2410_{\text{base }5} = 2 \cdot 5^3 + 4 \cdot 5^2 + 1 \cdot 5 + 0 = 250 + 100 + 5 + 0 = 355$. The two quantities are equal.

30. (A) Quantity A is the number of cupcakes Zoe bought. Work backward from the information in the question. She had 2 left over. Adding the 1 she gave to her brother makes 3. Adding the 1 she ate on the way home makes 4, which is what she had after she gave half away. Multiplying by 2 gives 8, the number of cupcakes Zoe bought. Quantity A is greater.

31. (B) The smallest possible stacks are 1, 2, and 4. Hence, the exact number of blocks needed to make the smallest possible stacks is 7 (Quantity A). Quantity B is greater.

32. (A) Eliminate (D) because only numbers are involved. Quantity A is:

$$\frac{55 \text{ miles}}{1 \text{ hour}} \times \frac{5280 \text{ feet}}{1 \text{ mile}} \times \frac{1 \text{ hour}}{3600 \text{ seconds}} \approx 80.7 \text{ feet per second} > 80 \text{ feet per second (Quantity B)}.$$

Quantity A is greater.

33. (B) Let $x =$ the greater number and $y =$ the lesser number. Then (1) $x + y = 45$ and (2) $x - y = 23$. Adding the two equations yields $2x = 68$, $x = 34$ (Quantity B). Because $x = 34$, $x + y = 45$ implies $y = 11$, $3y = 33$ (Quantity A). Quantity B is greater.

34. (B) The simple interest formula is $I = PRT$, where I is the interest earned, P is the amount of the investment, R is the annual interest rate, and T is the time of the investment (in years). Let $x =$ the amount invested at 2%, annually. Make a chart to organize the information in the question.

P	R	T (in years)	I = PRT
x	2%	1	2%x(1)
$20,000	3%	1	3%($20,000)(1)
N/A	N/A	Total:	$900

Quantity B is $20,000. Determine Quantity A by using the information in the chart to set up an equation and solve for x (omitting units for convenience):

$$2\%x + 3\%(20,000) = 900$$

$$0.02x + 0.03(20,000) = 900$$

$$0.02x + 600 = 900$$

$$0.02x = 300$$

$$x = \$15,000 \text{ (Quantity A)}$$

Quantity B is greater.

35. (B) You can work this problem two ways.

Method 1: In a "work" problem, it is usually necessary to determine the rate at which someone or something does a task or job. The rate equals the amount of work done divided by the total time worked. Let $t =$ the time (in hours) it will take Willard and Jada, working together, to paint the room. Make a chart to organize the information in the question.

Worker	Rate	Time (in hours)	Amount of work (in rooms)
Willard	$\frac{1 \text{ room}}{6 \text{ hr.}} = \frac{1}{6}$ room/hr.	t	$\frac{1}{6}t$
Jada	$\frac{1 \text{ room}}{4 \text{ hr.}} = \frac{1}{4}$ room/hr.	t	$\frac{1}{4}t$
N/A	N/A	Total:	1

Using the information in the chart, set up an equation and solve for t:

$$\frac{1}{6}t + \frac{1}{4}t = 1$$

$$\frac{2}{12}t + \frac{3}{12}t = 1$$

$$\frac{5}{12}t = 1$$

$$\frac{\cancel{12}}{\cancel{5}} \cdot \frac{\cancel{5}}{\cancel{12}}t = 1 \cdot \frac{12}{5}$$

$$t = \frac{12}{5}$$

Thus, Quantity A $= \dfrac{12}{5}$ hours $= 2.4$ hours $< 2\dfrac{1}{2}$ hours (Quantity B).

Method 2: When you have *only two* workers, a handy shortcut for finding the time it will take the two of them to do a job, working together, is to divide the *product* of their times working alone by the *sum* of their times working alone. Thus, Quantity A $=$
$$\frac{(\text{Willard's time working alone})(\text{Jada's time working alone})}{(\text{Willard's time working alone}) + (\text{Jada's time working alone})} = \frac{(6)(4)}{6+4} = \frac{24}{10} = 2.4 \text{ hours} <$$
$2\dfrac{1}{2}$ hours (Quantity B).

36. **(D)** Substitute values for x. If $x = 0$, Quantity A is $\dfrac{x^3}{5} = \dfrac{0^3}{5} = 0$ and Quantity B is $\left(\dfrac{x}{5}\right)^3 = \left(\dfrac{0}{5}\right)^3 = 0$. In this case, the two quantities are equal. If $x = 2$, Quantity A is $\dfrac{x^3}{5} = \dfrac{2^3}{5} = \dfrac{8}{5}$ and Quantity B is $\left(\dfrac{x}{5}\right)^3 = \dfrac{x^3}{125} = \dfrac{2^3}{125} = \dfrac{8}{125}$. In this case, Quantity A is greater. Because you found different results (one when the two quantities were equal and one when Quantity A was greater), the relationship cannot be determined from the information given.

37. **(B)** Substitute values for x. If $x = -10$, Quantity A is $5x = 5(-10) = -50$, and Quantity B is $2x = 2(-10) = -20$. In this case, Quantity B is greater. If $x = -100$, Quantity A is $5x = 5(-100) = -500$, and Quantity B is $2x = 2(-100) = -200$. In this case, (again) Quantity B is greater. Clearly, substituting any value x, such that $x < -8$, will yield $2x > 5x$. Quantity B is greater.

38. **(A)** Let $x =$ length in feet of the shorter piece. Then $x + 14 =$ length in feet of the longer piece. Write an equation and solve for x:

$$x + x + 14 = 50$$
$$2x = 36 \qquad \text{(Quantity A)}$$
$$x = 18$$
$$x + 14 = 32 \qquad \text{(Quantity B)}$$

Quantity A is greater.

39. (D) Let $x =$ the number of home team fans and $y =$ the number of visiting team fans. Then, $x + y = 6000$. From the question information, you know that $20\%(6000) = 1200$ fans are from out of town, but you cannot assume that all of these fans are visiting team fans nor can you assume that all of the remaining 4800 fans are home team fans, so further information is needed to determine x (Quantity A) and y (Quantity B). Thus, the relationship cannot be determined from the information given.

40. (C) $\sqrt{4ab} = 12$ implies $4ab = 144$, $ab = 36$. You are given $a + b = 13$. Find two numbers whose product is 36 and sum is 13. The numbers are 4 and 9 (Quantity A). Quantity B is $2 \cdot 4 + 1 = 8 + 1 = 9$. The two quantities are equal.

41. (B) Quantity A is $f(g(-1)) = f(3) = -4$. Quantity B is $g(f(-1)) = g(2) = -3$. Quantity B is greater.

42. (A) Make a table of possible paired values for x and y.

x	1	2	3	4	5	6	7	8	9
y	9	8	7	6	5	4	3	2	1

Only one pair, $x = 6$ (Quantity A) and $y = 4$ (Quantity B), satisfies the double inequality, $37 < 5x + 2y < 41$. Quantity A is greater.

43. (C) The nth term of an arithmetic sequence can be written as $a_n = a_1 + (n-1)d$, where $n =$ the number of terms in the sequence and $d =$ the common difference. For the sequence given, $d = 7 - 2 = 5$. Write and solve the following equation.

$$247 = 2 + (n-1) \cdot 5$$
$$247 = 2 + 5n - 5$$
$$250 = 5n$$
$$n = 50 \text{ (Quantity A)}$$

The two quantities are equal.

44. (D) Let $n =$ the number of nickels, $d =$ the number of dimes, and $q =$ the number of quarters. Then, $n + d + q = 58$ and $\$0.05n + \$0.10d + \$0.25q = \$5.00$, which (because you have three unknowns and only two equations) does not yield unique values for n, d, and q. For instance, if $n = 25$, $d = 30$, and $q = 3$, $n + d + q = 25 + 30 + 3 = 58$ and $\$0.05n + \$0.10d + \$0.25q = \$0.05(25) + \$0.10(30) + \$0.25(3) = \$5.00$. Then Quantity A is $30 + 3 = 33$ and Quantity B is 25. In this case, Quantity A is greater. If $n = 40$, $d = 10$, and $q = 8$, $n + d + q = 40 + 10 + 8 = 58$ and $\$0.05n + \$0.10d + \$0.25q = \$0.05(40) + \$0.10(10) + \$0.25(8) = \$5.00$. Then Quantity A is $10 + 8 = 18$ and Quantity B is 40. In this case, Quantity B is greater. Because you found different results (one when Quantity A was greater and one when Quantity B was greater), the relationship cannot be determined from the information given.

45. (A) $y < z$ implies $\dfrac{1}{y} > \dfrac{1}{z}$, and, thus, $\dfrac{x}{y} > \dfrac{x}{z}$. $x > w$ implies $\dfrac{x}{z} > \dfrac{w}{z}$. Combining $\dfrac{x}{y} > \dfrac{x}{z}$ and $\dfrac{x}{z} > \dfrac{w}{z}$ gives $\dfrac{x}{y} > \dfrac{w}{z}$. Quantity A is greater.

46. (C) Let $c=$ the original cost, $m=$ the markup $=25\%c=0.25c$, and $s=c+25\%c=1.25c=$ the selling price. Then Quantity A is $\dfrac{m}{s}\cdot100\%=\dfrac{0.25}{1.25}\cdot100\%=0.20\cdot100\%=20\%$. The two quantities are equal.

47. (D) $(3^p)^p=81$ implies that $3^{p^2}=3^4$. Thus, $p^2=4$, $p=\pm2$. If $p=-2$, Quantity B is greater. If $p=2$, the two quantities are equal. Because you found different results (one when Quantity B was greater and one when the quantities were equal), the relationship cannot be determined from the information given.

48. (B) Substituting $x=-5$ into $x^2+x-k=5$ yields

$$(-5)^2+(-5)-k=5$$

$$25-5-k=5$$

$$-k=-15$$

$$k=15\ \text{(Quantity A)}$$

Quantity B is greater.

49. (C) Divide every term in $\dfrac{x+z}{x-z}$ by z to obtain $\dfrac{\frac{x}{z}+1}{\frac{x}{z}-1}$. Substitute $\dfrac{x}{z}=5$ to obtain $\dfrac{5+1}{5-1}=\dfrac{6}{4}=\dfrac{3}{2}$ (Quantity A). The two quantities are equal. Select (C).

50. (B) Let $x=$ the number in the group who have taken postgraduate courses and $y=$ the number in the group who have not taken postgraduate courses. From the question information, (1) $x+y=180$, $y=180-x$; and (2) $x=\dfrac{1}{5}y$. Substitute (1) $y=180-x$ into (2) and solve.

$$x=\frac{1}{5}y$$

$$x=\frac{1}{5}(180-x)$$

$$\frac{5}{1}\cdot x=\frac{\cancel{5}}{1}\cdot\frac{1}{\cancel{5}}(180-x)$$

$$5x=(180-x)$$

$$5x=180-x$$

$$6x=180$$

$$x=30\ \text{(Quantity A)}$$

Quantity B is greater.

51. (B) In a geometric sequence, you multiply by a common ratio, r, to get the next term. From the consecutive terms 8 and 16, $r = \dfrac{16}{8} = 2$. Using 2 as the common ratio, the terms are 2, 4, 8, 16, 32, 64, 128. Thus, the list includes 7 terms. Hence, Quantity B is 7. Quantity A is $a_1 + a_2 = 2 + 4 = 6$. Quantity B is greater. Select (B).

52. (A) Let $f =$ the number of female members in the club and $m =$ the number of male members in the club. The question information yields two equations: (1) $f + m = 56$ and (2) $\dfrac{m+4}{56+4} = \dfrac{5}{12}$. Solve (2) for m.

$$\frac{m+4}{56+4} = \frac{5}{12}$$

$$12(m+4) = 5(60)$$

$$12m + 48 = 300$$

$$12m = 252$$

$$m = 21$$

Substituting $m = 21$ into (1) gives $f + 21 = 56$, $f = 35$ (Quantity A). Quantity A is greater. Select (A). *Tip:* Be sure to read the question carefully. Quantity A is the number of female members in the club, not the number of male members.

53. (C) Quantity B is:

$$\frac{x^3 + x^2 + x + 1}{x+1} = \frac{x^2(x+1) + (x+1)}{x+1} = \frac{(x+1)(x^2+1)}{x+1} = x^2 + 1$$

The two quantities are equal.

54. (C) Let $s =$ the amount of money Sofía has and $z =$ the amount of money Zayn has. The question information yields two equations: (1) $s - \$5 = z + \$5$, $s - z = \$10$; and (2) $s + \$5 = 2(z - \$5)$, $s + \$5 = 2z - \$10$, $s - 2z = -\$15$, $-s + 2z = \$15$. Adding (1) $s - z = \$10$ and (2) $-s + 2z = \$15$ gives $z = \$25$. Thus, Zayn has $25. Then $s - z = \$10$ implies $s - \$25 = \$10$, $s = \$35$. So Sofía has $35 (Quantity A). Quantity B is $\$25 + \$10 = \$35$. The two quantities are equal.

55. (B) Substitute $t = 2s - 1$ into the first equation and solve for s.

$$4s + 3t = 27$$

$$4s + 3(2s - 1) = 27$$

$$4s + 6s - 3 = 27$$

$$10s = 30$$

$$s = 3 \text{ (Quantity A)}$$

$$t = 2s - 1 = 2(3) - 1 = 5 \text{ (Quantity B)}$$

Quantity B is greater.

56. (C) Let x = the lesser number and y = the greater number. The question information yields two equations: (1) $3x + y = 35$; and (2) $y - 5x = 75$, $5x - y = -75$. Adding (1) $3x + y = 35$ and (2) $5x - y = -75$ yields $8x = -40$, $x = -5$. Then $3x + y = 35$ implies $3(-5) + y = 35$, $-15 + y = 35$, $y = 50$. Quantity A is 10 percent of y, which is $10\%(50) = 5$. Quantity B is the absolute value of x, which is $|-5| = 5$. The two quantities are equal.

57. (D) Solve the equation.

$$2x^2 - 5x = -2$$
$$2x^2 - 5x + 2 = 0$$
$$(2x - 1)(x - 2) = 0$$
$$x = \frac{1}{2},\ 2$$

If $x = \frac{1}{2}$, then Quantity B is greater. If $x = 2$, then Quantity A is greater. Because you found different results (one when Quantity B was greater and one when Quantity A was greater), the relationship cannot be determined from the information given.

58. (C) The discriminant of a quadratic equation is $b^2 - 4ac$. Quantity A is $b^2 - 4ac = 1^2 - 4(1)(1) = -3$. Quantity B is $b^2 - 4ac = (-1)^2 - 4(1)(1) = -3$. The two quantities are equal.

59. (B) Solve the equation.

$$\frac{x+2}{2} = \frac{12}{x}$$
$$x(x+2) = 24$$
$$x^2 + 2x - 24 = 0$$
$$(x+6)(x-4) = 0$$
$$x = -6,\ 4$$

If $x = -6$, then Quantity B is greater. If $x = 4$, then (again) Quantity B is greater. Thus, Quantity B is greater.

60. (C) In a coordinate plane, the distance between points (x_1, y_1) and (x_2, y_2) is $d = \sqrt{(x_2 - x_1)^2 + (y_2 - y_1)^2}$. Quantity A is $\sqrt{(5-2)^2 + (7-3)^2} = \sqrt{3^2 + 4^2} = \sqrt{25} = 5$. Quantity B is $\sqrt{(1-(-2))^2 + (1-5)^2} = \sqrt{3^2 + (-4)^2} = \sqrt{25} = 5$. The two quantities are equal.

61. (B) In a coordinate plane, the midpoint between points (x_1, y_1) and (x_2, y_2) is $\left(\frac{x_1 + x_2}{2}, \frac{y_1 + y_2}{2}\right)$. Thus, $7 = \frac{a+6}{2}$, $a + 6 = 14$, $a = 8$ (Quantity A); and $7 = \frac{b+5}{2}$, $b + 5 = 14$, $b = 9$ (Quantity B). Quantity B is greater. Select (B).

62. (D) The slope between points (x_1, y_1) and (x_2, y_2) is $\frac{y_2 - y_1}{x_2 - x_1}$. The slope of the line through (x, y) and $(-5, 5)$ is $\frac{5 - y}{-5 - x}$. If $(x, y) = (0, 1)$, then Quantity A is $\frac{5 - y}{-5 - x} = \frac{5 - 1}{-5 - 0} = \frac{4}{-5} = -0.8$. In this case, Quantity B is greater. If $(x, y) = (1, 5)$, then Quantity A is $\frac{5 - y}{-5 - x} = \frac{5 - 5}{-5 - 1} = \frac{0}{-6} = 0$. In this case, the two quantities are equal. Because you found different results (one when Quantity B was greater and one when the quantities were equal), the relationship cannot be determined from the information given.

63. (A) Two lines that are perpendicular have slopes that are negative reciprocals of each other. The slope between points (x_1, y_1) and (x_2, y_2) is $\frac{y_2 - y_1}{x_2 - x_1}$. The slope between $(2, 3)$ and $(k, 4)$ is $\frac{4 - 3}{k - 2} = \frac{1}{k - 2}$. Rewrite $3x + y = 10$ in slope-intercept form as $y = -3x + 10$. Hence, the slope of the line with equation $3x + y = 10$ is -3, which has negative reciprocal $\frac{1}{3}$. Thus, $\frac{1}{k - 2} = \frac{1}{3}$, $k - 2 = 3$, $k = 5$. Quantity A is greater.

64. (C) Substitute $y = x^2 - x$ into $y = x - 1$ and solve.

$$x^2 - x = x - 1$$

$$x^2 - 2x + 1 = 0$$

$$(x - 1)^2 = 0$$

$$x = 1 \text{ (Quantity A)}$$

The two quantities are equal.

65. (B) In triangle KLM, $\overline{LM}$ is opposite the largest angle, so it is longer than $\overline{KM}$. Quantity B is greater.

66. (A) Let $AX = x =$ the width of the river. Right triangles AXY and ACB are similar because they have common angle A. Set up a proportion based on corresponding sides and solve.

$$\frac{x}{x + 30} = \frac{60}{80} = \frac{3}{4}$$

$$4x = 3(x + 30)$$

$$4x = 3x + 90$$

$$x = 90 \text{ (Quantity A)}$$

Quantity A is greater. *Tip:* Simplifying $\frac{60}{80}$ to lowest terms $\left(\frac{3}{4}\right)$ makes the calculations easier to do in this problem.

67. (D) Without additional information (such as lines m and n are parallel), the relationship cannot be determined from the information given. *Tip:* The lines m and n appear parallel, but the question does not state that is the case.

68. (C) Because angles b and c are supplementary, lines l and m are parallel. Therefore, $\angle a \cong \angle d$ (because corresponding angles of parallel lines are congruent) and their measures are equal. The two quantities are equal.

69. (A) The sides of the two triangles are in the ratio 3:1, so the areas of the two triangles are in the ratio $3^2 : 1^2 = 9:1$. Thus, the area of the larger triangle is $9 \times (25$ square inches$) = 225$ square inches. Quantity A is greater.

70. (A) $m\angle ACB = 180° - 65° - 70° = 45°$ and $m\angle DCA = 60° + 45° = 105°$. The measure of an exterior angle of a triangle equals the sum of the measures of the remote interior angles. Thus, $m\angle DCA = 105° = 30° + m\angle E$. Hence, $m\angle E = 105° - 30° = 75°$. $m\angle B = 70°$. Thus, $m\angle B < m\angle E$. Quantity A is greater.

71. (D) $\angle A$ is a common angle in the two right triangles ABC and ADE. Thus, the two triangles are similar (because corresponding angles are congruent). However, without further information, you cannot determine AD. Therefore, the relationship cannot be determined from the information given.

72. (C) Sketch a figure.

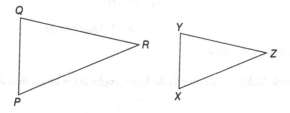

In the two triangles, two pairs of corresponding sides are proportional, and the included angles are congruent. Therefore, the triangles are similar. $m\angle R$ equals $m\angle Z$ (because corresponding angles of similar triangles are congruent). The two quantities are equal.

73. (D) Let $l =$ the length and $w =$ the width of the rectangular region. Then, its area $= lw = 24$ and its perimeter $= 2(l+w)$. If $l = 24$ and $w = 1$, then $lw = 24 \cdot 1 = 24$ and perimeter $= 2(l+w) = 2(24+1) = 50$. In this case, Quantity A is greater. If $l = 12$ and $w = 2$, then $lw = 12 \cdot 2 = 24$ and perimeter $= 2(l+w) = 2(12+2) = 28$. In this case, Quantity B is greater. Because you found different results (one when Quantity A was greater and one when Quantity B was greater), the relationship cannot be determined from the information given.

74. (B) Make a sketch.

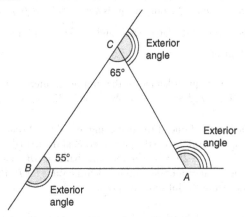

The exterior angle at B measures $180° - 55° = 125°$. The exterior angle at C measures $180° - 65° = 115°$. The exterior angle at A measures $55° + 65° = 120°$ (the measure of an exterior angle of a triangle equals the sum of the measures of the remote interior angles). Therefore, for all possible exterior angles, Quantity B is greater.

75. (C) Sketch a figure, labeling the vertices.

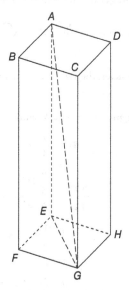

The greatest possible distance is the length of a diagonal across the center of the box. Without loss of generality, you can designate $\overline{AG}$ as this diagonal. $\overline{AG}$ is the hypotenuse of a right triangle with legs $AE = 12$ and EG, where $\overline{EG}$ is the hypotenuse of a right triangle with legs $EF = 3$ and $FG = 4$. Thus, $EG = \sqrt{3^2 + 4^2} = \sqrt{25} = 5$. Then, $AG = \sqrt{12^2 + 5^2} = \sqrt{169} = 13$. The two quantities are equal.

76. (A) Quantity A, the area of the shaded region, is the area of the larger circle minus the area of the smaller circle. Thus, Quantity A equals $\pi R^2 - \pi r^2 = \pi(6^2) - \pi(4^2) \approx 62.8$, where $R = \frac{1}{2}(12) = 6$ is the radius of the larger circle and $r = \frac{1}{2}(8) = 4$ is the radius of the smaller circle. Quantity A is greater.

77. (B) $JKLM$ is a convex quadrilateral, so the sum of its interior angles is $(n-2)180° = (4-2)180° = 360°$. Thus, $m\angle J + m\angle K + m\angle M = 360° - 30° = 330°$. Quantity B is greater.

78. (D) Let $x =$ the length of one of the two congruent sides of triangle ABC and $y =$ the length of the noncongruent side. Then the perimeter, P, of the triangle is $P = 2x + y$. If $AB = x$ and $BC = y$, then $P = 2 \cdot 15 + 20 = 50$. On the other hand, if $AB = y$ and $BC = x$, then $P = 2 \cdot 20 + 15 = 55$. Hence, you cannot determine a definite value for P. Thus, the relationship cannot be determined from the information given.

79. (C) Triangle XYZ is a right triangle. Using the question information, write and solve the following equation.

$$y(y+7) = 120$$
$$y^2 + 7y - 120 = 0$$
$$(y+15)(y-8) = 0$$
$$y = -15 \text{ (Reject because length is nonnegative); } y = 8, \; y + 7 = 15$$

Using the Pythagorean theorem, $z = \sqrt{8^2 + 15^2} = \sqrt{289} = 17$ (Quantity A). The two quantities are equal.

80. (B) Let $d =$ the sphere's diameter, then $d = 2r$, where r is its radius. Set up the following equality and solve for r.

$$\text{Surface area of sphere} = \text{Volume of sphere}$$
$$4\pi r^2 = \frac{4}{3}\pi r^3$$
$$\frac{4\pi r^2}{4\pi r^2} = \frac{\frac{4}{3}\pi r^3}{4\pi r^2}$$
$$1 = \frac{1}{3}r$$
$$3 = r$$
$$d = 2r = 6 \text{ (Quantity A)}$$

Quantity B is $2\pi \approx 2(3.14) = 6.28$. Quantity B is greater.

81. (A) Let $h =$ the height of the shorter jar, then $2h =$ the height of the taller jar. Let $r =$ the radius of the taller jar, then $2r =$ the radius of the shorter jar (the relationship between the radii is the same as that between the diameters). Quantity A is the capacity of the shorter jar $= \pi(2r)^2(h) = 4\pi r^2 h$. Quantity B is the capacity of the taller jar $= \pi(r^2)(2h) = 2\pi r^2 h$. Quantity A is greater.

82. (B) The degree measure of a semicircle is $180°$. Hence, $m\angle ACE + m\angle DCE = (x° + 90°) + (2x°) = 180°$, $3x° + 90° = 180°$, $3x° = 90°$, $x° = 30°$. Then, $m\angle ACB = 180° - (3x° + 10°) = 180° - (3 \cdot 30° + 10°) = 180° - (90° + 10°) = 80°$. The degree measure of an arc equals the measure of the central angle that intercepts the arc. Thus, the degree measure of minor arc $AB = 80°$. Quantity B is greater. *Tip:* Two points lying on a circle define two arcs. The shorter is the *minor arc* and the longer one is the *major arc*. In the figure for this question, $\overset{\frown}{AB}$ could mean either one, so the question specifies that $\overset{\frown}{AB}$ refers to the minor (shorter) arc. (Although, typically if "minor" or "major" is not explicitly stated, it is assumed that the reference is to the minor arc.)

83. (D) $m\angle CAB = y°$ (alternate interior angles of parallel lines are congruent). Hence, $x° + y° = 50°$. If $ABCD$ is a rhombus, then $x° = y°$ (the diagonals of a rhombus bisect the vertex angles). Otherwise, $x° \neq y°$. Thus, the relationship cannot be determined from the information given.

84. (C) $AD = BE$ implies $AB + BD = BD + DE$. Subtracting BD from both sides yields AB (Quantity A) $= DE$ (Quantity B). The two quantities are equal. Select (C).

85. (B) In a triangle, the sum of the lengths of any two sides must be greater than the length of the third side (triangle inequality). Hence, $15 + 6 = 21$ (Quantity B) is greater than the length of the third side (Quantity A). Quantity B is greater.

86. (A) The area of an equilateral triangle is $\dfrac{s^2\sqrt{3}}{4}$, where s is the length of one of the sides of the triangle. Thus, Quantity A is $\dfrac{s^2\sqrt{3}}{4} = \dfrac{4^2\sqrt{3}}{4} = 4\sqrt{3} \approx 6.9$. Quantity A is greater.

87. (C) Construct an altitude from vertex Z to $\overline{WX}$.

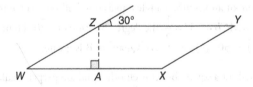

In right triangle WAZ, $\angle W = 30°$ (corresponding angles of parallel lines are congruent) and $WZ = XY = 8$ (opposite sides of a parallelogram are congruent). The length of the side opposite the $30°$ angle in a $30°$-$60°$-$90°$ right triangle is half the length of the hypotenuse. Hence, $ZA = 4$. Quantity A is the area of $WXYZ = bh = 10 \cdot 4 = 40$. The two quantities are equal.

88. (A) $x° > m\angle ADB$ (the measure of an exterior angle of a triangle is greater than the measure of either nonadjacent interior angle). $m\angle ADB = y°$ (alternate interior angles of parallel lines are congruent). Hence, $x° > y°$ and $x > y$. Quantity A is greater.

89. (A) $55° > 45° = \frac{1}{8}(360°)$. The length of an arc of the circle corresponding to $45°$ is $\frac{1}{8}(2\pi r) = \frac{1}{8}(2\pi \cdot 4) = \pi$. Thus, the length of minor arc PQ (Quantity A) is greater than π (Quantity B). Quantity A is greater. (See the Tip for Question 82 for an explanation of minor arc.)

90. (D) If the right triangle is isosceles, then $a = b$. In this case, $\frac{a}{10}$ (Quantity A) = $\frac{b}{10}$ (Quantity B). If the right triangle is not isosceles, then $a \neq b$. In this case, $\frac{a}{10}$ (Quantity A) $\neq \frac{b}{10}$ (Quantity B). Thus, the relationship cannot be determined from the information given.

91. (C) Construct radius $\overline{CQ}$.

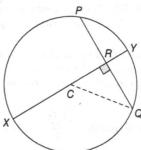

In right triangle CRQ, CQ (the hypotenuse) = 13, $RQ = \frac{1}{2}PQ = \frac{1}{2}(24) = 12$ (a radius that is perpendicular to a chord bisects the chord). Using the Pythagorean theorem, CR (Quantity A) = $\sqrt{13^2 - 12^2} = \sqrt{169 - 144} = \sqrt{25} = 5$. The two quantities are equal.

92. (B) The measure of an inscribed angle equals one-half the degree measure of its intercepted arc. Thus, $m\angle ACB = 75° = \frac{1}{2}$(the degree measure of $\overarc{AB}$). Hence, the degree measure of $\overarc{AB} = 2(75°) = 150°$ (Quantity A). Quantity B is greater.

93. (A) The diagonals of a square bisect each other and are perpendicular. In right triangle AEB, AB (the hypotenuse) is the length of a side of the square; $EA = EB = \frac{1}{2}(12) = 6$; and $\angle EAB = \angle EBA = 45°$. In a $45°$-$45°$-$90°$ right triangle, the hypotenuse is $\sqrt{2}$ times the length of one of the legs. Hence, $AB = 6\sqrt{2}$ (Quantity A). Quantity A is greater.

94. (B) Because $\overline{AB}$ and $\overline{CD}$ are two chords intersecting at E, then $(AE)(EB) = (CE)(ED)$. Thus, $(6)(10) = (9)(ED)$, $ED = \frac{60}{9} = \frac{20}{3} = 6\frac{2}{3}$ (Quantity A). Quantity B is greater.

95. (C) Congruent chords have congruent arcs, so $\overline{PQ} \cong \overline{PR}$ implies $\overarc{PQ} \cong \overarc{PR}$. Let x = the degree measure of minor arc PQ = the degree measure of minor arc PR. Then $2x + 100° = 360°$, $2x = 260°$, $x = 130°$ (Quantity A). The two quantities are equal. (See the Tip for Question 82 for an explanation of minor arc.)

96. (A) The *fundamental counting principle* states that for a sequence of k tasks, if a first task can be done in any one of n_1 different ways, and for each of these ways, a subsequent task can be done in any one of n_2 different ways, and for each of these ways, a following task can be done in any one of n_3 different ways, and so on to the kth task, which can be done in any one of n_k different ways, then the total number of different ways the sequence of k tasks can be done is $n_1 \times n_2 \times n_3 \times \cdots \times n_k$. Applying this principle to four tasks, the number of possible lunches that can be selected is the product of the number of ways to select a salad, the number of ways to select an entrée, the number of ways to select a beverage, and the number of ways to select a desert. Hence, Quantity A is $4 \times 2 \times 3 \times 5 = 120$. Quantity A is greater.

97. (C) For both Quantity A and Quantity B, there are five positions to fill: first, second, third, fourth, and fifth. The number of arrangements of the five people (or the five letters) is the product of the number of ways to fill each position. There are 5 people (or letters) from which to choose to fill the first position. Following that selection, there are 4 people (or letters) from which to choose to fill the second position. Following that selection, there are 3 people (or letters) from which to choose to fill the third position. Following that selection, there are 2 people (or letters) from which to choose to fill the fourth position. Following that selection, there is 1 person (or letter) to fill the fifth position. Therefore, Quantity A = Quantity B = $5 \times 4 \times 3 \times 2 \times 1 = 120$. The two quantities are equal.

98. (B) In a three-digit number there are three positions to fill: hundreds place, tens place, and units place. Quantity A is $5 \times 4 \times 3 = 60$ (because digits may not repeat). Quantity B is $5 \times 5 \times 5 = 125$ (because repetitions are allowed). Quantity B is greater.

99. (C) Use the *combination* formula to determine Quantity A and Quantity B. A *combination* is a selection from a set of objects without regard to order; that is, different arrangements of the same objects are considered to be the same selection. The number of combinations of r objects from n distinct objects, denoted $_nC_r$ or $\begin{pmatrix} n \\ r \end{pmatrix}$ is $\dfrac{n!}{(n-r)!r!}$. *Note:* The symbol "!" is read "factorial"; $n!$ is the product of all positive integers less than or equal to n (except $0! = 1$). The order in which committee members are selected is immaterial. Quantity A is:

$$_5C_2 = \frac{5!}{(5-2)!2!} = \frac{5!}{(3)!2!}. \text{ Quantity B is } _5C_3 = \frac{5!}{(5-3)!3!} = \frac{5!}{(2)!3!}$$

The two quantities are equal.

100. (B) Quantity A is:

$$\frac{\text{number of vowels in } graduate}{\text{number of letters in } graduate} = \frac{4}{8} = \frac{1}{2}$$

Quantity B is:

$$\frac{\text{number of letters other than } a \text{ or } d \text{ in } graduate}{\text{number of letters in } graduate} = \frac{5}{8}$$

Quantity B is greater. *Tip:* A shortcut for this question is to recognize that the probabilities will have the same denominator, so you need to compare only the numerators of the two quantities.

101. (B) Quantity A is:

$$\frac{\text{number of primes or even numbers in the set}}{\text{number of elements in the set}} = \frac{3}{5}$$

Quantity B is greater.

102. (B) The probability of Team X losing to Team Y is $1 - \frac{2}{3} = \frac{1}{3}$. The probability of Team X losing to Team Z is $1 - \frac{1}{4} = \frac{3}{4}$. Quantity A, the probability that Team X wins both games, is $\frac{2}{3} \cdot \frac{1}{4} = \frac{1}{6}$. Quantity B, the probability that Team X loses both games, is $\frac{1}{3} \cdot \frac{3}{4} = \frac{1}{4}$. Quantity B is greater.

103. (A) To ensure that the probability of winning a prize is 2 percent, only 2% of the tickets printed should be marked as winners. Thus, Quantity A is $2\%(1500) = 0.02(1500) = 30$. Quantity A is greater.

104. (D) If exactly two sides of triangle ABC are congruent, there are three possibilities for the congruent sides: $AB \cong AC$, $AB \cong BC$, or $AC \cong BC$. The altitude drawn from A to $\overline{BC}$ is congruent to the median drawn from A to $\overline{BC}$ in only one (when $AB \cong AC$) of these three possibilities. In this case, Quantity A, the probability that the altitude drawn from A to $\overline{BC}$ is congruent to the median drawn from A to $\overline{BC}$, is $\frac{1}{3}$, so the two quantities are equal.

If the triangle is equilateral, then the altitude drawn from A to $\overline{BC}$ is always congruent to the median drawn from A to $\overline{BC}$, so the probability that the altitude drawn from A to $\overline{BC}$ is congruent to the median drawn from A to $\overline{BC}$ is 1. In this case, Quantity A is greater. Because you found different results (one when the quantities were equal and one when Quantity A was greater), the relationship cannot be determined from the information given.

105. (B) Let w = the original number of white marbles and b = the original number of black marbles. Write two equations (1) $\frac{w}{w+b} = \frac{7}{8}$, $8w = 7w + 7b$, $w = 7b$; (2) $\frac{w+6}{w+b+6} = \frac{x}{y}$. From (2) you can reason that when 6 white marbles are added to the box, the probability of drawing a white marble is greatest if there is only 1 black marble in the box to begin with. Substituting (1) $w = 7b$ into (2) yields:

$$\frac{7b+6}{7b+b+6} = \frac{7b+6}{8b+6} = \frac{x}{y}. \text{ When } b = 1, \frac{x}{y} = \frac{7b+6}{8b+6} = \frac{7(1)+6}{8(1)+6} = \frac{13}{14}.$$

Thus, when $b \geq 1$, Quantity A is $\frac{x}{y} \leq \frac{13}{14} \approx 0.929$. Quantity B is $\frac{14}{15} \approx 0.933$. Quantity B is greater.

106. (A) *Note:* This question uses the combination formula. Refer to Question 99 for an explanation of the formula. For both Quantity A and Quantity B, the probability is computed using the same denominator. The denominator is the number of ways to select four people from the nine (five women + four men) available people. Hence, determine and compare only the numerators. For Quantity A, the numerator is the number of ways to select two women and two men on the committee. Thus, Quantity A is the following product:

(the number of ways to select two × (the number of ways to select
of the five women)   two of the four men)

$$= {}_5C_2 \times {}_4C_2 = \frac{5!}{(5-2)!2!} \times \frac{4!}{(4-2)!2!} = \frac{5!}{(3)!2!} \times \frac{4!}{(2)!2!}$$

For Quantity B, the numerator is the number of ways to select three women and one man on the committee. Thus, Quantity B is the following product: (the number of ways to select three of the five women) × (the number of ways to select one of the four men) =

$$ {}_5C_3 \times {}_4C_1 = \frac{5!}{(5-3)!3!} \times \frac{4!}{(4-1)!1!} = \frac{5!}{(2)!3!} \times \frac{4!}{(3)!1!}$$

By inspection, the numerators of Quantity A and Quantity B have a common factor of $\frac{5!}{(3)!2!} = \frac{5!}{(2)!3!}$, which you can divide out. Now, compare $\frac{4!}{(2)!2!} = \frac{4 \cdot 3 \cdot 2!}{(2 \cdot 1)2!} = 6$ and $\frac{4!}{(3)!1!} = \frac{4 \cdot 3!}{3!(1)} = 4$. Because $6 > 4$, Quantity A is greater.

107. (C) After the data are put in order (from least to greatest or greatest to least), the *median* is the middle value (for an odd number of data values) or the average of the two middle values (for an even number of data values). Quantity A is the median of $2, 4, 8, 15, 25 = 8$. Quantity B is the median of $-20, 4, 8, 15, 200 = 8$. The two quantities are equal.

108. (B) The *mean* $= \dfrac{\text{sum of data values}}{\text{number of data values}}$

By inspection, the sum of the five numbers in Quantity A is less than the sum of the five numbers in Quantity B. Thus, Quantity B is greater.

109. (A) The standard deviation is a measure of the deviation of the data values from their mean. For both sets of data, the mean is 8. For Quantity B, the standard deviation is 0 because none of the data values deviate from 8. The data in Quantity A exhibit some deviation from the mean of 8. Thus, Quantity A is greater. *Tip:* For the GRE quantitative comparison questions, rather than trying to calculate a standard deviation by formula, simply look at the data. The standard deviation of data that cluster closely around the mean is less than the standard deviation of data that are spread out away from the mean.

110. (B) Let s = the standard deviation of the distribution. Then, $60 = 50 + 2s$, $10 = 2s$, $s = 5$. Quantity B is greater.

111. (C) The number of workers who have $100,000 or more in total savings and investments is $(6\% + 2\%)(2000) = 8\%(2000) = 160$. The two quantities are equal.

112. (B) The *mode* is the data value (or values) that occurs most often. Thus, Quantity A is 54. In an ordered set of n data values, the location of the median is the $\dfrac{n+1}{2}$ position. For the stem-and-leaf plot, $n = 44$, so $\dfrac{n+1}{2} = \dfrac{44+1}{2} = \dfrac{45}{2} = 22.5$. Thus, the median is halfway between the 22nd and the 23rd data values. Hence, Quantity B is $\dfrac{54+55}{2} = 54.5$. Quantity B is greater.

113. **(A)** Fifty percent of the employees have salaries greater than $48,000 (the median). Because $55,000 is above the median, the percent of employees with salaries greater than $55,000 (the mean) is less than 50 percent. Thus, the number of employees with salaries greater than $48,000 (Quantity A) is greater than the number of employees with salaries greater than $55,000 (Quantity B).

114. **(D)** Without further information (such as the percent of the numbers below 15), the percent of the numbers between 15 and 20 cannot be determined. Thus, the relationship cannot be determined from the information given.

115. **(A)** Because there are equal numbers in each set, the average of the 40 numbers combined is the sum of the two averages given in the question divided by 2. Thus, Quantity A is $\dfrac{6.8+17.2}{2}=\dfrac{24}{2}=12$. When the two sets are combined and put in order from least to greatest, the two middle values are 10 and 11. The median is the average of these two values. Thus, Quantity B is $\dfrac{10+11}{2}=\dfrac{21}{2}=10.5$. Quantity A is greater.

116. **(C)** The Rth percentile is a value at or below which lie R% of the data values. To find the Rth percentile for a data set, first put the data in order. Next compute k, using the formula $k=n\left(\dfrac{R}{100}\right)$, where n is the number of data values. If k is an integer, the Rth percentile is the average of the kth and $(k+1)$th data values. If k is *not* an integer, round k up to the next greatest integer, say l, and then the Rth percentile is the lth data value. *Tip:* Do not confuse *percentiles* with *percents*. A percentile is a value that acts as cut point for a specified percent.

For the data presented in Quantity A, the value of k for the 90th percentile is $k=n\left(\dfrac{R}{100}\right)=10\left(\dfrac{90}{100}\right)=9$ (an integer). Thus, the 90th percentile is halfway between the ninth and tenth values. Hence, Quantity A is $\dfrac{100+1400}{2}=\dfrac{1500}{2}=750$. The two quantities are equal. *Tip:* In some other publications and online materials, a slightly different definition of percentile from the one given in this answer explanation is given. In those publications/online materials, the Rth percentile is a value *below which* lie R% of the data values. For continuous distributions (such as the normal curve), the two definitions are equivalent. For the GRE, just think of the Rth percentile as a value that splits the data into two parts so that R% is at or below that value and $(100-R)$% is at or above it.

117. **(B)** Refer to Question 116 for an explanation of percentiles. $59,700 is the 75th percentile and $51,500 is the 50th percentile. *Note:* The median is the 50th percentile (because it divides the data into two halves). Thus, 25% (75% − 50%) of the 500 teachers have salaries between $51,500 and $59,700. Hence, Quantity A is 25%(500) = 125. Quantity B is greater.

118. **(A)** The distribution of a data set that has the shape shown is *right-skewed*. Notice that the distribution is not symmetrical because it tapers off to the right. This tapering indicates the presence of a few very high data values that are not balanced by corresponding very low data values. The result of this situation is that when these very high data values are averaged with the other data values, the mean of the distribution will be artificially high compared to the median. The median is not affected by the very high data values because it is determined by its position as the 50th percentile. Therefore, when a distribution is *right-skewed*, the mean is greater than the median. Quantity A is greater. *Tip:* In a *left-skewed* distribution (one that tapers off to the left), the mean is less than the median. For a *symmetrical* distribution, the mean and median coincide.

119. (B) The total number of points needed to obtain an average of 90 on five tests is $5(90) = 450$ points. The student has accumulated $90+92+78+95 = 355$ points. Hence, Quantity A is $450-355 = 95$. Quantity B is greater.

120. (B) The standard deviation is a measure of the deviation of the data values from their mean. For both sets of data, the data values are symmetric about 50, which is the mean (by inspection). For Distribution X, the data are clustered closer around 50 than are the data in Distribution Y, indicating less deviation from the mean in Distribution X's data. Thus, Quantity B is greater.

121. (A) The interquartile range (IQR) for a data set is the difference between the 75th percentile, denoted Q_3, and the 25th percentile, denoted Q_1 (refer to Question 116 for an explanation of percentiles); that is, $IQR = Q_3 - Q_1$. The coffee shop data has $n = 16$ data values. For the data's 25th percentile, $k = n\left(\dfrac{R}{100}\right) = 16\left(\dfrac{25}{100}\right) = 4$ (an integer). Hence, Q_1 is halfway between the fourth and fifth data values. Both data values are 6, so $Q_1 = 6$. For the data's 75th percentile, $k = n\left(\dfrac{R}{100}\right) = 16\left(\dfrac{75}{100}\right) = 12$ (an integer). Hence, Q_3 is halfway between the 12th and 13th data values: $= \dfrac{13+15}{2} = \dfrac{28}{2} = 14$. Thus, Quantity A equals $IQR = Q_3 - Q_1 = 14-6 = 8$. The *range* of the data is the difference between the maximum value (max) and the minimum value (min). Quantity B equals $\dfrac{\max - \min}{2} = \dfrac{19-5}{2} = \dfrac{14}{2} = 7$. Quantity A is greater.

122. (C) A *normally distributed* data set has special characteristics. The distribution (called a *normal distribution*) is bell-shaped and symmetric about its mean, and the mean, median, and mode coincide. A normal distribution is completed defined by its mean and standard deviation. The mean determines its center and the standard deviation determines whether it is tall and thin (corresponding to small standard deviations) or short and wide (corresponding to large standard deviations). The total area under the curve is 1. The bell shape of the curve means that most of the data will fall in the middle of the distribution with the amount of data tapering off evenly in both directions as you move away from the center of the distribution. The horizontal axis is marked off in equal intervals from the center (mean). The length of each interval is one standard deviation. Because the total area under the curve is 1, the area under the curve to the left of a value along the horizontal axis is the proportion of the distribution that is below that value. Similarly, the area under the curve to the right of a value along the horizontal axis is the proportion of the distribution that is above that value. And, the area under the curve between any two values along the horizontal axis equals the proportion of the distribution between those two values. These proportions can be interpreted as probabilities as well.

For the problem at hand, you can make a rough sketch of a normal distribution with mean 75 and standard deviation 10. Mark 75 as the mean (center). Mark 55 as two standard deviations below 75 (because $55 = 75 - 20 = 75 - 2(10) =$ mean minus two standard deviations). Mark 95 as two standard deviations above 75 (because $95 = 75 + 20 = 75 + 2(10) =$ mean plus two standard deviations). Shade the area under the curve to the left of 55 to indicate the area of probability that a score is less than 55. Shade the area under the curve to the right of 95 to indicate the area of probability that a score is greater than 95.

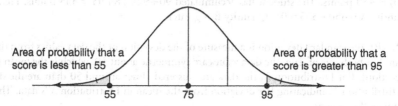

Compare the shaded areas. You can see that because the curve is symmetric, the area to the left of 55 equals the area to the right of 95. Thus, Quantity A, the probability that a score will be less than 55, and Quantity B, the probability that a score will be greater than 95, are equal.

123. (A) Quantity B, an IQ score at the 50th percentile, is the median, which equals the mean in a normal distribution. (Refer to Question 122 for a discussion of characteristics of normally distributed data.) Thus, Quantity B is 100. Quantity A is greater.

124. (B) Refer to Question 122. Make a sketch of a normal distribution with mean 25 and standard deviation 2. Mark 25 as the mean (center). Mark 21 as two standard deviations below 25 (because $21 = 25 - 4 = 25 - 2(2) =$ mean minus two standard deviations). Mark 23 as one standard deviation below 25 (because $23 = 25 - 2 = 25 - 1(2) =$ mean minus one standard deviation). Mark 27 as one standard deviation above 25 (because $27 = 25 + 2 = 25 + 1(2) =$ mean plus one standard deviation). Shade the area under the curve between 21 and 23 to indicate the proportion of the distribution between 21 and 23. Shade the area under the curve between 25 and 27 to indicate the proportion of the distribution between 25 and 27.

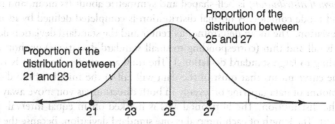

By inspection, the proportion of the distribution between 21 and 23 is less than the proportion of the distribution between 25 and 27. Thus, Quantity A, the percent of the distribution between 21 and 23, is less than Quantity B, the percent of the distribution between 25 and 27. Quantity B is greater.

125. (A) Refer to Question 122. Quantity A, the probability of scoring above 600 on Exam X, is illustrated in the following sketch of a normal distribution with mean 500 and standard deviation 100. The score 600 is one standard deviation above the mean (because $600 = 500 + 100 = 500 + 1(100) =$ mean plus one standard deviation).

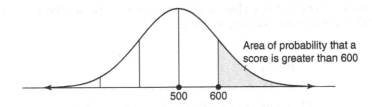

Area of probability that a score is greater than 600

500　600

Quantity B, the probability of scoring above 31 on Exam Y, is illustrated in the following sketch of a normal distribution with mean 21 and standard deviation 5. The score 31 is two standard deviations above the mean (because $31 = 21 + 10 = 21 + 2(10) =$ mean plus two standard deviations).

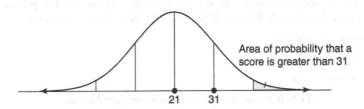

Area of probability that a score is greater than 31

21　31

By inspection of the two sketches, Quantity A, the probability of scoring above 600 on Exam X, is greater than Quantity B, the probability of scoring above 31 on Exam Y.

Chapter 2: Numeric Entry Questions

126. $\dfrac{3}{10}$ The grandson inherits $\dfrac{1}{4}$ of the land, so the two granddaughters inherit $1 - \dfrac{1}{4} = \dfrac{3}{4}$ of the land. Let $x =$ the portion inherited by the younger granddaughter. Then $x + 50\%x =$ the portion inherited by the older granddaughter. Now, write and solve the following equation:

$$x + (x + 50\%x) = \frac{3}{4}$$

$$x + x + \frac{1}{2}x = \frac{3}{4}$$

$$\frac{5}{2}x = \frac{3}{4}$$

$$\frac{\cancel{2}}{\cancel{5}} \cdot \frac{\cancel{5}}{\cancel{2}}x = \frac{2}{5} \cdot \frac{3}{4}$$

$$x = \frac{6}{20} = \frac{3}{10}$$

127. 100 The lcm$(n, 50) = 100$, so n cannot be 25 or 50, because lcm$(25, 50) = 50$ and lcm$(50, 50) = 50$. Therefore, $n \geq 100$. Thus, $n = 100$, because lcm$(100, 50) = 100$.

128. $\dfrac{3}{8}$ Let $x =$ the number of white rose plants; then $55 - x =$ the number of red rose plants. The number of red rose plants is 10 more than twice the number of white rose plants. Write and solve the following equation:

$$55 - x = 2x + 10$$
$$45 = 3x$$
$$x = 15, \text{ the number of white rose plants}$$
$$55 - x = 55 - 15 = 40, \text{ the number of red rose plants}$$

Thus, the ratio of white rose plants to red rose plants $= \dfrac{15}{40} = \dfrac{3}{8}$.

129. \$180,000 Let $x =$ the amount invested in municipal bonds; then $\$300,000 - x =$ the amount invested in oil stocks. The amount invested in oil stocks is 150 percent of the amount invested in municipal bonds. Write and solve the following equation:

$$\$300,000 - x = 150\% x$$
$$\$300,000 - x = 1.5x$$
$$\$300,000 = 2.5x$$
$$x = \$120,000, \text{ the amount invested in municipal bonds}$$
$$\$300,000 - x = \$300,000 - \$120,000 = \$180,000, \text{ the amount invested in oil stocks}$$

Tip: When you have two unknowns and a first unknown is described in terms of a second unknown, it is usually easier to let the variable equal the second unknown. In this question, you have two unknowns: the amount of money invested in municipal bonds and the amount of money invested in oil stocks. The amount invested in oil stocks is described in terms of the amount invested in municipal bonds, so let x equal the amount invested in municipal bonds. But because the question asks for the amount invested in oil stocks, remember to solve for this amount after you find x.

130. $\dfrac{2}{3}$ You know the number of green marbles is 5. Let $x =$ the number of black marbles and $y =$ the number of red marbles. The probability of drawing a black or red marble is $\dfrac{x+y}{15}$. You have 15 marbles altogether, so $15 = x + y + 5$, from whence you can determine that $x + y = 15 - 5 = 10$. Thus, the probability of drawing a black or red marble is $\dfrac{x+y}{15} = \dfrac{10}{15} = \dfrac{2}{3}$.

Tip: Notice that to determine the solution, you do not need the specific values of x and y, only their sum, $x + y$.

131. 4 Let $r =$ the amount spent on rent, $f =$ the amount spent on food $= \dfrac{2}{5}r$, and $c =$ the amount spent on clothing $= \dfrac{1}{4}f = \dfrac{1}{4} \cdot \dfrac{2}{5}r = \dfrac{1}{10}r$. Then, the average of the total amounts spent on food and clothing is $\dfrac{f+c}{2} = \dfrac{\frac{2}{5}r+\frac{1}{10}r}{2}$. To answer the question, you

need to determine $r + \left(\dfrac{\frac{2}{5}r+\frac{1}{10}r}{2} \right)$. This expression is a ratio, and it looks a bit complicated.

However, you can write it as $\dfrac{r}{\left(\dfrac{\frac{2}{5}r+\frac{1}{10}r}{2}\right)} = \dfrac{r}{r\left(\dfrac{\frac{2}{5}+\frac{1}{10}}{2}\right)}$ and see that r will cancel

out. Therefore, you can put in a convenient value for r. The ratio will be the same regardless of the value of r you choose. Let $r = \$100$. This value for r would yield $f=\dfrac{2}{5}r=\dfrac{2}{5}\cdot\$100=\$40$ and $c=\dfrac{1}{4}f=\dfrac{1}{4}\cdot\$40=\$10$. Therefore, if the amount spent on rent were $\$100$, the average of f (the amount spent on food) and c (the amount spent on clothing) is $\dfrac{f+c}{2}=\dfrac{\$40+\$10}{2}=\dfrac{\$50}{2}=\$25$. Thus, $r+\left(\dfrac{f+c}{2}\right)=\$100+\$25=4$. *Tip:* Picking a convenient number to work with can simplify a problem.

132. 20%

$$\text{The percent increase} = \frac{\text{the amount the sale price increased}}{\$125}\cdot 100\%$$

$$= \frac{\$25}{\$125}\cdot 100\% = \frac{1}{5}\cdot 100\% = 20\%$$

133. 45 grams Let $x =$ the number of grams of tin in the alloy. You know the number of grams of copper in the alloy is 36. You must determine $x+36$ to answer the question. Given that the ratio of tin to copper in the alloy is 1 to 4, $\dfrac{x}{36}=\dfrac{1}{4}$. Thus, $4x = 36$. Hence, $x = 9$ and $x+36 = 9+36 = 45$.

134. $20,012.50 You calculate the amount in the account at the end of the first month by adding I_1, the interest earned in one month, to P_0, the initial investment of $\$20,000$. To obtain I_1 multiply $\$20,000$ by the monthly interest rate, which is $\dfrac{0.75\%}{12}=\dfrac{0.0075}{12}=$ 0.000625. You divide the annual rate, 0.75%, by 12 to obtain the monthly rate. Thus, $P_0+I_1 = A = \$20,000+\$20,000\left(\dfrac{0.75}{12}\right)= \$20,000+\$20,000(0.000625) = 20,000 + \$12.50 = \$20,012.50$.

135. $134.96 Let $t =$ the number of hours the friends will be charged at $\$19.99$ per hour, and $d =$ the total mileage the friends will be charged at $\$0.55$ per mile. Then the cost, C, for the truck rental is $\$19.99t + \$0.55d$. From the question information, $d = 100$ miles and $t = 4$ hours (because they are charged a full hour for a portion of an hour). Therefore, $C = \$19.99t + \$0.55d = \$19.99(4)+\$0.55(100) = \$134.96$.

136. 2 hours The distance traveled for the first half of the trip is 63 mph · 2 hours = 126 miles, so the distance traveled for the second half of the trip is 266 miles − 126 miles = 140 miles and the time, t, for the second half of the trip is $t = \dfrac{140 \text{ miles}}{70 \text{ mph}} = 2$ hours.

137. 47 Let n, $n+2$, and $n+4$ be the three consecutive odd integers. Given that the sum is 147, write and solve the following equation:

$$n+(n+2)+(n+4)=147$$
$$3n+6=147$$
$$3n=141$$
$$n=47, \text{ the least of the integers}$$

138. 8 Because $\gcd(m,n)=2$, then both m and n have at least one factor of 2, so you can write $m=2y$ and $n=2z$. Then $x=6m^2+4n^2=6(2y)^2+4(2z)^2=6\cdot 2^2 y^2+4\cdot 2^2 z^2 = 2\cdot 3\cdot 2^2 y^2+2^2\cdot 2^2 z^2=2^3\cdot 3\cdot y^2+2^3\cdot 2\cdot z^2$, from which you can determine that the greatest even number that *must* be a factor of x is $2^3=8$.

139. 400 The number of part-time positions is $3600\left(\dfrac{1}{x}\right)$. This number is reduced by $\dfrac{1}{x}$, so the number of part-time positions lost is $3600\left(\dfrac{1}{x}\right)\left(\dfrac{1}{x}\right)=\dfrac{3600}{x^2}$. Given that $x^2=9$, you have $\dfrac{3600}{x^2}=\dfrac{3600}{9}=400$.

140. 20 The number of ways to pair 5 teams is five things taken two at a time, which equals $\begin{pmatrix} 5 \\ 2 \end{pmatrix}=\dfrac{5!}{2!3!}=\dfrac{5\cdot 4\cdot \cancel{3!}}{2\cdot 1\cdot \cancel{3!}}=10$. Thus, the total games played during the season is $2\cdot 10=20$.

Tip: You also can figure out the number of ways to pair 5 teams by designating the teams as A, B, C, D, and E. Then systematically list all of the 10 ways to match the teams two at a time, yielding AB, AC, AD, AE, BC, BD, BE, CD, CE, and DE.

141. $\dfrac{1}{3}$ To answer the question, determine $y=\dfrac{k}{360}$. From $\dfrac{2}{9}=\dfrac{k}{540}$, $k=\dfrac{(2)(540)}{9}=120$. Thus, $y=\dfrac{k}{360}=\dfrac{120}{360}=\dfrac{1}{3}$.

142. $68.00 Let $x=$ the marked-down price. The original price of the jacket is $85. The original price of the jacket plus the sales tax on the original price is the amount the customer would have paid. The marked-down price plus the sales tax on the marked-down price is the amount the customer actually paid. The difference between the amount the customer would have paid and the amount the customer actually paid is $18.36. Write and solve the following equation:

$$(\$85.00+8\%\cdot \$85.00)-(x+8\%x)=\$18.36$$
$$(\$85.00+0.08\cdot \$85.00)-(x+0.08x)=\$18.36$$
$$\$91.80-1.08x=\$18.36$$
$$-1.08x=-\$73.44$$
$$x=\$68.00$$

143. 5 Let x = the number of vases with 10 flowers, and $8 - x$ = the number of vases with 8 flowers. Write and solve the following equation:

$$10x + 8(8 - x) = 74$$

$$10x + 64 - 8x = 74$$

$$2x = 10$$

$$x = 5$$

144. 9 Let x = the number of matches played. Then $x - 21$ = the number of matches lost. The team won 70% (100% − 30%) of their matches. Thus, $70\%x = 21$; $x = \dfrac{21}{0.7} = 30$. Therefore, the team lost $30 - 21 = 9$ matches. *Tip:* Remember to answer the question asked. In this question, you were to find the number of matches lost.

145. 45% The percent strength of the solution is

$$\left(\frac{\text{number of liters (L) of alcohol in the solution}}{\text{total volume of the solution}}\right) \cdot 100\% = \frac{20\%(30\text{ L}) + 60\%(50\text{ L})}{30\text{ L} + 50\text{ L}} \cdot 100\%$$

$$= \frac{6\text{ L} + 30\text{ L}}{80\text{ L}} \cdot 100\%$$

$$= \frac{36\text{ L}}{80\text{ L}} \cdot 100\% = 0.45 \cdot 100\%$$

$$= 45\%$$

146. $\dfrac{20}{3}$ Substitute into the formula and solve for R_2.

$$\frac{1}{R} = \frac{1}{R_1} + \frac{1}{R_2}$$

$$\frac{1}{4} = \frac{1}{10} + \frac{1}{R_2}$$

$$40R_2 \cdot \left(\frac{1}{4}\right) = 40R_2\left(\frac{1}{10}\right) + 40R_2\left(\frac{1}{R_2}\right)$$

$$10R_2 = 4R_2 + 40$$

$$6R_2 = 40$$

$$R_2 = \frac{40}{6} = \frac{20}{3}$$

Tip: When an equation contains fractions, you can remove fractions by multiplying both sides of the equation by the least common denominator of the fractions in the equation.

147. 45 Let x = Morgan's age now, and $x + 5$ = Morgan's age 5 years from now. Write and solve the following equation, and then compute $x + 5$:

$$x - 20 = \frac{1}{3}(x + 20)$$

$$3(x - 20) = 3 \cdot \frac{1}{3}(x + 20)$$

$$3x - 60 = x + 20$$

$$2x = 80$$

$$x = 40$$

$$x + 5 = 45$$

Tip: Be sure to answer the question asked. In this question, you must find Morgan's age five years from now, not his current age.

148. 10 Let m = the number of male guests at the party and $25 - m$ = the number of female guests. Write and solve the following equation:

$$\frac{25 - m}{m} = \frac{3}{2}$$

$$2(25 - m) = 3m$$

$$50 - 2m = 3m$$

$$50 = 5m$$

$$m = 10$$

149. 6 miles per hour Let r = the jogger's average jogging speed in miles per hour. Then $r = \dfrac{8 \text{ miles}}{t}$, where t is the total time jogging (in hours). From the question information, t = 10:20 a.m. – 9:00 a.m. = 1 hour 20 minutes $= 1\frac{1}{3}$ hours $= \frac{4}{3}$ hours. Therefore, $r = \dfrac{d}{t} = \dfrac{8 \text{ miles}}{\frac{4}{3} \text{ hours}} = 6$ miles per hour.

150. 63 Let x, $y = 3x$, and $z = 5x$ be the three integers. Then their sum is $x + 3x + 5x = 9x$. Because $z - y = 14$, write and solve the following equation, and then compute $9x$:

$$5x - 3x = 14$$

$$2x = 14$$

$$x = 7$$

$$9x = 63$$

151. \$7 Let p = the price of one papaya and m = the price of one mango. Then $p + 2m$ is the price of one papaya and two mangoes. *Tip:* Notice that to answer the question, you do not need the specific values of p and m. You need only the value of the sum, $p + 2m$. From the information about Pierre's purchase, $10m + 5p = \$35$, which simplifies to $p + 2m = \$7$.

152. 22 Let x, $x+1$, and $x+2$ be the three consecutive integers. Write and solve the following equation, and then compute $x+2$:

$$2(x+x+1+x+2)=71+\frac{5}{2}(x+2)$$

$$2(3x+3)=71+\frac{5}{2}x+5$$

$$6x+6=76+2.5x$$

$$3.5x=70$$

$$x=\frac{70}{3.5}=20$$

Thus, the greatest integer is $x+2=22$.

Tip: Make sure you answer the question asked. In this question, after you obtain x, you must calculate $x+2$ to answer the question.

153. 124

$$324_{\text{base }6}=3\cdot6^2+2\cdot6+4=3\cdot36+2\cdot6+4=108+12+4=124$$

154. 11 In this question, use the divisibility property that if an integer divides both b and c, then it divides $bx+cy$, where x and y are any two integers. Because m divides both $(7n+3)$ and $(35n+26)$, then m divides $1\cdot(35n+26)-5(7n+3)=35n+26-35n-15=11$. The only divisors of 11 are 1 and 11; $m\neq1$, so $m=11$.

155. 4896 If a and b are positive integers and $ab\neq0$, then the least positive common multiple of a and b is their product divided by their greatest common divisor. Thus, the least positive common multiple of 51 and 288 is $\dfrac{51\cdot288}{3}=4896$.

156. 12 Factor 72 into primes using exponents: $72=2^3\cdot3^2$. Then add 1 to each of the exponents and multiply the results. This gives you the number of positive divisors of 72. Thus, 72 has $(3+1)(2+1)=4\cdot3=12$ positive divisors.

157. 0 When $y=3$, $(2^x)(4^y)=(2^x)(4^3)=2^x\cdot64$. This final expression equals 64 if and only if $2^x=1$, which implies that $x=0$.

Tip: Another way to work this problem is to rewrite the equation as follows:

$$(2^x)(2^{2y})=2^6$$

$$2^{x+2y}=2^6$$

Thus, $x+2y=6$; $x=6-2y$. When $y=3$, $x=6-2y=6-2\cdot3=6-6=0$.

158. 26 Let $x=$ the number of dimes in the collection. Then, $33-x=$ the number of quarters in the collection. Organize the information in the question.

Coin	Face value	Number of coins	Value
dime	$0.10	x	$0.10x$
quarter	$0.25	$(33-x)$	$0.25(33-x)$
mixed collection	N/A	33	$4.35

Using the previous information, write and solve the following equation (omitting units for convenience):

$$0.10x + 0.25(33 - x) = 4.35$$
$$0.10x + 8.25 - 0.25x = 4.35$$
$$-0.15x = -3.90$$
$$x = 26$$

159. 96% Let $x =$ original price. Then $x - 20\%x = \$120$, new price. Hence, $80\%x = \$120$; $x = \dfrac{\$120}{80\%} = \dfrac{\$120}{0.80} = \$150$, the original price. After the electronics store raises the new price by 20%, the final price is $\$120 + 20\%(\$120) = \$120 + 0.20(\$120) = \$120 + \$24 = \$144$. Calculate the percent, R, as follows:

$$R = \frac{P}{B} = \frac{\$144 \text{ (final price)}}{\$150 \text{ (original price)}} = 0.96 = 96\%$$

160. 1

$$\sqrt{3x+3} = \sqrt{3x} + 1; \text{ square both sides.}$$
$$(\sqrt{3x+3})^2 = (\sqrt{3x} + 1)^2$$
$$3x + 3 = (\sqrt{3x})^2 + 2\sqrt{3x} + 1$$
$$3x + 3 = 3x + 2\sqrt{3x} + 1$$
$$2 = 2\sqrt{3x}$$
$$1 = \sqrt{3x}; \text{ square both sides.}$$
$$1 = 3x$$

161. 20 Let $x =$ the greater number; $35 - x =$ the smaller number. Write and solve the following equation:

$$x(35 - x) = 300$$
$$35x - x^2 = 300$$
$$-x^2 + 35x - 300 = 0$$
$$x^2 - 35x + 300 = 0$$
$$(x - 20)(x - 15) = 0$$
$$x = 20 \text{ or } x = 15$$

Choose $x = 20$ because x is the greater number.

162. $\dfrac{3}{10}$ Solve this problem by finding the simultaneous solution of the following two equations:

$$(1)\ \frac{n+2}{d}=\frac{1}{2};\ 2n+4=d$$

$$(2)\ \frac{n}{d+5}=\frac{1}{5};\ 5n=d+5,\ 5n-5=d$$

Substituting (2) into (1) gives $2n+4=5n-5; 9=3n; n=3;$ then $d=2n+4=2\cdot3+4=10;$
$\dfrac{n}{d}=\dfrac{3}{10}.$

163. 92 Let $p =$ the number of paperback books sold from the used book bin last week, and $h =$ the number of hardcover books sold from the used book bin last week. Write and solve simultaneously the following two equations:

$$(1)\ p=2h+42;\ (2)\ 2p+5h=309$$

Substituting (1) into (2) yields

$$2(2h+42)+5h=309$$
$$4h+84+5h=309$$
$$9h=225$$
$$h=25;\ \text{then}\ p=2h+42=2\cdot25+42=92$$

164. 45 From the question information, $b=a+1$ and $c=a+2$. Write and solve the following equation, and then compute $c=a+2$:

$$\frac{1}{2}\big(a+(a+1)+(a+2)\big)=a+23$$
$$\frac{1}{2}(3a+3)=a+23$$
$$3a+3=2a+46$$
$$a=43$$
$$c=a+2=43+2=45$$

165. 25 Let $x =$ Caleb's age now, $2x =$ Marisha's age now, and $2x+5 =$ Marisha's age 5 years from now. Write and solve the following equation, and then compute $2x+5$:

$$x+2x=30$$
$$3x=30$$
$$x=10$$
$$2x+5=2\cdot10+5=25$$

166. 4 Rewrite the given equation as follows:

$$x^2 - 4x = 12$$
$$x^2 - 4x + 4 = 12 + 4$$
$$(x-2)^2 = 16$$

Thus, $|x-2| = 4$

167. −8 Let $x =$ the larger number and $y =$ the smaller number. Write and solve simultaneously the following two equations:

$$(1)\ x - y = 4;\ x - 4 = y$$
$$(2)\ xy = 96$$

Substituting (1) into (2) yields

$$x(x-4) = 96$$
$$x^2 - 4x - 96 = 0$$
$$(x-12)(x+8) = 0$$
$$x = 12\ (\text{reject});\ x = -8$$

168. 14 meters Let $w =$ the rectangle's width, and $l = w + 3 =$ the rectangle's length. Write and solve the following equation, and then compute $l = w + 3$:

$$w(w+3) = 154$$
$$w^2 + 3w - 154 = 0$$
$$(w+14)(w-11) = 0$$
$$w = -14\ (\text{reject});\ w = 11$$
$$l = w + 3 = 11 + 3 = 14$$

169. 25 Given that $b = 10$, you have

$$x^2 + 10x + c = (x+h)^2 \text{ or equivalently}$$
$$x^2 + 10x + c = x^2 + 2hx + h^2$$

Hence, $10 = 2h$ and $c = h^2$ (because corresponding coefficients are equal). Thus, $h = 5$ and $c = h^2 = 5^2 = 25$.

170. 2 hours Let $x=$ the time it takes Ian to paint the room working alone. Organize the question information.

Worker	Rate	Time worked	Amount of work done
Laetitia	$\dfrac{1\text{ room}}{3\text{ hours}}=\dfrac{1}{3}$ room/hr	1.2 hr	$\left(\dfrac{1}{3}\text{ room/hr}\right)(1.2\text{ hr})=0.4$ room
Ian	$\dfrac{1\text{ room}}{x\text{ hours}}=\dfrac{1}{x}$ room/hr	1.2 hr	$\left(\dfrac{1}{x}\text{ room/hr}\right)(1.2\text{ hr})=\dfrac{1.2}{x}$ room
Together	*Do not add rates*	1.2 hr	1 room

Using the previous information, solve the following equation (omitting units for convenience):

$$0.4+\frac{1.2}{x}=1$$
$$0.4x+1.2=x$$
$$1.2=0.6x$$
$$x=2\text{ hours}$$

171. $1372 Write and solve the following equation:

$$1\%x=\$13.72$$
$$0.01x=\$13.72$$
$$x=\$1372$$

172. $(-\infty,-2)$

$$-\left(\frac{1}{2}x+1\right)>0$$
$$-\frac{1}{2}x-1>0$$
$$-\frac{1}{2}x>1$$
$$\frac{1}{2}x<-1$$

Tip: Reverse the direction of the inequality when you multiply both sides by a negative number. $x<-2$, which is $(-\infty,-2)$ in interval notation.

173. 7.5 liters The amount of alcohol before mixing equals the amount of alcohol after mixing. Therefore, write and solve the following equation:

$$60\%x + 10\%(30) = 20\%(x + 30)$$
$$0.6x + 0.1(30) = 0.2(x + 30)$$
$$0.6x + 3 = 0.2x + 6$$
$$0.4x = 3$$
$$x = 7.5 \text{ liters}$$

174. $1\dfrac{1}{3}$ Solve equations (1) $\dfrac{4}{3a} + \dfrac{x}{2a} = 1$ and (2) $\dfrac{x}{a} = \dfrac{2}{3}$ simultaneously. Simplify each equation:

(1) $\dfrac{4}{3a} + \dfrac{x}{2a} = 1$ 　　　　　　(2) $\dfrac{x}{a} = \dfrac{2}{3}$

(1) $6a\left(\dfrac{4}{3a}\right) + 6a\left(\dfrac{x}{2a}\right) = 6a(1)$ 　　(2) $3x = 2a$

(1) $8 + 3x = 6a$ 　　　　　　(2) $3x - 2a = 0$

(1) $3x - 6a = -8$

Eliminate a by multiplying (2) by -3 and adding to (1):

$$3x - 6a = -8$$
$$\underline{-9x + 6a = 0}$$
$$-6x = -8$$
$$x = 1\dfrac{1}{3}$$

175. 2 Let $x =$ the smaller number and $y = 5x =$ the larger number. Write and solve the following equation:

$$\frac{1}{x} + \frac{1}{5x} = \frac{3}{5}$$
$$5x\left(\frac{1}{x} + \frac{1}{5x}\right) = 5x\left(\frac{3}{5}\right)$$
$$5 + 1 = 3x$$
$$3x = 6$$
$$x = 2$$

176. 500 Let $x =$ the number of balcony seats sold, and $y =$ the number of orchestra seats sold. Write and solve simultaneously the following two equations:

(1) $x + y = 800$

(2) $\$50x + \$80y = \$49,000$

Solve (1) for y and substitute into (2). Omit units and solve for x.

$$50x + 80(800 - x) = 49,000$$
$$50x + 64,000 - 80x = 49,000$$
$$-30x = -15,000$$
$$x = 500$$

177. $\dfrac{1}{6}$ Let $w =$ the number of white marbles in the box, $b = 2w =$ the number of black marbles in the box, and $r = b + 50\%b = 1.5b = 1.5(2w) = 3w =$ the number of red marbles in the box. Then the probability, P, of randomly drawing a white marble from the box is:

$$P = \frac{w}{w + b + r} = \frac{w}{w + 2w + 3w} = \frac{w}{6w} = \frac{1}{6}$$

178. −13 Let $n =$ the lesser integer, and $n + 1 =$ the greater integer. Write and solve the following equation:

$$n(n + 1) = 182$$
$$n^2 + n - 182 = 0$$
$$(n + 14)(n - 13) = 0$$

Thus, n is −14 with $n + 1 = -13$ or $n = 13$ (reject).

179. 300 $x^2 + xy = 100 - y^2 - xy$, which can be rewritten as follows:

$$x^2 + 2xy + y^2 = 100$$
$$(x + y)^2 = 100$$

Thus, $(x\sqrt{3} + y\sqrt{3})^2 = (\sqrt{3})^2(x + y)^2 = 3(x + y)^2 = 3(100) = 300$.

180. 0.125

$\sqrt[5]{a} = 2 \Rightarrow a = 2^5 \Rightarrow a^{-0.6} = (2^5)^{-0.6} = 2^{-3} = \dfrac{1}{2^3} = \dfrac{1}{8} = 0.125$. *Note:* $\Rightarrow$ means "implies."

181. 4 days Let d = the number of days it will take the five machines to do the job and r = the rate at which one machine could do the job working alone. 10 days times 2 machines times r equals 1 job, from which you have $20r = 1$ (omitting units). Thus, $r = \dfrac{1}{20}$; that is, each machine does $\dfrac{1}{20}$ of the job per day. Therefore, if 5 machines working together for d days complete the job, then d times 5 machines times $\dfrac{1}{20}$ job per machine = 1 job. Omitting units and solving for d yields $d \cdot 5 \cdot \dfrac{1}{20} = 1$

$$\frac{d}{4} = 1$$
$$d = 4 \text{ days}$$

182. –4

$$f(g(-1)) = f(3) = -4$$

183. 2 Observe that in simplified form $y = \dfrac{(x-2)^2(x+3)}{(x-2)^3(x+3)} = \dfrac{1}{x-2}$, which will have a vertical asymptote when $x - 2 = 0$; that is, when $x = 2$.

184. 97 $a_{20} = a_1 + (20-1)d = a_1 + (19)d$, so you need the values of a_1 and d to determine a_{20}. Write and simultaneously solve the following two equations:
   (1) $a_4 = 17 = a_1 + 3d$ and (2) $a_{10} = 47 = a_1 + 9d$. Multiply (2) by –1 and add to (1) to obtain $-6d = -30$; $d = 5$. Substitute $d = 5$ into (1) to obtain $a_1 = 2$. Thus, $a_{20} = a_1 + (19)d = 2 + (19)(5) = 97$.

185. 3 hours Let t = the number of hours in which the two vehicles will be 390 miles apart, x = the speed of the first vehicle in miles per hour, and $x - 10$ = the speed of the second vehicle. When the two vehicles are 390 miles apart, the second vehicle has gone a distance of 180 miles, so the first vehicle has gone a distance of 390 miles – 180 miles = 210 miles. Organize the question information.

Vehicle	Rate	Time	Distance
1	x	t	$xt = 210$ miles
2	$x - 10$	t	$(x-10)t = 180$ miles
Together	*Do not add rates*	t	390 miles

From the chart, you can write and solve simultaneously the following two equations:

   (1) $xt = 210$ and   (2) $(x-10)t = 180$, $xt - 10t = 180$

Substitute (1) into (2) and solve for t.

$$xt - 10t = 180$$
$$210 - 10t = 180$$
$$-10t = -30$$
$$t = 3 \text{ hours}$$

186. 800 The expected deer population in 20 years is $P(20) = P_0 \cdot 2^{0.25(20)} = P_0 \cdot 2^5$. Given that $P(12) = 200$, then $P_0 \cdot 2^{0.25(12)} = P_0 \cdot 2^3 = P_0 \cdot 8 = 200$; $P_0 = 25$. Thus, $P(20) = P_0 \cdot 2^{0.25(20)} = 25 \cdot 2^5 = 25 \cdot 32 = 800$.

187. 3
Substitute $(x, y) = (5, -1)$ into the equation $(x-2)^2 + (y+1)^2 = r^2$ and then solve for r.

$$(5-2)^2 + (-1+1)^2 = r^2$$

$$(3)^2 + (0)^2 = r^2$$

$$r = 3$$

188. 6 Each of the points (u, v) and $(u+3, v+k)$ must satisfy the equation $y = 2x + 5$. Write and solve simultaneously the following two equations:

(1) $v = 2u + 5$ and   (2) $(v+k) = 2(u+3) + 5$

Substituting (1) into (2) yields

$$2u + 5 + k = 2u + 6 + 5;\ k = 6.$$

189. 17 The distance d between two points (x_1, y_1) and (x_2, y_2) in a coordinate plane is $d = \sqrt{(x_2 - x_1)^2 + (y_2 - y_1)^2}$. Substituting the coordinates of P and Q into the formula yields $d = \sqrt{(3-(-5))^2 + (20-5)^2} = \sqrt{(8)^2 + (15)^2} = \sqrt{64 + 225} = \sqrt{289} = 17$.

190. 90° $\overrightarrow{XZ}$ and $\overrightarrow{XY}$ are perpendicular because their slopes are negative reciprocals of each other. Thus, $\angle ZXY$ is a right angle with measure 90°.

191. 50° Sketch a figure.

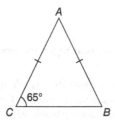

Tip: Sketches help you organize the question information, but do not spend unnecessary time making them. They should be quick and rough. $m\angle C = m\angle B = 65°$ because they are base angles of an isosceles triangle. $m\angle A = 180° - 2(65°) = 50°$.

192. 8.4 The perimeter, P, of triangle ABC is $P = AB + BC + AC$. From the figure, $AB = 3.5$, $BC = 2.1$, and triangle ABC is a right triangle with $\angle C = 90°$. Using the Pythagorean theorem, $AC = \sqrt{(3.5)^2 - (2.1)^2} = \sqrt{7.84} = 2.8$. Therefore, $P = AB + BC + AC = 3.5 + 2.1 + 2.8 = 8.4$.

193. 126 Angle *DEC* is an exterior angle of triangle *BEC*. Thus, $y° = 88° + 38° = 126°$ (the measure of an exterior angle of a triangle equals the sum of the measures of the remote interior angles).

194. 48 From the figure, polygon *A* is a pentagon and polygon *B* is a hexagon. Compute the sum of the measures of the interior angles of each of these polygons using the formula $(n-2)180°$, where *n* is the number of sides. The sum of the measures of the interior angles of polygon *A* is $(5-2)180° = 3 \cdot 180° = 540°$, and of polygon *B* is $(6-2)180° = 4 \cdot 180 = 720°$. To organize the angle information in this question, label relevant angles in the figure.

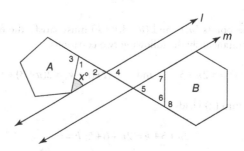

In a regular polygon, all interior angles are congruent. Thus, $m\angle 3 = \dfrac{540°}{5} = 108°$, and $m\angle 8 = \dfrac{720°}{6} = 120°$. From the figure, $\angle 1$ and $\angle 3$ are supplementary, so $m\angle 1 = 180° - 108° = 72°$. Also, $x° + m\angle 1 + m\angle 2 = 180°$, which implies that $x° + 72° + m\angle 2 = 180°$. $\angle 6$ and $\angle 7$ are each supplementary with an interior angle of polygon *B*. Thus, $m\angle 6 = m\angle 7 = 180° - 120° = 60°$. Hence, $m\angle 5 = 180° - 2 \cdot 60° = 60°$ (sum of the angles of a triangle is $180°$). Then $m\angle 4 = m\angle 5 = 60°$ (corresponding angles of parallel lines are congruent). Also, $m\angle 4 = m\angle 2 = 60°$ (vertical angles are congruent). Thus, $x° + m\angle 1 + m\angle 2 = x° + 72° + 60° = 180°$; $x° + 132° = 180°$; $x° = 48°$.

195. 22.5

$m\angle POM = 115° = 2z° + 70°$ (vertical angles are congruent); $2z° = 45°$; $z° = 22.5°$

196. 8 $\angle A \cong \angle B$, so $AC = BC = n$. From the triangle inequality, $n + 15 > n$, and $15 + n > n$, and $n + n > 15$. The first two statements are true for any value of *n*. Using $n + n > 15$ yields $2n > 15$; $n > 7.5$. Thus, the smallest possible value for the whole number *n* is 8.

197. 1758 centimeters In one revolution, the cylindrical barrel will roll a distance equal to its circumference, $\pi d = \pi(56 \text{ cm})$. Thus, in 10 revolutions, the barrel will roll a distance of $10\pi d = 10\pi \cdot (56 \text{ cm}) \approx 10(3.14)(56 \text{ cm}) = 1758.4 \text{ cm}$.

198. 113 square inches The area equals $\pi r^2 \approx (3.14)(6 \text{ in})^2 = 113.04 \text{ in}^2$.

199. 50 cubic centimeters By counting the grid marks on the figure, you can determine that the box will have length 5 cm, width 5 cm, and height 2 cm. The volume, V, is length times width times height. Thus, $V = (5\text{ cm})(5\text{ cm})(2\text{ cm}) = 50\text{ cm}^3$.

200. 180 inches The length, l, of the shawl in inches is 6(9 inches) = 54 inches. Its width, w, is 4(9 inches) = 36 inches. Its perimeter, P, is $2l + 2w$. Thus,

$$P = 2(54\text{ inches}) + 2(36\text{ inches}) = 180\text{ inches}$$

201. 30 The medians in a triangle intersect at a point that is two-thirds the distance from each vertex to the midpoint of the opposite side. Thus, $FB = \dfrac{2}{3}DB$ and $DF = 15 = \dfrac{1}{3}DB$. Hence, $FB = \dfrac{2}{3}DB = 2\left(\dfrac{1}{3}DB\right) = 2(15) = 30$.

202. $\dfrac{16}{9}$ The ratio of the area of $ABCDE$ to the area of $HIJKL$ is the square of the ratio of corresponding sides; $\left(\dfrac{4}{3}\right)^2 = \dfrac{16}{9}$.

203. 67 revolutions per minute In one revolution, the wheel will travel a distance equal to its circumference, $\pi d \approx (3.14)(25\text{ inches})$. Converting 5 $\dfrac{\text{miles}}{\text{hour}}$ into revolutions per minute (rpm) $= 5\ \dfrac{\cancel{\text{miles}}}{\cancel{\text{hour}}} \cdot \dfrac{5280\ \cancel{\text{feet}}}{1\ \cancel{\text{mile}}} \cdot \dfrac{12\ \cancel{\text{inches}}}{1\ \cancel{\text{foot}}} \cdot \dfrac{1\ \cancel{\text{hour}}}{60\text{ minutes}} \cdot \dfrac{1\text{ revolution}}{(3.14)(25\ \cancel{\text{inches}})} \approx 67\text{ rpm}$.

204. 62 Triangle ABC is an equilateral triangle. Using the formula for the area of an equilateral triangle, the area =

$$A = \frac{s^2\sqrt{3}}{4} = \frac{12^2\sqrt{3}}{4} \approx 62$$

Tip: If you do not recall that the area of an equilateral triangle is $\dfrac{s^2\sqrt{3}}{4}$, you can construct an altitude of the triangle. The altitude divides the equilateral triangle into two 30°-60°-90° right triangles. You can use one of these right triangles to determine that the length of the altitude is $\dfrac{s\sqrt{3}}{2}$, and thus:

$$A = \frac{1}{2}bh = \frac{1}{2}sh = \frac{1}{2}s\left(\frac{s\sqrt{3}}{2}\right) = \frac{s^2\sqrt{3}}{4}$$

205. 8 Let $n =$ the number of sides of the polygon. The sum of the measures of the exterior angles of any convex polygon is 360°. Thus, $\dfrac{360°}{n} = 45°$; $45n = 360$; $n = 8$.

206. 170° The sum of the measures of the interior angles of an n-sided convex polygon is $(n-2)180°$. For a pentagon, this sum is $(5-2)180° = (3)180° = 540°$. From the information in the figure, $6x+2°$ is the greatest of the measures of the angles. Write and solve the following equation, and then compute $6x+2°$:

$$(2x-14°)+(2x)+(6x+2°)+(4x-8°)+6x = 540°$$
$$20x-20° = 540°$$
$$20x = 560°$$
$$x = 28°$$
$$6x+2° = 6 \cdot 28°+2° = 170°$$

207. 5 The area of triangle $RYQ = 45 = \frac{1}{2}(RQ)(YQ)$, which implies that $(RQ)(YQ) = 90$. Also, the area of triangle $RPY = 90 = \frac{1}{2}(RQ)(PY)$, which implies that $(RQ)(PY) = 180$. Thus, $(RQ)(YQ) = \frac{1}{2}(RQ)(PY)$; $(YQ) = \frac{1}{2}(PY) = \frac{1}{2}(10) = 5$. From the figure, $XQ = XY + YQ = 10$. Substituting $YQ = 5$ gives $XY + 5 = 10$; $XY = 5$.

208. 8 feet The volume, V, of the cylindrical tank is $\pi r^2 h$, where r is the radius of its circular base and h is the height of the cylinder. From the question information, write and solve the following equation for r, and then compute $d = 2r$:

$$\frac{3}{4}V = \frac{3}{4}\pi r^2 h = \frac{3}{4}\pi r^2 (8 \text{ ft}) = 96\pi \text{ cubic feet}$$

Omitting units and solving for r,

$$\frac{3}{4}\pi r^2 (8) = 96\pi$$
$$r^2 = 16$$
$$r = 4$$
$$d = 2r = 2 \cdot 4 = 8 \text{ feet}$$

209. 21 From the figure, $XY = (z+12)+3$. Because $\overline{XY}$ and $\overline{UV}$ are intersecting chords in a circle, $(XW)(WY) = (UW)(WV)$. Solve the following equation, and then compute $XY = (z+12)+3$:

$$(z+12)(3) = (z+3)(z)$$
$$3z+36 = z^2 +3z$$
$$36 = z^2$$

$z = 6$ (because you can assume that, as a measurement of length, z is positive)

$$XY = (z+12)+3 = (6+12)+3 = 21$$

210. 14 Sketch a figure. The perimeter, P, is $P = 2l + 2w$, where the rectangle's length, l, is $AD = BC$, and its width, w, is $AB = DC$. Write and solve simultaneously the following two equations (assuming throughout that l and w are positive measures):

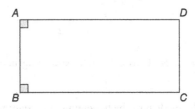

(1) $lw = 12$ and (2) $5^2 = l^2 + w^2$ (by the Pythagorean theorem)

Solve (2) for w: $w = \sqrt{25 - l^2}$.

Substitute into (1): $l\sqrt{25 - l^2} = 12$.

Square both sides: $l^2(25 - l^2) = 144$.

Simplify: $l^4 - 25l^2 + 144 = 0$.

Factor as you would a quadratic: $(l^2 - 9)(l^2 - 16)$.

Keeping in mind that l is positive, then from these two equations, $l = 3$ with $w = 4$ or $l = 4$ with $w = 3$. Either way, $P = 2l + 2w = 14$.

211. 5 The area of a square with sides of length, s, is s^2. The area of a parallelogram with base, b, and height, h, is bh. Write and solve the following equation:

$$10^2 = 20h$$
$$100 = 20h$$
$$h = 5$$

212. $\dfrac{1}{3}$ $\angle RCQ = \angle PCS = 120°$ (vertical angles are congruent). Thus, $\dfrac{2 \cdot 120°}{360°} = \dfrac{240°}{360°} = \dfrac{2}{3}$ of the circle is not shaded. Hence, $\dfrac{1}{3}$ of the circle is shaded.

213. 64° $m\angle A = m\angle DEB = 58°$ (corresponding angles of parallel lines are congruent). Because $\overline{BD} \cong \overline{DE}$, triangle BDE is isosceles. Thus, $m\angle B = m\angle DEB = 58°$ (base angles of an isosceles triangle are congruent). Thus, $m\angle C = 180° - 2(58°) = 64°$.

214. 72° Simplify $\frac{1}{3}y = b - 24°$:

$$3\left(\frac{1}{3}y\right) = 3(b - 24°)$$

$$y = 3b - 72°$$

From the figure, $x + y = 3b$ (vertical angles are congruent). Substituting yields $y = (x + y) - 72°$; $x = 72°$.

215. 13 The length of the median to the hypotenuse in a right triangle is half the length of the hypotenuse. Thus,

$$CM = \frac{1}{2}AB = \frac{1}{2}\sqrt{AC^2 + BC^2} = \frac{1}{2}\sqrt{24^2 + 10^2} = \frac{1}{2}\sqrt{676} = \frac{1}{2}(26) = 13$$

216. $\frac{3}{10}$ $3y° = m\angle 1 = 120°$ (corresponding angles of parallel lines are congruent); $y° = 40°$. Substitute into $5x° + 3y° = 180°$ (two consecutive angles of a parallelogram are supplementary) to obtain $5x° + 120° = 180°$; $5x° = 60°$; $x = 12$. Thus, $\frac{x}{y} = \frac{12}{40} = \frac{3}{10}$.

217. 60 Let x = the length of a side of the square. The perimeter, P, of the square is $P = 4x$. $\overline{BD}$ is a diagonal, so it divides the square into two isosceles right triangles. Because each of these triangles is a 45°-45°-90° right triangle, $BD = 15\sqrt{2} = x\sqrt{2}$; $x = 15$. Thus, $P = 4x = 4 \cdot 15 = 60$.

218. 10 $\angle R \cong \angle S$ (given), $\angle PTR \cong \angle QTS$ (vertical angles are congruent), and $\overline{PT} \cong \overline{QT}$ (T is the midpoint of $\overline{PQ}$), so $\triangle PTR \cong \triangle QTS$, by angle-angle-side. Thus, $QS = PR = 10$ (corresponding sides of congruent triangles are congruent).

219. 4.5 The diagonals of a parallelogram bisect each other, so (x_0, y_0) is the midpoint between $(0,0)$ and $(9,10)$, so $x_0 = \frac{0+9}{2} = 4.5$.

220. 12 Triangle XYZ is a 30°-60°-90° right triangle. Therefore, $x = \frac{1}{2}z = 4\sqrt{3}$; $z = 8\sqrt{3}$. And $y = \frac{\sqrt{3}}{2}z = \frac{\sqrt{3}}{2}(8\sqrt{3}) = 12$.

221. 14 Let x = the radius of circle K. Given that $\overline{AB}$ and $\overline{AKC}$ meet at point A exterior to circle K, then $(AD)(AB) = (AE)(AC)$. $AB = AD + BD$, so $24 = AD + 12$; $AD = 12$. $AKC = AE + x + x = 8 + 2x$. Substitute into $(AD)(AB) = (AE)(AC)$ and solve for x.

$$(12)(24) = (8)(8 + 2x)$$

$$288 = 64 + 16x$$

$$224 = 16x$$

$$14 = x$$

222. 72 Let $x =$ the number of customers who bought only a washer. Draw a Venn diagram, using the question information.

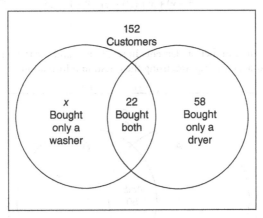

Using the diagram, write and solve the following equation:

$$x + 22 + 58 = 152$$
$$x + 80 = 152$$
$$x = 72$$

223. 4 Let $x =$ the number of students who like both orange and apple juice, $o =$ the number of students who like only orange juice, $a =$ the number of students who like only apple juice, and $g =$ the number of students who like only grape juice. Draw a Venn diagram, using the question information.

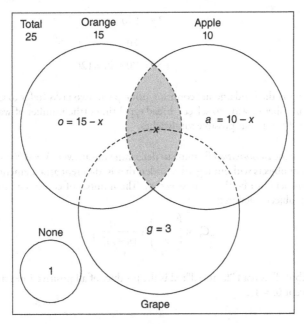

From the Venn diagram, write and solve the equation:

$$(15-x)+x+(10-x)+3+1=25$$

$$x=4$$

224. 120 Let x = the number of elements in set A only, and y = the number of elements in set B only. Draw a Venn diagram, using the question information.

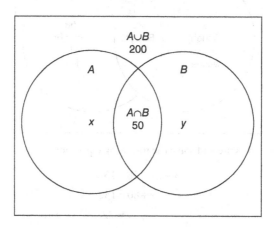

From the Venn diagram, $y+50$ = the number of elements in set B. Write and solve simultaneously the following two equations, and then compute $y+50$: (1) $x+50+y=200$ and (2) $x+50=y+50+10$. Simplify the equations: (1) $x+y=150$ and (2) $x-y=10$. Multiplying (2) by -1 and adding to (1) yields:

$$2y=140$$

$$y=70$$

$$y+50=70+50=120$$

225. 20 Applying the fundamental counting principle to two tasks (refer to Question 96), compute (the number of ways to select a bread type) times (the number of ways to select a filling) $= 4 \cdot 5 = 20$ different possible sandwiches.

226. 1140 Use the *combination* formula to determine the answer. A *combination* is a selection from a set of objects without regard to order; that is, different arrangements of the same objects are considered to be the same selection. The number of combinations of r objects from n distinct objects, denoted:

$$_nC_r \text{ or } \binom{n}{r} \text{ is } \frac{n!}{(n-r)!r!}$$

Note: The symbol "!" is read "factorial"; $n!$ is the product of all positive integers less than or equal to n (except $0! = 1$).

The order in which committee members are selected is immaterial. Therefore, the number of distinct committees is:

$$_{20}C_3 = \frac{20!}{(20-3)!3!} = \frac{20!}{(17)!3!} = \frac{20 \cdot 19 \cdot 18}{3 \cdot 2 \cdot 1} = 1140$$

227. 2700 Applying the fundamental counting principle to four tasks (refer to Question 96) yields $30 \cdot 6 \cdot 3 \cdot 5 = 2700$ different shoes in stock.

228. 24,360 There are 30 ways to fill the first position. After that position is filled, there are 29 ways to fill the second position. After the first and second positions are filled, there are 28 ways to fill the third position. Thus, there are $30 \cdot 29 \cdot 28 = 24,360$ different ways to fill the positions.

229. 64 Because repetitions are allowed, there are 4 ways to select the first digit, 4 ways to select the second digit, and 4 ways to select the third digit, yielding $4 \cdot 4 \cdot 4 = 64$ possible three-digit codes.

230. 60 For a 3-digit number, you must fill the hundreds place, the tens place, and the ones place. To be greater than 700, the hundreds digit must be 7, 8, or 9. Thus, there are 3 choices for the hundreds digit. After the hundreds digit is selected, 5 digits are available for the tens place. After the tens place is selected, 4 digits are available for the ones place. Therefore, there are $3 \cdot 5 \cdot 4 = 60$ such numbers.

231. 2 Let $b =$ the number of boys in the family and $g = b + 2 =$ the number of girls in the family. The total number of children is $b + (b + 2) = 2b + 2$. The probability, P, of randomly selecting a girl is:

$$P = \frac{\text{number of girls}}{\text{number of children}} = \frac{b+2}{2b+2} = \frac{2}{3}$$

Solve for b.

$$\frac{b+2}{2b+2} = \frac{2}{3}$$

$$3(b+2) = 2(2b+2)$$

$$3b+6 = 4b+4$$

$$b = 2$$

232. 0.32 There are two ways for Katniss to make exactly one of the next two foul shots. She can make the first foul shot, but miss the second foul shot, or she can miss the first foul shot, but make the second foul shot. The probability that Katniss will make the shot is 0.8 and the probability that she will miss is 0.2. The outcomes of the foul shots are independent, so the probability that Katniss will make exactly one of the next two foul-shot attempts is $(0.8)(0.2) + (0.2)(0.8) = 0.32$.

233. $\dfrac{1}{5}$ Let $x =$ the coordinate of point P.

Then the probability that the point selected is within 2 units of point P is
$$\dfrac{(x+2)-(x-2)}{AB}=\dfrac{4}{14+6}=\dfrac{4}{20}=\dfrac{1}{5}.$$

234. $30,000 Let $x =$ total amount of the investment. $45\%x - 30\%x = 15\%x$ is how much more money is invested in US stocks than in foreign stocks. From the graph and question information, you know that $5\%x = \$10,000$. Thus, $15\%x = 3(5\%x) = 3(\$10,000) = \$30,000$.

235. 18%

$$\text{The range is the maximum value minus the minimum value} =$$
$$8\% - (-10\%) = 8\% + 10\% = 18\%$$

236. 11%

$$\dfrac{17\% + 5\% + 4\% + 9\% + 9\% + 14\% + 19\%}{7} = 11\%$$

237. 22%

$$19\% - (-3\%) = 19\% + 3\% = 22\%$$

238. 16.6 years

$$\text{mean age} = \dfrac{2 \cdot 18 + 11 \cdot 17 + 12 \cdot 16}{2 + 11 + 12} = \dfrac{415}{25} = 16.6$$

239. 17 years The median position is $\dfrac{n+1}{2} = \dfrac{25+1}{2} = 13$. The number in the 13th position is 17, so 17 is the median age.

240. 16 years The age with the highest frequency is 16, so 16 is the mode age.

241. 98 Let $x =$ the required score for the fourth test. Write and solve the following the equation:

$$\dfrac{77+91+94+x}{4} = 90$$
$$\dfrac{262+x}{4} = 90$$
$$262+x = 360$$
$$x = 98$$

242. 75 kilograms Let $x=$ the weight of the fourth student. Write and solve the following equation:

$$\frac{3(55)+x}{4}=60$$

$$\frac{165+x}{4}=60$$

$$165+x=240$$

$$x=75$$

243. 4 The average is $\frac{a+b+c}{3}$. *Tip:* Notice that to answer the question, you do not need the specific values of a, b, and c. You need only the value of their sum, $a+b+c$. Adding the two equations yields the equation $6a+6b+6c=72$, which simplifies to $a+b+c=12$. Then $\frac{a+b+c}{3}=\frac{12}{3}=4$.

244. 165 Refer to Question 116 for an explanation of percentiles. For the data in the stem-and-leaf plot, the value of k for the 95th percentile is $k=n\left(\frac{R}{100}\right)=36\left(\frac{95}{100}\right)=34.2$. Round up 34.2 to get $l=35$. Thus, the 95th percentile is the 35th data value, which is 165.

245. 2.5 The interquartile range (IQR) is the difference between the third and first quartiles: $\text{IQR} = Q_3 - Q_1$. *Note:* Q_1 is the 25th percentile and Q_3 is the 75th percentile (refer to Question 116 for an explanation of percentiles). For the 25th percentile, $k=n\left(\frac{R}{100}\right)=48\left(\frac{25}{100}\right)=12$. So Q_1, the 25th percentile, is halfway between the 12th and 13th data values: $\frac{1+2}{2}=1.5$. For the 75th percentile, $k=n\left(\frac{R}{100}\right)=48\left(\frac{75}{100}\right)=36$. So Q_3, the 75th percentile, is halfway between the 36th and 37th data values: $\frac{4+4}{2}=4$. Thus, $\text{IQR}=Q_3-Q_1=4-1.5=2.5$.

246. 12.25 The variance is the square of the standard deviation. Thus, variance $= 3.5^2 = 12.25$.

247. 56.5 inches 54 inches $+1(2.5$ inches$) = 56.5$ inches.

248. 96% On the standard normal curve, 15 years (the mean) corresponds to 0, 6 years corresponds to −2 (because $15 - 2(4.5) = 15 - 9 = 6$), and 24 years corresponds to 2 (because $15 + 2(4.5) = 15 + 9 = 24$) as shown here.

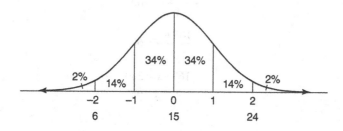

Thus, $14\% + 34\% + 34\% + 14\% = 96\%$ of the teachers have years of service between 6 years and 24 years.

249. 98% On the standard normal curve, 152 (the mean) corresponds to 0, and 170 corresponds to 2 (because $152 + 2(9) = 152 + 18 = 170$) as shown here.

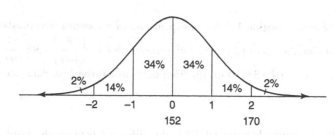

Thus, a test taker with a score of 170 does as well or better than $100\% - 2\% = 98\%$ of the test takers.

250. 16% On the standard normal curve, 183 (the mean) corresponds to 0, and 190 corresponds to 1 (because $183 + 1(7) = 183 + 7 = 190$) as shown here.

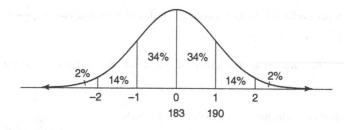

From the figure, $14\% + 2\% = 16\%$ of the scores are above 190, so the probability that Colin will bowl a score above 190 is 16%.

Chapter 3: Multiple-Choice Questions with One Correct Answer

251. (E) The squares between 2 and 100 that have units digit 6 are 16 and 36, so n is either 4 or 6. Suppose n is 4, then 9 is the units digit of $(n-1)^2 = 3^2 = 9$. Thus, n is not 4. If n is 6, 5 is the units digit of $(n-1)^2 = 5^2 = 25$. The units digit of $(n+1)^2 = 7^2 = 49$ is 9.

252. (B) Let m and n be the two positive integers, then $\sqrt{m \cdot n} = 15$, so $m \cdot n = 225$. The factors of 225 are 1, 3, 5, 9, 15, 25, 45, 75, and 225. The possible two-factor combinations for m and n, with a product of 225, are 1 and 225, 3 and 75, 4 and 45, 9 and 25, and 15 and 15. The possible sums for these two-factor combinations are 226, 78, 50, 34, and 30, which makes (B) the correct response.

253. (D)

$$20! = 20 \cdot 19 \cdot 18 \cdot 17 \cdot 16 \cdot 15 \cdot 14 \cdot 13 \cdot 12 \cdot 11 \cdot 10 \cdot 9 \cdot 8 \cdot 7 \cdot 6 \cdot 5 \cdot 4 \cdot 3 \cdot 2 \cdot 1$$

Hence, you can eliminate (A) because any positive integer ≤ 20 is a factor of 20. Eliminate (B) because it is a prime. Any positive integer > 20 that can be expressed as the product of factors of 20! is a factor of 20!. For instance, $36 = 2 \cdot 18$ is a factor of 20!, so you can eliminate (C). Choice (D), 46, is not a prime *and* $46 = 2 \cdot 23$ is not a factor of 20! because 23 is not a factor of 20! Thus, (D) is the correct response. You do not have to check choice E because $46 < 58$.

254. (B) The fraction of the land inherited by the older son and oldest daughter together is $\dfrac{1}{4} + \dfrac{1}{3} = \dfrac{3}{12} + \dfrac{4}{12} = \dfrac{7}{12}$. The fraction remaining is $1 - \dfrac{7}{12} = \dfrac{5}{12}$. The fraction inherited by each of the three remaining children (including the younger son) is $\dfrac{5}{12} \div 3 = \dfrac{5}{12} \times \dfrac{1}{3} = \dfrac{5}{36}$.

255. (D) Let b = the basketball coach's salary. Then $b + \dfrac{1}{4}b = 1\dfrac{1}{4}b$ = the football coach's salary. The basketball coach's salary is $\dfrac{1\frac{1}{4}b}{b} \cdot 100\%$ of the football coach's salary. Because b will cancel out of this latter expression, you can substitute any convenient value for b to determine the percent. The final answer will be the same no matter what amount for b you choose—even if it's a completely unrealistic amount. Let b = \$100. Then $\$100 + \dfrac{1}{4} \cdot \$100 =$ $\$125$ = the football coach's salary. Thus, the percent is $\dfrac{100}{125} \cdot 100\% = \dfrac{4}{5} \cdot 100\% = 80\%$.

Tip: Picking a number to work with (even if it is not realistic) can simplify a problem.

256. (A) Let x = the length (in centimeters) of the cricket scale drawing. Set up a proportion and solve for x.

$$\frac{x}{9 \text{ cm}} = \frac{1 \text{ cm}}{2.5 \text{ cm}}$$

$$x = \frac{(9 \text{ cm})(1 \text{ cm})}{2.5 \text{ cm}} = 3.6 \text{ cm}$$

Tip: In the proportion $\dfrac{a}{b} = \dfrac{c}{d}$, ad and bc are the *cross products*. You can shorten the process for solving a proportion by doing the following: Find a cross product that you can numerically calculate and divide it by the numerical term in the proportion that you did not use. For instance, in this problem, calculate (9 cm)(1 cm) and divide by 2.5 cm. Since you are allowed to use a calculator on the GRE, this is the quickest and most reliable way to solve a proportion on the test.

257. (B) Let x = the number of grams of zinc needed. Set up a proportion and solve for x.

$$\frac{x}{120} = \frac{2}{5}; \; x = \frac{(120)(2)}{5} = 48$$

258. (C) Let x = original price. Then:

$$x - 15\%x = \$119$$

$$85\%x = \$119$$

$$x = \frac{\$119}{85\%} = \frac{\$119}{0.85} = \$140 = \text{original price}$$

After the toy store raises the new price by 20%, the final price is $\$119 + 20\%(119) =$ $\$119 + 0.20(119) = \$119 + \$23.80 = \$142.80$. This amount is greater than $\$140$, so eliminate (A) and (B) because these percents are less than 100%. You can check (C), (D), and (E) by multiplying the percent times $\$140$ to see if the product is $\$142.80$, or you can calculate the percent, R, as follows (omitting units for convenience):

$$R = \frac{P}{B} = \frac{142.80}{140} = 1.02 = 102\%.$$

259. (D) Because the question indicates there is a longer and a shorter piece, you know that the rope was *not* cut in half. Therefore, the longer piece has to be longer than 25 feet (half of 50 feet). Hence, you can eliminate (A), (B), and (C). Now, check the remaining choices. Checking (D): If the longer piece is 30 feet, then the shorter piece is 20 feet. Because 30 = $150\%(20) = 1.5(20)$, (D) is the correct response. There is no need to check (E). Move on to the next question.

260. (B) Working backward is the best strategy for this problem. In the fourth week, the student worked 20% more hours than in the third week, so write the following percent equation and solve for x, where x is the number of hours worked in the third week: $42 = 120\%x$. Thus, $x = \dfrac{42}{120\%} = \dfrac{42}{1.2} = 35$ (the number of hours worked in the third week). In the third week, the student worked 25% more hours than in the second week, so write the following percent equation and solve for y, where y is the number of hours worked in the second week: $35 = 125\%y$. Thus, $y = \dfrac{35}{125\%} = \dfrac{35}{1.25} = 28$ (the number of hours worked in the second week).

In the second week, the student worked 40% more hours than in the first week, so write the following percent equation and solve for z, where z is the number of hours worked in the first week: $28 = 140\%z$. Thus, $z = \dfrac{28}{140\%} = \dfrac{28}{1.4} = 20$ (the number of hours worked in the first week). *Tip:* Use the provided calculator wisely. Changing percents to decimals in this problem simplified the calculator computations.

261. (C) $\sqrt{400} = 20$, so choice C is the correct response because $(\sqrt{20})^2 = 20$.

262. (D) In February, the electricity cost is $\$1420 - 0.025(\$1420) = (\$1420)(1 - 0.025) =$ $(\$1420)(0.975)$. Thus, in March, the electricity cost is $(\$1420)(0.975)(1 - 0.025) =$ $(\$1420)(0.975)(0.975)$.

263. (E) It is useful to know that, in general, if the prime factorization of a positive integer is $p_1^{k_1} p_2^{k_2} \cdots p_n^{k_n}$, where the p's are distinct positive prime numbers and the k's are their corresponding exponents, then the number of positive divisors of that integer is the product $(k_1 + 1)(k_2 + 1) \cdots (k_n + 1)$. Thus, the number of positive divisors of $m = a^4 b^2 c^5 d$ is $(4 + 1)(2 + 1)(5 + 1)(1 + 1) = (5)(3)(6)(2) = 180$. *Tip:* Knowing simple tricks about integers such as how to quickly determine the number of positive divisors of a positive integer (as demonstrated in this question) can turn what, at first, looks like a difficult question into an easy computation exercise.

264. (B) Calculate the initial number of college students: $\dfrac{1}{4} \times 4800 = 1200$. Calculate $\dfrac{1}{3}$ of this number: $\dfrac{1}{3} \times 1200 = 400$. Calculate the number of college students remaining: $1200 - 400 = 800$. Calculate the number of total residents remaining: $4800 - 400 = 4400$. Calculate the portion of the total remaining that are college students: $\dfrac{800}{4400} = \dfrac{2}{11}$.

265. (D) For convenience, suppose the investment is $\$100$. In 10 years, its value will be $3 \cdot \$100 = \$300$. In 20 years, its value will be $3 \cdot \$300 = \$900$. Finally, in 30 years, the value of the investment will be $3 \cdot \$900 = \$2700$. Because $\$2700$ is 27 times $\$100$, the investment increased by a factor of 27. *Tip:* Picking a convenient amount for the investment is a useful strategy in problems like this one.

266. (C) The total percent invested in stocks, the mutual fund, and bonds is $50\% + 25\% + 20\% = 95\%$. Thus, the percent invested in certificates of deposit is $100\% - 95\% = 5\%$. Write the following percent equation and solve for x, the total amount invested: $5\%x = \$20,000$. Hence,

$$x = \frac{\$20,000}{5\%} = \frac{\$20,000}{0.05} = \$400,000$$

267. (D)

$$\text{Percent increase} = \frac{\text{New value} - \text{Old value}}{\text{Old value}} = \frac{\$375 - \$300}{\$300} = \frac{\$75}{\$300} = \frac{1}{4} = 25\%$$

268. (D) Find all the positive integers that will divide into 19 and leave a remainder of 3. These integers are 4, 8, and 16, the sum of which is 28.

269. (E) Looking for a pattern is the best strategy for this problem. Calculate powers of 3:

$$3^0 = 1, 3^1 = 3, 3^2 = 9, 3^3 = 27, 3^4 = 81, 3^5 = 243.$$

Because the units digit of 3^5 is 3, the next power, 3^6, will have units digit 9, and 3^7 will have units digit 7. Thus, the units digit for powers of 3 has the pattern 1, 3, 9, 7, 1, 3, 9, 7, and so on. Therefore, 3^{4n} has units digit 1, 3^{4n+1} has units digit 3, 3^{4n+2} has units digit 9, and 3^{4n+3} has units digit 7. Hence, $3^{102} = 3^{4\cdot25+2} = 3^{4n+2}$ has units digit 9.

270. (C) For convenience, designate the locations A, B, C, D, and E with tokens in the ratio 5:3:2:4:1, respectively. Let x be the number of tokens in E. Then A, B, C, D, and E have $5x$, $3x$, $2x$, $4x$, and x tokens, respectively. The minimum number of tokens needed to win is $\dfrac{1}{8}$ of the combined tokens in B, C, and E (because these locations have the fewest tokens):

$\dfrac{1}{8}\cdot 3x + \dfrac{1}{8}\cdot 2x + \dfrac{1}{8}\cdot x = \dfrac{6x}{8} = \dfrac{3}{4}x$. The total number of tokens is $5x + 3x + 2x + 4x + x = 15x$.

The minimum percent needed to win is $\dfrac{\frac{3}{4}x}{15x}$, which you can calculate two ways:

$\dfrac{\frac{3}{4}\cancel{x}}{15\cancel{x}} = \dfrac{3}{4} \div 15 = \dfrac{\cancel{3}}{4} \times \dfrac{1}{\cancelto{5}{15}} = \dfrac{1}{4} \times \dfrac{1}{5} = \dfrac{1}{20} = 5\%$ or, equivalently, $\dfrac{\frac{3}{4}\cancel{x}}{15\cancel{x}} = \dfrac{0.75}{15} = 0.05 = 5\%.$

Tip: You are provided a basic calculator, so changing common fractions to decimals before performing computations is an efficient strategy (as demonstrated in the preceding calculation). Take some time to make sure you know familiar equivalents (such as $\dfrac{1}{2} = 0.5$, $\dfrac{1}{4} = 0.25$, $\dfrac{3}{4} = 0.75$, $\dfrac{1}{5} = 0.2$, and so on).

271. (B)

$$\dfrac{\$800,000,000}{1} \times \dfrac{1\text{ second}}{\$1} \times \dfrac{1\text{ hour}}{3600\text{ seconds}} \times \dfrac{1\text{ day}}{24\text{ hours}} \times \dfrac{1\text{ year}}{365\text{ days}} =$$

$$\dfrac{\cancel{\$}800,000,000}{1} \times \dfrac{1\text{ \cancel{second}}}{\cancel{\$}1} \times \dfrac{1\text{ \cancel{hour}}}{3600\text{ \cancel{seconds}}} \times \dfrac{1\text{ \cancel{day}}}{24\text{ \cancel{hours}}} \times \dfrac{1\text{ year}}{365\text{ \cancel{days}}} \approx 25\text{ years}$$

Tip: Because the answer choices are not close to each other, round the numbers in this problem to estimate the answer as follows:

$$\frac{800{,}000{,}000}{1} \times \frac{1}{4000} \times \frac{1}{20} \times \frac{1}{400} = \frac{\overset{200}{\cancel{800{,}000{,}000}}}{1} \times \frac{1}{\underset{1}{\cancel{4000}}} \times \frac{1}{\underset{2}{\cancel{20}}} \times \frac{1}{\underset{4}{\cancel{400}}}$$

$$= \frac{\overset{100}{\cancel{200}}}{1} \times \frac{1}{\underset{1}{\cancel{2}}} \times \frac{1}{4} = \frac{100}{4} = 25.$$

272. (D) Checking the answers is a good strategy for this problem. Checking (A): At $30 per ticket, 200 people will attend, yielding $200 \times \$30 = \$6000$ in ticket sales. Checking (B): At $45 per ticket, 175 people will attend, yielding $175 \times \$45 = \$7875$ in ticket sales. Checking (C): At $60 per ticket, 150 people will attend, yielding $150 \times \$60 = \$9000$ in ticket sales. Checking (D): At $75 per ticket, 125 people will attend, yielding $125 \times \$75 = \$9375$ in ticket sales. Checking (E): At $90 per ticket, 100 people will attend, yielding $100 \times \$90 = \$9000$ in ticket sales. Thus, (D) is the correct response.

273. (D) Let $2x$, $5x$, and $6x$ equal the weights (in grams) of ingredients X, Y, and Z, respectively, in the mixture. Then,

$$2x + 5x + 6x = 7.8 \text{ grams}$$

$$13x = 7.8 \text{ grams}$$

$$x = 0.6 \text{ grams}$$

$$2x = 1.2 \text{ grams of ingredient } X$$

$$6x = 3.6 \text{ grams of ingredient } Z$$

$$3.6 \text{ grams} - 1.2 \text{ grams} = 2.4 \text{ grams}$$

274. (B) The vehicle traveled 5 hours at 50 miles per hour (mph), so the distance, d, from City A to City B is $d = rt = (50 \text{ mph})(5 \text{ hours}) = 250$ miles. At 65 mph, the time would be $t = \dfrac{d}{r} = \dfrac{250 \text{ miles}}{65 \text{ mph}} \approx 3.846$ hours ≈ 3 hours, 51 minutes. 9 a.m. plus 3 hours 51 minutes = 12:51 p.m.

275. (A) For convenience, let the value of the pendant in 2010 equal $100. In 2011, the value of the pendant was $\$100 - 10\%(\$100) = \$90$. In 2012, the value of the pendant was $\$90 + 20\%(\$90) = \$108$. In 2013, the value of the pendant was $\$108 - 10\%(\$108) = \$97.20$. The percent change is:

$$\frac{\text{New value} - \text{Old value}}{\text{Old value}} = \frac{\$97.20 - \$100}{\$100} = \frac{-2.80}{100} = -2.8\%,$$

which is a 2.8% decrease in value.

276. (C) According to the chart, the total number of students is $950 + 1450 + 1040 + 560 = 4000$. The number of students 21 or over is $1040 + 560 = 1600$. The percent of students 21 or over is $\dfrac{1600}{4000} = 40\%$.

277. (A) The percent water by weight in the initial solution is $100\% - 20\% = 80\%$. For convenience, suppose initially the solution weighed 100 grams (g). Then it would contain 20 g (20% of 100 g) of sugar and 80 g (80% of 100 g) of water. After evaporation, the number of grams of sugar is still 20 g. This represents 60% of the evaporated solution by weight. Write the following percent equation and solve for x, the new weight (after evaporation) of the solution: $60\% x = 20$ g. Thus, $x = \dfrac{20\ \text{g}}{60\%} = \dfrac{20\ \text{g}}{.6} = \dfrac{100\ \text{g}}{3} = 33\dfrac{1}{3}$ g. The weight of water in the evaporated solution is $33\dfrac{1}{3}$ g $- 20$ g $= 13\dfrac{1}{3}$ g $= \dfrac{40}{3}$ g. Thus, the ratio of the final weight of water to the initial weight of water in the mixture is:

$$\dfrac{\dfrac{40}{3}\ \text{g}}{80\ \text{g}} = \dfrac{40}{3} \div \dfrac{80}{1} = \dfrac{\cancel{40}}{3} \times \dfrac{1}{\cancel{80}_2} = \dfrac{1}{6}\ \text{or 1 to 6.}$$

Tip: You should eliminate (D) and (E) from the outset because these ratios imply that the weight of water after evaporation was more than the weight before evaporation. This result does not make sense in the real world.

278. (D) $\left(\sqrt{5+\sqrt{17}} - \sqrt{5-\sqrt{17}}\right)^2 = \left(\sqrt{5+\sqrt{17}}\right)^2 - 2\sqrt{5+\sqrt{17}}\sqrt{5-\sqrt{17}} + \left(\sqrt{5-\sqrt{17}}\right)^2 =$

$5 + \sqrt{17} - 2\sqrt{25 - (\sqrt{17})^2} + 5 - \sqrt{17} = 10 - 2\sqrt{25-17} = 10 - 2\sqrt{8} = 10 - 4\sqrt{2}$.

279. (E) When you divide a number by 6, your remainder can be 0, 1, 2, 3, 4, or 5. Thus, any non-negative integer must be of the form $6k$, $6k+1$, $6k+2$, $6k+3$, $6k+4$, or $6k+5$. Because n is not divisible by 2 or 3, then n must have the form $6k+1$ or $6k+5$ ($k = 0, 1, 2, \ldots$). So the remainder when n is divided by 6 is either 1 or 5. Thus, (E) is the correct response.

280. (A) The number on the left of the equal sign is expressed in the base-7 system, while the number on the right is expressed in the base-12 system. To find the value of b, expand the numbers in their respective bases to convert them to the base-10 system and then solve for b.

$$5b2_{\text{base 7}} = 187_{\text{base 12}}$$
$$5\cdot 7^2 + b\cdot 7 + 2 = 1\cdot 12^2 + 8\cdot 12 + 7$$
$$5\cdot 49 + 7b + 2 = 1\cdot 144 + 8\cdot 12 + 7$$
$$7b + 247 = 247$$
$$7b = 0$$
$$b = 0$$

281. (B) You will find it helpful to know that the least common multiple of two positive integers is their product divided by their greatest common divisor. Thus, $756 = \dfrac{84n}{12}$; $756 = 7n$; $n = 108$. *Tip:* This question demonstrates the use of a well-known fact about the relationship between least common multiple and greatest common divisor.

282. (D) Let $x =$ Effie's total sales last week.

$$\$350 + 6\%x = \$920$$

$$6\%x = \$570$$

$$x = \frac{\$570}{6\%} = \frac{\$570}{0.06} = \$9500$$

283. (D) Let $x =$ Shirin's age now. Then $2x =$ Mario's age now. Make a chart to organize the information in the question.

When?	Shirin's Age	Mario's Age	Sum
Now	x	$2x$	?
5 years from now	$x + 5$	$2x + 5$	52

Using the information in the chart, set up an equation and solve for x.

$$(x + 5) + (2x + 5) = 52$$

$$x + 5 + 2x + 5 = 52$$

$$3x = 42$$

$$x = 14, \text{ Shirin's age now}$$

$$2x = 28, \text{ Mario's age now}$$

$$28 + 10 = 38, \text{ Mario's age 10 years from now}$$

Tip: Make sure you answer the question asked. In this question, after you obtain Shirin's age now, you must calculate Mario's age 10 years from now.

284. (C)

$$(m+n)^2 - 2 + 2(m+n) + \frac{m+n}{3} = (-6)^2 - 2 + 2(-6) + \frac{-6}{3} = 36 - 2 - 12 - 2 = 20$$

285. (C)

$$\left(\frac{x^{-5}}{x^{-9}}\right)^{\frac{1}{2}} = (x^{-5+9})^{\frac{1}{2}} = (x^4)^{\frac{1}{2}} = x^2$$

286. (D)

$$z = \frac{1.2y}{x^2}$$

$$zx^2 = 1.2y$$

$$x^2 = \frac{1.2y}{z}$$

$$x = \pm\sqrt{\frac{1.2y}{z}}$$

287. (D)

$$10x = 10(1+(2+3^{-1})^{-1})^{-1} = 10\left(1+\left(2+\frac{1}{3}\right)^{-1}\right)^{-1} = 10\left(1+\left(\frac{7}{3}\right)^{-1}\right)^{-1} = 10\left(1+\frac{3}{7}\right)^{-1}$$

$$= 10\left(\frac{10}{7}\right)^{-1} = 10\left(\frac{7}{10}\right) = 7$$

288. (A) Let x = number of pounds of \$2.50 per pound candy. Then $90 - x$ = number of pounds of \$3.75 per pound candy. Make a chart to organize the information in the question.

Price	Number of Pounds	Value
\$2.50	x	\$2.50x
\$3.75	$90 - x$	\$3.75$(90 - x)$
\$3.00	90	\$3.00(90)

The value of the candy before it is mixed should equal the value after it is mixed. Using the information in the chart, set up an equation and solve for x (omitting units for convenience):

$$2.50x + 3.75(90 - x) = 3.00(90)$$

$$2.50x + 337.50 - 3.75x = 270.00$$

$$-1.25x = -67.5$$

$$x = 54$$

Tip: Think before you begin. If you use half of each type of candy, then the price would be the average of \$2.50 and \$3.75, which is about \$3.13, so you know that to bring the price down to \$3.00 per pound, you will need more than 45 pounds (half of 90 pounds) of the \$2.50 candy. So you can eliminate choices (C), (D), and (E) right away. You can check (A) and (B) in the first equation to determine that (A) is the correct response.

289. (E) Because the square of any real number is always nonnegative, then $(2x-3)^2 \geq 0$. Thus, $5-(2x-3)^2$ is less than or equal to 5 for all real numbers x.

290. (D)

$$(3 \otimes 2) = 2 \cdot 3 + 3 \cdot 2 = 12, \text{ so } (3 \otimes 2) \otimes 5 = 12 \otimes 5 = 2 \cdot 12 + 12 \cdot 5 = 24 + 60 = 84$$

291. (E)

$$12^x + 15^x = (3 \cdot 4)^x + (3 \cdot 5)^x = 3^x \cdot 4^x + 3^x \cdot 5^x = 3^x(4^x + 5^x)$$

292. (C)

$$(c^2+9)^{-\frac{1}{2}} = \frac{1}{(c^2+9)^{\frac{1}{2}}} = \frac{1}{\sqrt{c^2+9}}$$

293. (D)

$$\sqrt{3x+3} = \sqrt{3x}+1 \text{ Square both sides.}$$
$$(\sqrt{3x+3})^2 = (\sqrt{3x}+1)^2$$
$$3x+3 = (\sqrt{3x})^2 + 2\sqrt{3x} + 1$$
$$3x+3 = 3x + 2\sqrt{3x} + 1$$
$$2 = 2\sqrt{3x}$$
$$1 = \sqrt{3x} \text{ Square both sides.}$$
$$1^2 = (\sqrt{3x})^2$$
$$1 = 3x$$

294. (C) Solve the double inequality.

$$-7 < 2x+1 < 5$$
$$-7-1 < 2x+1-1 < 5-1$$
$$-8 < 2x < 4$$

$-4 < x < 2$, which corresponds to choice (C).

Tip: Because the inequalities in the problem are strictly "less than," the interval will not include endpoints. So you can eliminate (B) and (D) right off as these intervals include endpoints.

295. (E) If $a \neq 0$, $ax^2 + bx + c = 0$ is a quadratic equation. The quantity $b^2 - 4ac$ is its discriminant. The discriminant determines the nature of the roots of the equation. If $b^2 - 4ac < 0$, there are no real roots; if $b^2 - 4ac = 0$, there is exactly one real, rational root; and if $b^2 - 4ac > 0$ (as in this question), there are exactly two real roots. Both of these roots are rational if $b^2 - 4ac$ is a perfect square; otherwise, both are irrational. Because 17 is not a perfect square, the equation has exactly two real, irrational roots.

296. (C) Let $2x =$ the number of ounces of flaxseed in the mixture. Then $3x =$ the number of ounces of wheat germ in the mixture, and $5x =$ the number of ounces of cornmeal in the mixture. Using the information in the question, write an equation and solve for x.

$$2x + 3x + 5x = 30$$
$$10x = 30$$
$$x = 3$$
$$2x = 6$$

297. (D) Divide the numerator and denominator by y: $\dfrac{x}{y+z} = \dfrac{\dfrac{x}{y}}{\dfrac{y}{y}+\dfrac{z}{y}} = \dfrac{\dfrac{x}{y}}{1+\dfrac{z}{y}}$. Substitute the information from the question and simplify: $\dfrac{20}{1+\dfrac{1}{10}} = \dfrac{20}{11/10} = \dfrac{10(20)}{10\left(11/10\right)} = \dfrac{200}{11}$.

298. (E)

$$3(x+1)(x-1) + \frac{x(4x-6)}{2} = 3(x^2-1) + \frac{4x^2-6x}{2} = 3(x^2-1) + \frac{\cancel{2}(2x^2-3x)}{\cancel{2}}$$
$$= 3x^2 - 3 + 2x^2 - 3x = 5x^2 - 3x - 3$$

299. (B) First, let $x = 5$ and solve for k.

$$x^2 - 2x + k = 12$$
$$5^2 - 2 \cdot 5 + k = 12$$
$$25 - 10 + k = 12$$
$$k = -3$$

Next, let $k = -3$ and solve for x.

$$x^2 - 2x - 3 = 12$$
$$x^2 - 2x - 15 = 0$$
$$(x-5)(x+3) = 0$$
$$x = 5 \text{ or } x = -3$$

Tip: Once you know that the equation is $x^2 - 2x - 3 = 12$, you can substitute in the answer choices to determine that (B) is the correct response.

300. (D) For convenience, number the equations.

$$(1)\ 4x+5y\qquad=-2$$
$$(2)\ -4x+3y+5z=13$$
$$(3)\ 2x+5y-\ z=5$$

Proceed systematically. First, eliminate x from the three equations. Add (1) and (2):

$$4x+5y\qquad=-2$$
$$\underline{-4x+3y+5z=13}$$
$$(4)\qquad 8y+5z=11$$

Add 2 times (3) to (2):

$$4x+10y-2z=10$$
$$\underline{-4x+\ 3y+\ 5z=13}$$
$$(5)\qquad 13y+3z=23$$

Now, eliminate z from (4) and (5) by adding 5 times (5) and –3 times (4), and then solve for y.

$$65y+15z=115$$
$$\underline{-24y-15z=-33}$$
$$41y\qquad=82$$
$$y\qquad=2$$

301. (D) $2t(t-2)=1$

$$2t^2-4t-1=0$$

$$t=\frac{-b\pm\sqrt{b^2-4ac}}{2a}=\frac{4\pm\sqrt{16+8}}{4}=\frac{4\pm\sqrt{24}}{4}=\frac{4\pm2\sqrt{6}}{4}=\frac{2\pm\sqrt{6}}{2}$$

302. (A) A function is a set of ordered pairs for which each first element is paired with *one and only one* second element. In other words, in a function no two ordered pairs have the same first element but different second elements. Only the set of ordered pairs in (A) fails to satisfy the definition of a function. The ordered pairs $(1,2)$ and $(1,5)$ have the same first element but different second elements.

303. (A) $\dfrac{f(1)}{g(4)}=\dfrac{1^2+1+1}{\sqrt{4}}=\dfrac{3}{2}$ *Tip:* Remember the square root symbol always indicates the nonnegative root of a number. This root is the *principal square root*.

304. (A) Using the table, $f(4)=2$, so $g(f(4))=g(2)=1$.

305. (D) $\left(\sqrt{\sqrt{\sqrt{x}}}\right)^6 = \left(\left(\left((x)^{\frac{1}{2}}\right)^{\frac{1}{2}}\right)^{\frac{1}{2}}\right)^6 = x^{\frac{1}{2}\frac{1}{2}\frac{1}{2}\frac{6}{1}} = x^{\frac{6}{8}} = x^{\frac{3}{4}}$

306. (B) $\dfrac{m}{m^2-n^2} - \dfrac{n}{m^2+mn} = \dfrac{m}{(m+n)(m-n)} - \dfrac{n}{m(m+n)}$

$$= \dfrac{m \cdot m}{m(m+n)(m-n)} - \dfrac{n(m-n)}{m(m+n)(m-n)}$$

$$= \dfrac{m^2}{m(m+n)(m-n)} - \dfrac{nm-n^2}{m(m+n)(m-n)} = \dfrac{m^2-mn+n^2}{m(m+n)(m-n)}$$

Tip: Apply a minus sign preceding a fraction to each term of the numerator.

307. (C) $\left|2x-1\right| > 7$ if and only if ($\Leftrightarrow$)

$$2x-1 < -7 \text{ or } 2x-1 > 7 \Leftrightarrow$$
$$2x < -6 \text{ or } 2x > 8 \Leftrightarrow$$
$$x < -3 \text{ or } x > 4 \Leftrightarrow$$
$$(-\infty,-3)\cup(4,\infty)$$

308. (B) $f(g(t)) = \dfrac{\left(1+\dfrac{1}{g(t)}\right)^2}{\left(1-\dfrac{1}{g(t)}\right)} = \dfrac{\left(1+\dfrac{1}{\frac{1}{t}}\right)^2}{\left(1-\dfrac{1}{\frac{1}{t}}\right)} = \dfrac{\left(1+\dfrac{t(1)}{t\left(\frac{1}{t}\right)}\right)^2}{\left(1-\dfrac{t(1)}{t\left(\frac{1}{t}\right)}\right)} = \left(\dfrac{1+t}{1-t}\right)^2 = \dfrac{(1+t)^2}{(1-t)^2}$

$$= \dfrac{(t+1)^2}{(t-1)^2} = \left(\dfrac{t+1}{t-1}\right)^2$$

Tip: $(1-t)^2 = ((-1)(t-1))^2 = (-1)^2(t-1)^2 = 1(t-1)^2 = (t-1)^2$.

309. (A) The distance formula is $d = rt$, where d is the distance traveled at a uniform rate of speed, r, for a length of time, t. Let t = the time in hours. Make a chart to organize the information in the question.

Vehicle	Rate (in mph)	Time (in hours)	Distance
Vehicle 1	r	t	rt
Vehicle 2	$r + 10$	t	$(r + 10)t$
N/A	N/A	Total:	d

Using the information in the chart, set up an equation and solve for t (omitting units for convenience):

$$rt+(r+10)t = d$$
$$t(r+r+10) = d$$
$$t(2r+10) = d$$
$$t = \frac{d}{2r+10}$$

310. (C) Let x = number of milliliters of distilled water to be added. Make a chart to organize the information in the question.

Alcohol strength of solution	Number of milliliters	Amount of alcohol
0% (distilled water)	x	0%x
80%	600	80%(600)
50%	$x + 600$	50%($x + 600$)

The amount of alcohol before mixing equals the amount of alcohol after mixing. Using the information in the chart, set up an equation and solve for x.

$$0\%x+80\%(600) = 50\%(x+600)$$
$$0.8(600) = 0.5(x+600)$$
$$480 = 0.5x+300$$
$$180 = 0.5x$$
$$360 = x$$

Tip: You should eliminate (E) at the outset because adding 600 milliliters to a 600 milliliter 80% alcohol solution would dilute it to a 40% alcohol solution.

311. (E) Determine the rate at which one device works. Let r = rate of 1 device, then when 2 devices work together for 6 hours, you have:

$$2 \cdot r \cdot 6 = 1 \text{ (task)}$$
$$12r = 1$$
$$r = \frac{1}{12} \text{ task per hour}$$

You can reason that if one device working alone can do $\frac{1}{12}$ of the task in one hour, then it will take 12 hours for it to do the task. You also can arrive at this answer as follows:

Let $t =$ number of hours it will take one device to do the task working alone:

$$(1 \text{ device}) \cdot \left(\frac{1}{12} \text{ task per hour} \right) \cdot t = 1 \text{ (task)}$$

$$\frac{1}{12} t = 1 \text{ (omitting units for convenience)}$$

$$12 \cdot \frac{1}{12} t = 12 \cdot 1$$

$$t = 12 \text{ hours}$$

Tip: You should eliminate (A), (B), and (C) at the outset because it doesn't make sense that one device working alone would take the same time or less time than two devices working together to do the task.

312. (C) Because the lines are parallel their slopes are equal. The slope of $Ax + By = C$ is $-\frac{A}{B}$. The line with equation $6x + 5y = 10$ has slope $-\frac{6}{5}$. Therefore, the line through $(3,1)$ must have slope $-\frac{6}{5}$. By inspection, you can eliminate (B), (D), and (E) because these equations do not yield slope equal to $-\frac{6}{5}$.

Now check whether $(3, 1)$ satisfies (A) or (C). Checking (A): $6 \cdot 3 + 5 \cdot 1 = 18 + 5 = 23 \neq 21$, so eliminate (A). Choice (C) is correct, so move on to the next question.

313. (A) Parallel lines have equal slopes. The slope of the line through points (x_1, y_1) and (x_2, y_2) is $m = \frac{y_2 - y_1}{x_2 - x_1}$. Set up an equation and solve for k.

slope of line through $(-8, k)$ and $(2, 1)$ = slope of line through $(11, -1)$ and $(7, k+1)$

$$\frac{1-k}{2-(-8)} = \frac{(k+1)-(-1)}{7-11}$$

$$\frac{1-k}{2+8} = \frac{k+1+1}{7-11}$$

$$\frac{1-k}{10} = \frac{k+2}{-4}$$

$$-4(1-k) = 10(k+2)$$

$$-4 + 4k = 10k + 20$$

$$-6k = 24$$

$$k = -4$$

Tip: When calculating slope, enclose negative values in parentheses to avoid making a sign error.

314. (C) The parabola turns upward, so the coefficient of x^2 is positive. Therefore, eliminate (D) and (E). The graph does not intersect the x-axis, so $b^2 - 4ac < 0$. Check the remaining answer choices. Checking (A): $b^2 - 4ac = 2^2 - 4 \cdot 1 \cdot -3 > 0$, so eliminate (A). Checking (B): $b^2 - 4ac = (-2)^2 - 4 \cdot 1 \cdot -3 > 0$, so eliminate (B). Thus, choice (C) is correct, so move on to the next question.

315. (D) θ and $3x + 50°$ are congruent because they are vertical angles; θ and $2x + 70°$ are congruent because they are corresponding angles of parallel lines. Thus, $\theta = 3x + 50° = 2x + 70°$, so $x = 20°$. Thus, $\theta = 3x + 50° = 3 \cdot 20° + 50° = 110°$. *Tip:* Make sure you answer the question. The question asks for the measure of angle θ, not the measure of x.

316. (E) Make a sketch, filling in the question information.

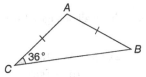

Angles C and B are base angles of an isosceles triangle, so they are equal: $\angle B = \angle C = 36°$. The sum of the angles of a triangle is $180°$. Thus, $\angle A = 180° - 2(36°) = 180° - 72° = 108°$.

317. (B)

$$\angle AQC = \angle AQB + \angle BQC$$

$$m\angle AQP + m\angle AQB + m\angle BQC + m\angle CQR = 180°$$

Given $\angle AQP \cong \angle AQB$ and $\angle BQC \cong \angle CQR$, then $2(m\angle AQB) + 2(m\angle BQC) = 180°$. Thus, $m\angle AQB + m\angle BQC = 90° = m\angle AQC$.

318. (C) $\angle 3$ is congruent to the vertical angle between $\angle 1$ and $\angle 2$. Therefore, $m\angle 1 + m\angle 2 + m\angle 3 = 180°$. Thus, $65° + 85° + m\angle 3 = 180°$, so $m\angle 3 = 30°$.

319. (C) List the triangles, proceeding systematically. You have triangles *ABC, ABD, ABE, ACD, ADE, BCD, BCE,* and *CDE* for a total of 8 triangles.

320. (C) Make a sketch, filling in the question information.

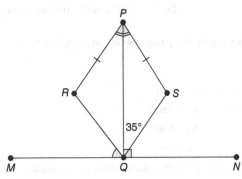

$\overline{RP} \cong \overline{PS}$, $\angle RPQ \cong \angle SPQ$, and $\overline{PQ} \cong \overline{PQ}$. Therefore, $\triangle PQR \cong \triangle PQS$ because two sides and the included angle of $\triangle PQR$ are congruent to the corresponding parts of $\triangle PQS$. Thus, $m\angle PQR = \underline{m\angle PQS} = 35°$ (corresponding parts of congruent triangles are congruent). Given that $\overline{PQ}$ is perpendicular to $\overline{MN}$, $m\angle RQM = 90° - 35° = 55°$.

321. (A) In a triangle, the sum of the lengths of any two sides must be *greater* than the length of the third side (triangle inequality). The lengths given in (A) satisfy this criterion. The lengths given in the other answer choices do not.

322. (D) Triangle ABC is isosceles, so $m\angle ABC = m\angle ACB$. Given that $\angle ABC \cong ADE$ and $m\angle ADE = 63°$, then $m\angle ABC = m\angle ACB = 63°$. Thus, $m\angle A = 180° - 2(63°) = 54°$.

323. (C) Let $2x =$ the measure of the smallest angle. Then the measures of the other two angles are $3x$ and $5x$. Thus,

$$2x + 3x + 5x = 180°$$
$$10x = 180°$$
$$x = 18°$$
$$2x = 36°$$

324. (E) Let $x =$ the length of the third side of the triangle. Of the lengths 3, 7, and x, the longest side is either 7 or x. If the longest side is 7, by the triangle inequality, $3 + x > 7$, which implies $x > 4$. If the longest side is x, by the triangle inequality, $3 + 7 > x$, which implies $10 > x$. Therefore, the third side must have a length between 4 and 10. The possible whole number lengths are 5, 6, 7, 8, and 9, so five triangles are possible.

325. (D) Let $x = m\angle B$. Then $x + 25° = m\angle A$. And $2x - 9° = m\angle C$. Write an equation and solve for x.

$$x + (x + 25°) + (2x - 9°) = 180°$$
$$x + x + 25° + 2x - 9° = 180°$$
$$4x = 164°$$
$$x = 41° = m\angle B$$
$$x + 25° = 66° = m\angle A$$
$$2x - 9° = 73° = m\angle C, \text{ the largest angle}$$

326. (A) Consecutive angles of a parallelogram are supplementary, so write an equation and solve for x.

$$(x - 30°) + (2x + 60°) = 180°$$
$$x - 30° + 2x + 60° = 180°$$
$$3x = 150°$$
$$x = 50°$$
$$x - 30° = 20°, \text{ the measure of the smaller angle}$$

327. (E) For any triangle, if P, Q, and R are the midpoints of the sides, the perimeter of triangle PQR is one-half the perimeter of the original triangle because the segment between the midpoints of any two sides of a triangle is half as long as the third side. Thus, the perimeter of the triangle formed by connecting the midpoints of the sides of triangle ABC is 30.

328. (A) The median of a trapezoid is one-half the sum of its bases. Thus,

$$TU = 14 = \frac{1}{2}(SR + PQ) = \frac{1}{2}(SR + 22). \text{ Solve } 14 = \frac{1}{2}(SR + 22) \text{ for } SR.$$

$$14 = \frac{1}{2}SR + 11$$

$$3 = \frac{1}{2}SR$$

$$6 = SR$$

329. (C) Make a sketch, filling in the question information.

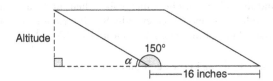

The area is base times height. Angle $\alpha = 180° - 150° = 30°$. The indicated altitude is the side opposite the 30° angle in a 30°-60°-90° right triangle. The sides of a 30°-60°-90° right triangle are in the ratio $1 : \sqrt{3} : 2$. Thus, the altitude's length in inches is $\frac{1}{2} \cdot 16 = 8$. Therefore, the area in square inches is $16 \cdot 8 = 128$.

330. (D) The length of the wall is $(8 \text{ ft}) \left(\frac{12 \text{ in}}{1 \text{ ft}} \right) = 96$ in and its width is $(6 \text{ ft}) \left(\frac{12 \text{ in}}{1 \text{ ft}} \right) =$ 72 in. The area of the wall in square inches is $(96 \text{ in})(72 \text{ in}) = 6912 \text{ in}^2$. The area of one tile in square inches is $(4 \text{ in})(4 \text{ in}) = 16 \text{ in}^2$. The number of tiles needed is $\frac{\text{area of wall (in in}^2)}{\text{area of 1 tile (in in}^2)} = \frac{6912 \text{ in}^2}{16 \text{ in}^2} = 432$ tiles.

331. (D) Let $x =$ the length in centimeters of a side of the square. Then $x^2 =$ the area of the square = the area of the rectangle = $lw = 16 \text{ cm} \cdot 25 \text{ cm} = 400 \text{ cm}^2$. Thus, $x^2 = 400 \text{ cm}^2$, so $x = 20$ cm. Thus, the square's perimeter is $4 \cdot 20 \text{ cm} = 80$ cm.

332. (D) In a right triangle, the square of the length of the hypotenuse is equal to the sum of the squares of the lengths of the legs (Pythagorean theorem). In (D) $7^2 + 10^2 = 149 \neq 169 = 13^2$. The lengths in the other answer choices satisfy the Pythagorean theorem.

333. **(D)** Let d = the distance in miles from camp. Make a sketch, filling in the question information.

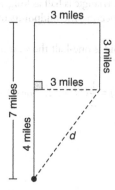

From the sketch, d is the length of the hypotenuse of a right triangle with legs of lengths 3 miles and 4 miles. Therefore, d is 5 miles. *Tip:* Knowing Pythagorean triples (such as 3, 4, 5) can be very helpful when working with right triangles.

334. **(E)** First, find the volume of one 4-inch cube. Then, find the volume of the crate by multiplying the volume of one 4-inch cube by 81. The volume of one 4-inch cube is $(4 \text{ in})^3 = 64 \text{ in}^3$. The volume of the crate is $(81)(64 \text{ in}^3) = 5184 \text{ in}^3$.

335. **(D)** Make a sketch, filling in the question information.

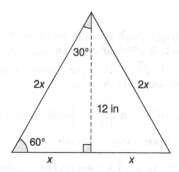

The angles in an equilateral triangle each measure 60°. Also, in an equilateral triangle, an altitude bisects the angle at the vertex from which it is drawn and the side to which it is drawn. The altitude shown is the leg opposite the 60° angle in a 30°-60°-90° right triangle. The sides of a 30°-60°-90° right triangle are in the ratio $1 : \sqrt{3} : 2$. Omitting units for convenience, set up a proportion and solve for x and $2x$.

$$\frac{x}{12} = \frac{1}{\sqrt{3}}; \text{ so } x = \frac{12}{\sqrt{3}} = \frac{12\sqrt{3}}{3} = 4\sqrt{3} \text{ and } 2x = 8\sqrt{3}.$$

Hence, the area $= \frac{1}{2}(8\sqrt{3})(12) = 48\sqrt{3}$.

336. (D) Make a quick sketch and mark on the figure as shown.

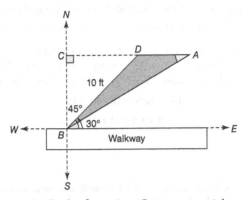

Constructing the perpendicular from A to C creates two right triangles, $\triangle DCB$ and $\triangle ACB$. Angle CBD measures 45° (90° − 45°) because $\overline{BD}$ makes a 45° angle with the walkway. Given that $\overline{DA}$ is parallel to the walkway, $m\angle CAB$ is 30° because it is congruent with the 30° angle that $\overline{BA}$ makes with the walkway (alternate interior angles of parallel lines are congruent). Thus, $\triangle DCB$ is a 45°-45°-90° right triangle and $\triangle ACB$ is a 30°-60°-90° right triangle. The perimeter, P, of the flower bed in feet equals $10 + BA + DA$. In $\triangle DCB$, $\overline{CB}$ and $\overline{CD}$ are the legs of a 45°-45°-90° right triangle whose hypotenuse is 10. Because the sides of a 45°-45°-90° right triangle are in the ratio $\sqrt{2} : \sqrt{2} : 2$, $CB = CD = \dfrac{10}{2}\sqrt{2} = 5\sqrt{2}$. In 30°-60°-90° right triangle ACB, $\overline{CB}$ is the side opposite the 30° angle and $\overline{CA}$ is the side opposite the 60° angle. Because the sides of a 30°-60°-90° right triangle are in the ratio $1 : \sqrt{3} : 2$, $BA = 2(5\sqrt{2}) = 10\sqrt{2}$ and $CA = \sqrt{3}(5\sqrt{2}) = 5\sqrt{6}$. Thus, $DA = 5\sqrt{6} - 5\sqrt{2} = 5(\sqrt{6} - \sqrt{2})$. Therefore, $P = 10 + 10\sqrt{2} + 5(\sqrt{6} - \sqrt{2}) = 5(2 + 2\sqrt{2} + \sqrt{6} - \sqrt{2}) = 5(2 + \sqrt{2} + \sqrt{6})$. *Tip:* This question illustrates the value of making an astute construction on a figure. When you are given angle values of 30° and/or 45°, look for ways you can make 30°-60°-90° and/or 45°-45°-90° right triangles. Also, the explanation for this question is lengthy, but in reality, once you create the two special right triangles, the computations are straightforward and can be done quickly—even mentally.

337. (B) Make a sketch, filling in the question information.

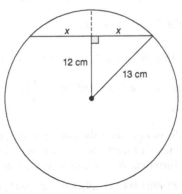

In a circle, a radius that is perpendicular to a chord bisects the chord. Let $x =$ one-half the length of the chord. Then $2x =$ the length of the chord. Using the Pythagorean theorem,

$$x^2 = 13^2 - 12^2 = 169 - 144 = 25; \text{ so } x = 5 \text{ and } 2x = 10.$$

338. (B) Because $\overline{PQ}$ and $\overline{RS}$ are two chords in C intersecting at T, then $(PT)(TQ) = (RT)(TS)$. $PQ = PT + TQ$, so $4x + 6 = PT + 5$; $PT = 4x + 1$. $RS = RT + TS$, so $6x + 8 = RT + 3$; $RT = 6x + 5$. Substitute into $(PT)(TQ) = (RT)(TS)$ and solve for x.

$$(4x+1)(5) = (6x+5)(3)$$
$$20x + 5 = 18x + 15$$
$$2x = 10$$
$$x = 5$$

339. (B) In a right triangle, the altitude to the hypotenuse separates the triangle into two triangles that are similar to each other and to the original triangle. Therefore, $\triangle ACD \approx \triangle ABC$. Set up a proportion based on corresponding sides of similar triangles and solve for AD.

$$\frac{AD}{AC} = \frac{AC}{AB}$$
$$\frac{AD}{6} = \frac{6}{18}$$
$$AD = \frac{6 \cdot 6}{18} = \frac{36}{18} = 2$$

340. (B) The volume of the molten metal in one of the three smaller cubes is $\dfrac{(18 \text{ cm})^3}{3} = \dfrac{18^3 \text{ cm}^3}{3}$. Omitting units, the length of an edge of one of the cubes equals:

$$\sqrt[3]{\frac{18^3}{3}} = 18\sqrt[3]{\frac{1}{3}} = 18\sqrt[3]{\frac{1 \cdot 3^2}{3 \cdot 3^2}} = 18\sqrt[3]{\frac{9}{3^3}} = \frac{18}{3}\sqrt[3]{9} = 6\sqrt[3]{9}$$

341. (A) The perimeter of the figure $= AB + BC + \text{length of } \overset{\frown}{AC}$

$$AB = x$$
$$BC = \sqrt{x^2 + (2x)^2} = \sqrt{5x^2} = x\sqrt{5}$$
$$\text{length of } \overset{\frown}{AC} = \frac{1}{2}(2\pi x) = \pi x$$

Thus, the perimeter $= AB + BC + \text{length of } \overset{\frown}{AC} = x + x\sqrt{5} + \pi x$.

342. (C) The area (in square units) of figure $ABCDEF = \dfrac{1}{4}(\pi r^2) + l \cdot w = \dfrac{1}{4}(\pi \cdot 4^2) + 7 \cdot 3 = 4\pi + 21 \approx 4(3.14) + 21 \approx 34$.

343. (D) The capacity of the storage bin is the volume of the cylindrical top, with radius 7 feet and height 13 feet (25 feet − 12 feet), plus the volume of the conical base, with radius 7 feet and height 12 feet. Therefore, the capacity in cubic feet of the storage bin equals $\pi(7^2)(13) + \dfrac{1}{3}\pi(7^2)(12) = \pi(49)(13) + \dfrac{1}{3}\pi(49)(12) = \pi(49)(13) + \pi(49)(4)$. Rather than performing the calculations, get an approximate answer by rounding first:

$$\pi(49)(13)+\pi(49)(4) \approx 3(50)(10)+3(50)(4) = 2100.$$

Compare this result to the answer choices; so pick choice (D).

344. (A) Make a sketch, filling in the question information.

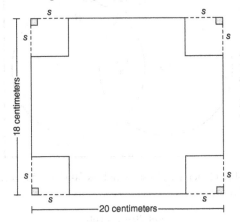

The volume of the box in cubic centimeters $= l \cdot w \cdot h = (20-2s)(18-2s)s = (360-76s+4s^2)s = 4s^3 - 76s^2 + 360s$.

345. (A) The perimeter of the triangle $= AB + BC + CA$. The distance between points (x_1, y_1) and (x_2, y_2) is $d = \sqrt{(x_2-x_1)^2 + (y_2-y_1)^2}$. Therefore:

$$AB = \sqrt{(-1-2)^2 + (-1-3)^2} = \sqrt{(-3)^2 + (-4)^2} = \sqrt{9+16} = \sqrt{25} = 5$$
$$BC = \sqrt{(3+1)^2 + (-4+1)^2} = \sqrt{(4)^2 + (-3)^2} = \sqrt{16+9} = \sqrt{25} = 5$$
$$CA = \sqrt{(2-3)^2 + (3+4)^2} = \sqrt{(-1)^2 + (7)^2} = \sqrt{1+49} = \sqrt{50} = \sqrt{25 \cdot 2} = 5\sqrt{2}$$

Thus, the perimeter $= AB + BC + CA = 5 + 5 + 5\sqrt{2} = 10 + 5\sqrt{2}$.

346. (C) Let $M =$ the set of students who said they like math and $S =$ the set of students who said they like science. Sketch a Venn diagram.

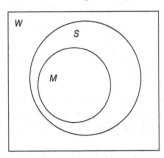

Because the set of students who said they like math is contained in the set of students who said they like science, then the number of students who said they like at least one of these subjects is 65.

347. (E) Sketch a Venn diagram and put in the problem information.

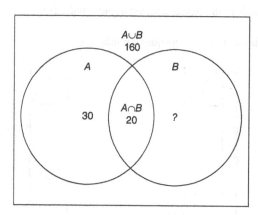

Notice that the number of elements in set A only is 30 (50 − 20). Let $x =$ the number of elements in set B only, then

$$30 + 20 + x = 160$$
$$x = 160 - 50 = 110$$

Thus, the number of elements in set $B = 110 + 20 = 130$.

348. (A) Applying the fundamental counting principle to three tasks (refer to Question 96), the number of possible different meals is $8 \cdot 5 \cdot 7 = 280$.

349. (C) There are 5 ways to go from A to B, 8 ways to go from B to C, 7 ways to go from C to B without retracing a path, and 4 ways to go from B to A without retracing a path for a total of $5 \cdot 8 \cdot 7 \cdot 4 = 1120$ ways to accomplish the task.

350. (E) The people are not assigned to particular seats, but are arranged relative to one another only. Therefore, for instance, the four arrangements shown in the following figure are the same because the people (P1, P2, P3, and P4) are in the same order clockwise.

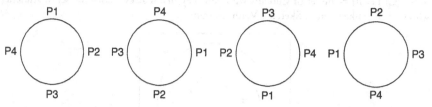

Hence, the position of P1 is immaterial. What counts is the positions of the other three people relative to P1. Therefore, keeping P1 fixed, there are $3 \cdot 2 \cdot 1 = 6$ different ways to arrange the other 3 people, so there are 6 different arrangements of the four people in a circle.

351. (D) The first prize can be given in 10 ways; when it is given, the second prize can be given in 9 ways; then following that, the third prize can be given in 8 ways. Hence, the number of ways of giving the three prizes is $10 \cdot 9 \cdot 8 = 720$.

352. (E) There are 17 favorable outcomes (7 black marbles plus 10 red marbles) out of 23 total outcomes. Thus, $P(\text{black or red}) = \dfrac{17}{23}$.

353. (D) For any one question, there are 3 wrong answers out of 4 total answers, so the probability of guessing wrong on a particular question is $\dfrac{3}{4}$. Because the student is randomly guessing, each guess on a question is independent of the guesses on the other questions, so the probability of getting all five questions wrong is $P(\text{none correct}) = \dfrac{3}{4} \cdot \dfrac{3}{4} \cdot \dfrac{3}{4} \cdot \dfrac{3}{4} \cdot \dfrac{3}{4} = \dfrac{243}{1{,}024}$.

Therefore, the probability of at least one correct is $1 - P(\text{none correct}) = 1 - \dfrac{243}{1{,}024} = \dfrac{781}{1024}$.

354. (D) After a red marble is drawn and not replaced, there are 7 red marbles and 6 blue marbles left in the box. Thus, the probability of drawing blue on the second draw is $\dfrac{6}{13}$.

355. (B) Fill in the missing probabilities. Thus, the probability that it snows and an Internet failure occurs $= (60\%)(15\%) = 9\%$.

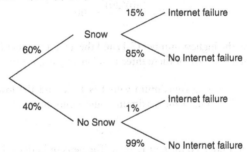

356. (B) The probability will be the area of the rectangular portion that lies in the second quadrant divided by the area of the entire rectangle. By inspection, you can see that the rectangular portion that lies in the second quadrant is $\dfrac{1}{3}$ the size of the rectangle. So the probability is $\dfrac{1}{3}$ that the x-coordinate of a randomly selected point in the rectangle will be negative.

357. (A) Complete the table by filling in the row and column totals.

Residence Status of Senior Students ($N = 250$)

	On-Campus	Off-Campus	Total
Female	52	86	138
Male	38	74	112
Total	90	160	250

The table shows that 52 of the 250 students are female on-campus students. Thus, the probability that a randomly selected student is a female on-campus resident $= \dfrac{52}{250} = 0.208 \approx 0.21$.

358. (B) You know the student is male (it's given). The table (see the answer explanation to Question 357) shows there are 112 male students and that 38 of those 112 male students reside on campus. Thus, the probability that a randomly selected student resides on campus, given that the student selected is a male student $= \dfrac{38}{112} \approx 0.34$.

359. (E) The table (see the answer explanation to Question 357), there are 138 female students and 90 on-campus students. However, 52 of the 90 on-campus students are female students. Thus, the probability that a randomly selected student is female or resides on campus $= \dfrac{138+90-52}{250} = 0.704 \approx 0.70$.

360. (B) If all the tagged turtles are still active in the lake when the second group of turtles is captured, the proportion of tagged turtles in the second group should equal the proportion of tagged turtles in the whole population, P, of turtles in the lake. Set up a proportion and solve for P.

$$\frac{6}{30} = \frac{20}{P}$$
$$P = \frac{(30)(20)}{6} = 100$$

361. (D) Discarding the highest number (7.1) and the lowest number (6.2) leaves 6.3, 6.4, and 6.5. The arithmetic average of these three numbers, by inspection, is 6.4.

362. (E) The highest reading (maximum value) is 15°F and the lowest reading (minimum value) is –20°F. The range is the maximum value – minimum value = 15°F – (–20°F) = 15°F + 20°F = 35°F.

363. (B) The percent budgeted for rent is 40%. The percent budgeted for food and clothing combined is 17% + 17% = 34%. The difference is 40% – 34% = 6%. Thus, 6% of $3,500 = 0.06($3,500) = $210 is how much more money is budgeted for rent than for food and clothing combined. *Tip:* Rather than working with the percentages first, you can compute the money amounts first, and then subtract the amounts budgeted for food and clothing from the amount budgeted for rent to obtain the same answer.

364. (E) Store 1 sold 20 units of product A, 40 units of product B, 20 units of product C, and 30 units of product D, for a total of 110 units sold. Store 4 sold 20 units of product A, 30 units of product B, 20 units of product C, and 10 units of product D, for a total of 80 units sold. The number of units sold by Store 1 is $\left(\dfrac{110}{80}\right)$(100%) = (1.375)(100%) = 137.5% of the number of units sold by Store 4. Thus, the number of units sold by Store 1 is 37.5% greater than the number of units sold by Store 4.

365. (B) The average of the student's unit exams is $\dfrac{78+81+75}{3} = 78$. Therefore, the student's numerical course grade is $\dfrac{50\%(78)+10\%(92)+40\%(75)}{100\%} = 78.2$.

366. (C) The new product received 8 ratings of 0, 4 ratings of 1, 8 ratings of 2, 6 ratings of 3, 19 ratings of 4, and 3 ratings of 5. In an ordered set of n data values, the location of the median is the $\frac{n+1}{2}$ position. For these data, $\frac{n+1}{2} = \frac{48+1}{2} = 24.5$, so the median is halfway between the 24th and the 25th data value. From the information in the graph, you can determine that the 24th data value = 25th data value = 3, so the median is 3.

367. (B) Refer to Question 116 for an explanation of percentiles. For the 25th percentile, $k = n\left(\frac{R}{100}\right) = 48\left(\frac{25}{100}\right) = 12$, an integer. Thus, the 25th percentile is halfway between the 12th and 13th data values: $\frac{1+2}{2} = 1.5$.

368. (E) Because 60 percent of the employees have salaries that are equal to or less than $57,500, 60% of 320 = 192 employees have salaries equal to or less than $57,500.

369. (D) $57,500 is the 60th percentile, and $48,000 is the 50th percentile. Thus, 10% (60% – 50%) of 320 = 32 employees have salaries between $48,000 and $57,500.

370. (C) To answer the question, find the mode for each answer choice. Eliminate (A) and (E). The scores in these choices have no mode because each score occurs the same number of times. Eliminate (B) because the mode for these scores is 96. Eliminate (D) because the mode for these scores is 84. Choice (C) is correct. The mode for these scores is 87.

371. (A) Compute the number of standard deviations from the mean for each exam.

Exam 1: $\dfrac{\text{exam score} - \text{mean}}{\text{standard deviation}} = \dfrac{75-65}{5} = 2$

Exam 2: $\dfrac{\text{exam score} - \text{mean}}{\text{standard deviation}} = \dfrac{87-88}{2} = -0.5$

Exam 3: $\dfrac{\text{exam score} - \text{mean}}{\text{standard deviation}} = \dfrac{92-86}{4} = 1.5$

Exam 4: $\dfrac{\text{exam score} - \text{mean}}{\text{standard deviation}} = \dfrac{70-60}{10} = 1$

Exam 5: $\dfrac{\text{exam score} - \text{mean}}{\text{standard deviation}} = \dfrac{90-85}{5} = 1$

With a score that is 2 standard deviations above the mean, the student performed best on Exam 1 relative to the performance of the student's classmates.

372. (E) A box plot, also called box-and-whiskers plot, graphically displays the following (in this order): the minimum value (Min), the 25th percentile (Q_1, the lower quartile), the median (Med), the 75th percentile (Q_3, the upper quartile), and the maximum value (Max) of a data set. The interquartile range (IQR), which contains the center 50 percent of the data, is the difference between the first and third quartiles $= Q_3 - Q_1 = 12.1 - 8.2 = 3.9$.

373. (A) Refer to Question 122 for a discussion of characteristics of normally distributed data. An IQ score of 130 is 2 standard deviations above the mean $\left(\dfrac{130-100}{15}=2\right)$. According to the standard normal distribution shown, 2% of the distribution is to the right of 2. Therefore, 2% of IQ scores are greater than 130.

374. (D) Refer to Question 122 for a discussion of characteristics of normally distributed data. A score of 400 is 1 standard deviation below the mean $\left(\dfrac{400-500}{100}=-1\right)$. According to the standard normal distribution shown, 84% of the distribution is to the right of −1. Therefore, the probability that a randomly selected test taker's score on the exam will be at least 400 (≥ 400) is 0.84.

375. (E) Refer to Question 122 for a discussion of characteristics of normally distributed data. A weight of 19 fat grams is 2 standard deviations above the mean $\left(\dfrac{19-16}{1.5}=2\right)$. According to the standard normal distribution shown, 98% of the distribution is to the left of 2. Therefore, the probability that a randomly selected signature sandwich will have no more than 19 fat grams (≤ 19) = 0.98.

Chapter 4: Multiple-Choice Questions with One or More Correct Answers

Remember: No credit is given unless you select *exactly* the number of correct choices specified in the question.

376. (A), (B), (C), (E), (F) (A) $2\dfrac{1}{2}+3\dfrac{3}{4}=\dfrac{5}{2}+\dfrac{15}{4}=\dfrac{\overset{1}{\cancel{5}}}{\cancel{2}}\times\dfrac{\overset{2}{\cancel{4}}}{\underset{3}{\cancel{15}}}=\dfrac{2}{3}$; (B) $\dfrac{1}{2}\times 1\dfrac{1}{3}=\dfrac{1}{2}\times\dfrac{4}{3}=\dfrac{2}{3}$

(Think: "Half of $\dfrac{4}{3}$ is $\dfrac{2}{3}$"); (C) $2\dfrac{1}{3}+3\dfrac{1}{2}=\dfrac{7}{3}+\dfrac{7}{2}=\dfrac{\overset{1}{\cancel{7}}}{3}\times\dfrac{2}{\cancel{7}}=\dfrac{2}{3}$; (D) $\dfrac{5}{24}+\dfrac{3}{8}=\dfrac{5}{24}+\dfrac{9}{24}=\dfrac{14}{24}=$
$\dfrac{7}{12}\neq\dfrac{2}{3}$; (E) $\dfrac{20}{21}-\dfrac{2}{7}=\dfrac{20}{21}-\dfrac{6}{21}=\dfrac{14}{21}=\dfrac{2}{3}$; (F) $2.5+3.75$ (equivalent to (A))

377. (A), (B), (D), (E) Let m and n be the two positive integers, then $\sqrt{m\cdot n}=14$, so $m\cdot n=196$. The factors of 196 are 1, 2, 4, 7, 14, 28, 49, 98, and 196. The possible two-factor combinations for m and n, with a product of 196, are 1 and 196, 2 and 98, 4 and 49, 7 and 28, and 14 and 14. The possible sums for these two-factor combinations are 197 (E), 100 (D), 53 (B), 35 (A), and 28.

378. (A), (B), (C), (D) Select (A) and (B) because if $0 < n \leq 33$, the smallest whole number that is greater than or equal to $\dfrac{n}{33}$ is 1. Select (C) and (D) because if $33 < n \leq 66$, the smallest whole number that is greater than or equal to $\dfrac{n}{33}$ is 2. Eliminate (E) because if n is 70, the smallest whole number that is greater than or equal to $\dfrac{n}{33}$ is 3.

379. (B), (D) (A) $1\frac{1}{4}\% = 1.25\% \neq 125\%$; (B) $1.25 = 125\%$; (C) $0.125 = 12.5\% \neq 125\%$;

(D) $\frac{5}{4} = 1.25 = 125\%$; (E) $12.5\% \neq 125\%$

Tip: You should eliminate (A), (C), and (E) right off because 125% is greater than 100% (= 1). The numbers in these answer choices are less than 100%.

380. (D), (E), (F) If $a^* 0.5 = 0.5$, then $a \leq 0.5$. Only (A), (B), and (C) satisfy this condition.

381. (A), (C), (D), (F) (A) $-\sqrt[5]{33} \approx -\sqrt[5]{32} = -2$; (B) $-\frac{17}{4} = -4.25$; (C) $-\pi \approx -3.14$;

(D) $\sqrt[3]{8} = 2$; (E) $\sqrt{5}$, between $\sqrt{4} = 2$ and $\sqrt{9} = 3$; (F) $\frac{\pi}{2} \approx \frac{3.14}{2} = 1.57$; (G) $\frac{13}{3} = 4\frac{1}{3}$

382. (A), (C), (E) Eliminate (B) and (D) because each of these numbers is the product of 2 and an even number. (A) 6 is 2×3 (an odd number) and it is an even multiple of 3; (C) 18 is 2×9 (an odd number) and it is 6×3, an even multiple of 3; (E) 30 is 2×15 (an odd number) and it is 10×3, an even multiple of 3.

383. (B), (C), (E) Eliminate (A) and (D) because 41 and 37 are prime numbers, so a cannot be a positive divisor of either -41 or 37. To check the other answer choices, use the divisibility property that if an integer divides both b and c, then it divides $bx + cy$, where x and y are any integers. (B) $1 \cdot 30 - 1 \cdot 42 = 30 - 42 = -12$, so a divides -12; (C) $-1 \cdot 30 + 1 \cdot 42 = -30 + 42 = 12$, so a divides 12; (E) $2 \cdot 30 + 1 \cdot 42 = 60 + 42 = 102$, so a divides 102.

384. (A), (C) List the possibilities:

1 five-dollar bill and 3 one-dollar bills = $8 (A)
2 five-dollar bills and 2 one-dollar bills = $12
3 five-dollar bills and 1 one-dollar bill = $16 (C)

Note: $4 (4 one-dollar bills) and $20 (4 five-dollar bills) are not possibilities because the question states that Kobe has five-dollar and one-dollar bills.

385. (B) Make a sketch. The contractor erected 5 flags (B).

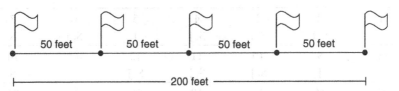

386. (C), (E) $m = 17q + 3$, where q is an integer. Check the answer choices. (A) $73 = 17q + 3$ implies q is not an integer; (B) $240 = 17q + 3$ implies q is not an integer; (C) $258 = 17q + 3$ implies $q = 15$; (D) $274 = 17q + 3$ implies q is not an integer; (E) $292 = 17q + 3$ implies $q = 17$.

387. (D) Only (D) must be true. (A) Not true if $x \leq 0$; (B) Not true if $x < 0$; (C) Not true because $-x = x$ when $x = 0$.

388. (C), (E) (A) $\left|6\right|-\left|-6\right|=6-6=0$ True; (B) $2\left|-5\right|=\left|-2\right|\left|-5\right|=2\cdot5=10$ True; (C) $\dfrac{\left|-10\right|}{\left|5\right|}=\dfrac{10}{5}=2\neq-\left|2\right|=-2$ False; (D) $\left|-4\right|\left|2\right|-\dfrac{\left|-16\right|}{\left|-2\right|}=4\cdot2-\dfrac{16}{2}=8-8=0$ True; (E) $\left|10\right|\left|-10\right|=10\cdot10=100\neq-100$ False.

389. (B), (C), (D) $w=60-r$, so $s=r-\dfrac{1}{4}w=r-\dfrac{1}{4}(60-r)=r-15+0.25r=1.25r-15$. You know that r is a whole number such that $0\leq r\leq60$. When $r=0$, the least score is $s=1.25r-15=1.25(0)-15=-15$, (B). When $r=60$, the greatest score is $s=1.25r-15=1.25(60)-15=75-15=60$. Therefore, eliminate (A) and (F). Solving $s=1.25r-15$ for r yields $r=\dfrac{s+15}{1.25}$. Now use $r=\dfrac{s+15}{1.25}$ to check the other answer choices to see whether r computes to be a whole number between 0 and 60. (C) $r=\dfrac{-5+15}{1.25}=8$; (D) $r=\dfrac{10+15}{1.25}=20$; (E) $r=\dfrac{32+15}{1.25}=37.6$, not a whole number.

390. (C) Check the answer choices. (A) $45:30=\dfrac{45}{30}=\dfrac{3}{2}\neq\dfrac{7}{6}$; (B) $1\dfrac{1}{8}:\dfrac{3}{8}=\dfrac{\frac{9}{8}}{\frac{3}{8}}=\dfrac{3}{1}\neq\dfrac{7}{6}$; (C) $1\dfrac{3}{4}:1\dfrac{1}{2}=\dfrac{\frac{7}{4}}{\frac{3}{2}}=\dfrac{\frac{7}{4}}{\frac{6}{4}}=\dfrac{7}{6}$; (D) $9.6:7.2=\dfrac{9.6}{7.2}=\dfrac{96}{72}=\dfrac{4}{3}\neq\dfrac{7}{6}$.

391. (A), (D), (F) Make a chart and fill in the information. Start with the most definite clue. You know that Box 1 contains black markers, so it is the box that Hiroshi opened. Thus, Box 1 is labeled "red markers." Each box has an incorrect label. Thus, Box 2, containing red markers, is labeled "blue markers," and Box 3, containing blue markers, is labeled "black markers."

	Actual Contents	Label
Box 1	black markers	red markers (A)
Box 2	red markers	blue markers (D)
Box 3	blue markers	black markers (F)

392. (C), (D) Mark a chart listing the 30 days in September. Mark the days on which each person works, using "S" for Shail and "J" for Jackwyn.

1	2	3	4	5	6	7
	S, J	S, J	S, J	J	S, J	S
8	9	10	11	12	13	14
S	J	S, J	S, J	S, J	J	S
15	16	17	18	19	20	21
S	S, J	J	S, J	S, J	S, J	
22	23	24	25	26	27	28
S	S, J	S, J	J	S, J	S, J	S
29	30					
	S, J					

According to the chart, Shail and Jackwyn were both off on September 21 (C) and 29 (D).

393. (A), (C), (E), (G) (A) $-\sqrt{36} = -6$, rational; (B) $-\sqrt{120}$, irrational; (C) $-\sqrt{\dfrac{4}{9}} = -\dfrac{2}{3}$, rational; (D) $\sqrt{\dfrac{1}{2}}$, irrational; (E) $\sqrt{0.49} = 0.7$, rational; (F) $\sqrt{40}$, irrational; (G) $\sqrt{400} = 20$, rational.

394. (A), (C), (D), (E) The units digit of $27^1 (= 27)$ is 7 (D); the units digit of $27^2 (= 27 \cdot 27)$ is 9 (E) because $7 \cdot 7 = 49$; the units digit of $27^3 (= 27^2 \cdot 27)$ is 3 (C) because $9 \cdot 7 = 63$; the units digit of $27^4 (= 27^3 \cdot 27)$ is 1 (A) because $3 \cdot 7 = 21$; the units digit of $27^5 (= 27^4 \cdot 27)$ is 7 because $1 \cdot 7 = 7$; the units digit of $27^6 (= 27^5 \cdot 27)$ is 9 because $7 \cdot 7 = 49$; and so on. Thus, possibilities for the units digit of 27^x are 7, 9, 3, and 1. *Tip:* Notice that this question requires only single-digit by single-digit multiplication.

395. (C), (D) In simplest form, $3\sqrt{18} = 3\sqrt{9 \cdot 2} = 9\sqrt{2} \approx 12.7279....$ By inspection, select (D) and eliminate (A) and (E). Check (B) and (C) using the calculator square root key. (B) $\sqrt{54} \approx 7.3$; (C) $\sqrt{162} \approx 12.7279...$ *Tip:* To find the square root of a number using the calculator provided for the test, key in the number and then press the square root key.

396. (A), (B), (C) In simplest form, $3\sqrt{8} + 6\sqrt{2} = 3\sqrt{4 \cdot 2} + 6\sqrt{2} = 6\sqrt{2} + 6\sqrt{2} = 12\sqrt{2} \approx 16.9706....$ By inspection, select (A) and eliminate (D) and (E). Check (B) and (C) using the calculator square root key. (B) $\sqrt{288} \approx 16.9706...$; (C) $2\sqrt{72} \approx 16.9706....$

397. (B), (E) (A) $(4\sqrt{3})(5\sqrt{12}) = 20\sqrt{36} = 20 \cdot 6$, rational; (B) $\left(\dfrac{1}{2}\sqrt{10}\right)(8\sqrt{5}) = 4\sqrt{50}$, irrational; (C) $(3\sqrt{32})(2\sqrt{2}) = 6\sqrt{64} = 6 \cdot 8$, rational; (D) $\left(\dfrac{2}{3}\sqrt{3}\right)^2 = \dfrac{4}{9} \cdot 3$, rational; (E) $(4\sqrt{3})(9\sqrt{6}) = 36\sqrt{18}$, irrational; (F) $\left(\dfrac{1}{2}\sqrt{8}\right)\left(\dfrac{1}{6}\sqrt{18}\right) = \dfrac{1}{12}\sqrt{144} = \dfrac{1}{12} \cdot 12$, rational.

Tip: As demonstrated in this question, avoid performing unnecessary computations.

398. (C), (F) Check the answer choices. (A) $\dfrac{\sqrt{11}}{\sqrt{121}} = \dfrac{\sqrt{11}}{11}$, irrational; (B) $\dfrac{\sqrt{18}}{\sqrt{25}} = \dfrac{\sqrt{18}}{5}$, irrational; (C) $\dfrac{\sqrt{50}}{\sqrt{2}} = \sqrt{\dfrac{50}{2}} = \sqrt{25} = 5$, rational; (D) $\dfrac{\sqrt{18}}{\sqrt{3}} = \sqrt{\dfrac{18}{3}} = \sqrt{6}$; irrational; (E) $\dfrac{\sqrt{5}}{\sqrt{16}} = \dfrac{\sqrt{5}}{4}$, irrational; (F) $\dfrac{\sqrt{9}}{\sqrt{64}} = \dfrac{3}{8}$, rational.

399. (A), (B), (C), (E) Let $3x =$ the lesser number and $4x =$ the larger number, where x is a whole number. Then $3x + 4x = 7x =$ the sum. Thus, the possible sums are multiples of 7. (A) $14 = 7 \cdot 2$; (B) $35 = 7 \cdot 5$; (C) $70 = 7 \cdot 10$; (D) 120, not a multiple of 7; (E) $140 = 7 \cdot 20$.

400. (A), (C), (D), (E) Check the answer choices. (A) If the ratio is 5:2, let $5x =$ larger integer and $2x =$ lesser integer. Then $5x - 2x = 3x =$ the difference. Thus, the difference must be a multiple of $5 - 2 = 3$. Select (A) because 30 is a multiple of 3. (B) If the ratio is 7:3, the difference must be a multiple of $7 - 3 = 4$. Eliminate (B) because 30 is not a multiple of 4.

(C) If the ratio is 8:5, the difference must be a multiple of $8 - 5 = 3$. Select (C) because 30 is a multiple of 3. (D) If the ratio is 9:4, the difference must be a multiple of $9 - 4 = 5$. Select (D) because 30 is a multiple of 5. (E) If the ratio is 11:1, the difference must be a multiple of $11 - 1 = 10$. Select (E) because 30 is a multiple of 10.

401. (A), (B), (E) Check the answer choices. (A) If the ratio is 2:1, let $2m = x$ and $1m = y$. Then, $x + y = 2m + 1m = 3m =$ the sum. Thus, the sum must be a multiple of $2 + 1 = 3$. From the figure, the two angles are supplementary, so the sum is 180. Select (A) because 180 is a multiple of 3. (B) If the ratio is 5:4, the sum must be a multiple of $5 + 4 = 9$. Select (B) because 180 is a multiple of 9. (C) If the ratio is 9:2, the sum must be a multiple of $9 + 2 = 11$. Eliminate (C) because 180 is not a multiple of 11. (D) If the ratio is 9:4, the sum must be a multiple of $9 + 4 = 13$. Eliminate (D) because 180 is not a multiple of 13. (E) If the ratio is 10:5, the sum must be a multiple of $10 + 5 = 15$. Select (E) because 180 is a multiple of 15.

402. (A), (C), (E) Check the answer choices. (A) If the ratio is 1:1:1, let $1m = x$, $1m = y$, and $1m = z$. Then, $x + y + z = 1m + 1m + 1m = 3m =$ the sum. Thus, the sum must be a multiple of $1 + 1 + 1 = 3$. The sum of the interior angles of a triangle is 180°. Select (A) because 180 is a multiple of 3. (B) If the ratio is 2:2:3, the sum must be a multiple of $2 + 2 + 3 = 7$. Eliminate (B) because 180 is not a multiple of 7. (C) If the ratio is 4:5:6, the sum must be a multiple of $4 + 5 + 6 = 15$. Select (C) because 180 is a multiple of 15. (D) If the ratio is 4:5:10, the sum must be a multiple of $4 + 5 + 10 = 19$. Eliminate (D) because 180 is not a multiple of 19. (E) If the ratio is 5:2:2, the sum must be a multiple of $5 + 2 + 2 = 9$. Select (E) because 180 is a multiple of 9.

403. (B), (E) In any proportion, $\dfrac{a}{b} = \dfrac{c}{d}$, $ad = bc$. Cross-multiply to check the answer choices. (A) $\dfrac{19}{15}, \dfrac{38}{25}$, $19 \cdot 25 \overset{?}{=} 15 \cdot 38$, $475 \neq 570$, not a proportion; (B) $\dfrac{1.6}{2.5}, \dfrac{64}{100}$, $1.6 \cdot 100 \overset{?}{=} 2.5 \cdot 64$, $160 = 160$; (C) $\dfrac{4}{3}, \dfrac{10}{5}$, $4 \cdot 5 \overset{?}{=} 3 \cdot 10$, $20 \neq 30$, not a proportion; (D) $\dfrac{14}{18}, \dfrac{18}{14}$, $14 \cdot 14 \overset{?}{=} 18 \cdot 18$, by inspection, not a proportion; (E) $\dfrac{3.6}{3}, \dfrac{18}{15}$, $3.6 \cdot 15 \overset{?}{=} 3 \cdot 18$, $54 = 54$.

404. (A), (B), (C), (E) $12\dfrac{1}{2}\%$ of $400 = (0.125)(400) = 50$. *Tip:* Assess this answer by thinking: "$12\dfrac{1}{2}\%$ of 400 should be close to 10% of 400, which is 40. So 50 is a reasonable answer." (A) 125% of $40 = (1.25)(40) = 50$; (B) $33\dfrac{1}{3}\%$ of $150 = \dfrac{1}{3} \times 150 = 50$; (C) 2.5% of $2000 = (0.025)(2000) = 50$; (D) $\dfrac{1}{8}\%$ of $4000 = \dfrac{1}{800} \times 4000 = 5$; (E) $\dfrac{1}{2}\%$ of $10{,}000 = \dfrac{1}{200} \times 10{,}000 = 50$; (F) 0.1% of $500 = (0.001)(500) = 0.5$.

405. (A), (B), (C), (D), (E) A ratio, r, of the measures of the corresponding sides equals the ratio of the perimeters. By inspection, $r = \dfrac{\text{sum of the sides}}{18}$ is a real number for choices (A) through (E).

406. (C), (D) The ratio of the areas of the two polygons is the square of the ratio of the perimeters, which equals $\left(\dfrac{5}{9}\right)^2 = \dfrac{25}{81}$. Select choice (C). For the other answer choices, write the ratio of the areas of the two polygons and then cross-multiply to determine whether the ratio equals $\dfrac{25}{81}$. (A) $\dfrac{20}{45} \overset{?}{=} \dfrac{25}{81}$, $20 \cdot 81 \overset{?}{=} 45 \cdot 25$, $1620 \neq 1125$; (B) $\dfrac{55}{99} \overset{?}{=} \dfrac{25}{81}$, $55 \cdot 81 \overset{?}{=} 99 \cdot 25$, $4455 \neq 2475$; (D) $\dfrac{100}{324} \overset{?}{=} \dfrac{25}{81}$, $100 \cdot 81 \overset{?}{=} 324 \cdot 25$, $8100 = 8100$; (E) $\dfrac{200}{360} \overset{?}{=} \dfrac{25}{81}$, $200 \cdot 81 \overset{?}{=} 360 \cdot 25$, $16,200 \neq 9000$. *Tip:* You can check equality of the ratios in other ways (e.g., reducing each ratio to simplest form). However, using the provided calculator to check by cross-multiplying is an efficient way to determine the correct choices.

407. (A) Simplify the expression. $\dfrac{6}{4+\sqrt{7}} = \dfrac{6}{\left(4+\sqrt{7}\right)} \cdot \dfrac{\left(4-\sqrt{7}\right)}{\left(4-\sqrt{7}\right)} = \dfrac{6\left(4-\sqrt{7}\right)}{16-7} = \dfrac{6\left(4-\sqrt{7}\right)}{9} = \dfrac{2\left(4-\sqrt{7}\right)}{3}$. By inspection, only choice (A) is correct.

408. (A), (B), (E), (F) A number is divisible by 8 (that is, leaves a remainder of 0 when divided by 8) if and only if its last three digits form a number that is divisible by 8. (A) 403,127,531,808 is divisible by 8 because 808 is divisible by 8; (B) 100,190,999,064 is divisible by 8 because 064 is divisible by 8; (C) 325,121,750,548 is not divisible by 8 because 548 is not divisible by 8; (D) 113,200,211,132 is not divisible by 8 because 132 is not divisible by 8; (E) 431,333,209,112 is divisible by 8 because 112 is divisible by 8; (F) 786,920,325,120 is divisible by 8 because 120 is divisible by 8.

409. (A), (B), (C), (E) Check the answer choices by factoring. (A) $y^3 - x^3 = -(x^3 - y^3) = -(x-y)(x^2+xy+y^2)$; (B) $(x^2-y^2)^5 = \left((x-y)(x+y)\right)^5$; (C) $x^3 - 3x^2y + 3xy^2 - y^3 = (x-y)^3$; (E) $x^4 - 2x^2y^2 + y^4 = (x^2-y^2)^2 = \left((x-y)(x+y)\right)^2$.

410. (A), (C), (E) $|2x-1| > 5$ if and only if $(2x-1) < -5$ or $(2x-1) > 5$. Solving each of these two inequalities yields $x < -2$ or $x > 3$. Select (A) because $-\pi < -2$; select (C) because $-\sqrt{10} \approx -3.2 < -2$; select (E) because $2\pi > 3$.

411. (C), (E)

$$\begin{cases} y = 3x - 5 \\ y = x^2 - x - 5 \end{cases}$$

Substitute $y = 3x - 5$ into the second equation and solve for x.

$$3x - 5 = x^2 - x - 5$$
$$0 = x^2 - 4x$$
$$0 = x(x-4)$$
$$x = 0 \text{ (C) or } x = 4 \text{ (E)}$$

412. (D) $16x^2 = 81$

Solve for x^2: $x^2 = \dfrac{81}{16}$.

Take the square root of both sides: $x = \dfrac{9}{4}$ (because $x > 0$).

Take the principal square root of both sides: $\sqrt{x} = \dfrac{3}{2}$ (D).

413. (B), (C), (D), (E) $n = \pm 4$ and $m = \pm 6$, so the difference could be -10 (B), -2 (C), 2 (D), or 10 (E).

414. (D) The square root symbol ($\sqrt{}$) always indicates the principal (nonnegative) square root. Thus,

$$x = \sqrt{\frac{(-4)^2}{7^2}} = \frac{4}{7} \ (D)$$

415. (A), (D) Substituting gives $x + x^2 = 2$, which is equivalent to $x^2 + x - 2 = 0$. Factoring the left side of this equation yields $(x+2)(x-1) = 0$, from which you have $x = -2$ (A) or $x = 1$ (D).

416. (B), (D) From $y^2 = 4$, y is 2 or -2. Substitute each y value into the equation and solve for the corresponding value of x.

Substituting $y = 2$ yields:

$$3.5x + 1.5(2) + 1 = -0.5(2) - 2.5x$$
$$3.5x + 3 + 1 = -1 - 2.5x$$
$$6x = -5$$
$$x = -\frac{5}{6} \ (B)$$

Substituting $y = -2$ yields:

$$3.5x + 1.5(-2) + 1 = -0.5(-2) - 2.5x$$
$$3.5x - 3 + 1 = 1 - 2.5x$$
$$6x = 3$$
$$x = \frac{1}{2} \ (D)$$

417. (E), (F) The graph of a parabola with vertex (h, k) that opens upward has equation $y = (x-h)^2 + k$. The graph in the figure is a parabola with vertex $(-2, 0)$, opening up. Thus, the equation is $y = (x+2)^2$. Select (E). Select (F) because $y = x^2 + 4x + 4$ implies that $y = (x+2)^2$.

418. (C), (D), (E) $|x+1| < 2$ implies $-3 < x < 1$. Thus, $x = -2, -1$, or 0. Substituting into $2x^2 - 5x + 3$ yields $2(-2)^2 - 5(-2) + 3 = 8 + 10 + 3 = 21$ (E), when $x = -2$; $2(-1)^2 - 5(-1) + 3 = 2 + 5 + 3 = 10$ (D), when $x = -1$; $2(0)^2 - 5(0) + 3 = 3$ (C), when $x = 0$.

419. (B), (C), (E) Let $n =$ the number of clients Ciara signs up. Then Ciara's monthly earnings, m, can be expressed as $m = \$5n + \$2(n-100) = \$7n - \$200$. Eliminate (A) because Ciara always signs up at least 100 clients. Thus, her monthly earnings cannot be less than $\$7(100) - \$200 = \$500$ (B). Omitting units and solving the equation $m = \$7n - \$200$ for n yields $n = \dfrac{m+200}{7}$. Because n is a whole number, $m + 200$ must be divisible by 7. Select (C) because $640 + 200 = 840$ is divisible by 7. Eliminate (D) because $800 + 200 = 1000$ is not divisible by 7. Select (E) because $850 + 200 = 1050$ is divisible by 7.

420. (A), (B) $2x + 3 < 7.5$ implies $x < 2.25$. Select (A) because $2.1 < 2.25$. Select (B) because $2.2 < 2.25$. Eliminate (C), (D), and (E) because 2.3, 2.4, and 2.5 are each greater than 2.25.

421. (C) Only choice (C) is equivalent to the statement. Eliminate (A) and (B) because "Fifteen less than four times a number x" is $4x - 15$, not $15 - 4x$. Eliminate (D) because "four times a number x" is $4x$, not $\dfrac{1}{4}x$.

422. (A), (E) The graph of a parabola with vertex (h, k) that opens downward has equation $y = -(x-h)^2 + k$. The graph in the figure is a parabola with vertex $(3, 4)$, opening down. Thus, the equation is $y = -(x-3)^2 + 4$. Select (E). Select (A) because $y = -(x-3)^2 + 4$ implies that $y = -(x^2 - 6x + 9) + 4 = -x^2 + 6x - 9 + 5 = -x^2 + 6x - 5$.

423. (B), (C), (D), (E) Simplify the equation:

$$ax^2 + bx + c = 3(x+1)(x-1) + \frac{x(4x-6)}{2}$$
$$ax^2 + bx + c = 3(x^2 - 1) + \frac{2x(2x-3)}{2}$$
$$ax^2 + bx + c = 3x^2 - 3 + 2x^2 - 3x$$
$$ax^2 + bx + c = 5x^2 - 3x - 3$$

Thus, $a = 5$, $b = -3$, $c = -3$, $a + b + c = 5 - 3 - 3 = -1$. Choice (A) only can equal $a + b + c$. The other choices cannot.

424. (A), (D), (E) According to the question information, $j = 3d + 7$. Then $d = \dfrac{j-7}{3}$. Thus, d is an integer only if $j - 7$ is divisible by 3. Select (A) because $10 - 7 = 3$ is divisible by 3. Eliminate (B) because $15 - 7 = 8$ is not divisible by 3. Eliminate (C) because $18 - 7 = 11$ is not divisible by 3. Select (D) because $22 - 7 = 15$ is divisible by 3. Select (E) because $40 - 7 = 33$ is divisible by 3.

425. (A), (D), (F) Check the answer choices. (A) $9^4 \cdot 9^3 = 9^7$, True because $x^m x^n = x^{m+n}$; (B) $2^2 \cdot 3^3 = 6^5$, False; (C) $5^4 \cdot 5^2 = 5^8$, False; (D) $10^4 \cdot 10 = 10^5$, True because $x^m x^n = x^{m+n}$; (E) $2^2 \cdot 3^3 = 6^6$, False; (F) $(2^3)^4 = 2^{12}$, True because $(x^m)^p = x^{mp}$.

426. (C), (D)

$$-3x(x-3)=6$$
$$-3x^2+9x-6=0$$
$$x^2-3x+2=0$$
$$(x-1)(x-2)=0$$
$$x=1 \text{ (C) or } x=2 \text{ (D)}$$

427. (A), (D) Check the answer choices. (A) $\dfrac{6^8}{3^4}=\dfrac{(2\cdot3)^8}{3^4}=\dfrac{2^8\cdot3^8}{3^4}=2^8\cdot3^4\neq2^4$, False;

(B) $\dfrac{5^6}{5^2}=5^4$, True; (C) $\dfrac{12^4}{4^4}=\dfrac{(3\cdot4)^4}{4^4}=\dfrac{3^4\cdot4^4}{4^4}=3^4$, True; (D) $\dfrac{4^5}{2^3}=\dfrac{(2^2)^5}{2^3}=\dfrac{2^{10}}{2^3}=2^7\neq2^2$,

False; (E) $\dfrac{9^2}{3^4}=\dfrac{81}{81}=1$, True; (F) $\dfrac{4^3}{2^3}=\dfrac{(2^2)^3}{2^3}=\dfrac{2^6}{2^3}=2^3$, True.

428. (A), (F) Check the answer choices. (A) $(-6)^0+2^{-4}=1+\dfrac{1}{2^4}=1+\dfrac{1}{16}=1\dfrac{1}{16}$,

True; (B) $6(3^{-3})=6\cdot\dfrac{1}{3^3}=\dfrac{6}{27}=\dfrac{2}{9}\neq-\dfrac{2}{9}$, False; (C) $10^{-2}=\dfrac{1}{10^2}=\dfrac{1}{100}\neq-100$, False;

(D) $4^5\cdot4^{-3}=4^2=16\neq\dfrac{1}{16}$, False; (E) $(2^3)^{-2}=2^{-6}\neq2$, False; (F) $(2^{-2})^{-2}=2^4=16$, True.

429. (A), (B), (C) On the GRE, measures (e.g., lengths) are greater than 0. Thus, $2x-30>0$, which implies $x>15$. Select (A), (B), and (C) because these values are not greater than 15.

430. (B), (D) The area is length times width $=(x+3)(x-9)=x^2-6x-27$. Select (D). By inspection, eliminate (A) and (E). Select (B) because $(x-3)^2-36=x^2-6x+9-36=x^2-6x-27$. Eliminate (C) because $(x-3)^2-18=x^2-6x+9-18=x^2-6x-9$.

431. (C), (E) Eliminate (A) because when $x=4$, $x^2-4=4^2-4=16-4=12\neq0$. Eliminate (B) because when $x=4$, $x^2=4^2=16\neq8$. Select (C) because when $x=4$, $x^2-16=4^2-16=16-16=0$ and when $x=-4$, $x^2-16=(-4)^2-16=16-16=0$. Eliminate (D) because when $x=-4$, $x^2-8x+16=(-4)^2-8(-4)+16=16+32+16\neq0$.

  Select (E) because when $x=4$, $2x^2=2(4)^2=2\cdot16=32$ and when $x=-4$, $2x^2=2(-4)^2=2\cdot16=32$.

432. (C), (D) Eliminate (A) because when $x=-10$, $x^2+6x=(-10)^2+6(-10)=100-60=40\neq-4$. Eliminate (B) because when $x=-4$, $x^2+6x=(-4)^2+6(-4)=16-24=-8\neq-4$. Select (C) because when $x=-3-\sqrt{5}$, $x^2+6x=(-3-\sqrt{5})^2+6(-3-\sqrt{5})=9+6\sqrt{5}+5-18-6\sqrt{5}=-4$. Select (D) because when $x=-3+\sqrt{5}$, $x^2+6x=(-3+\sqrt{5})^2+6(-3+\sqrt{5})=9-6\sqrt{5}+5-18+6\sqrt{5}=-4$. You have found two roots, so move on to the next question.

433. (B), (C) The graph of the equation $Ax^2+Ay^2+Cx+Dy+F=0$; $A\neq0$ is a circle. By inspection, select (B) and (C).

434. (C), (D) Choice (A) $7^2 + 10^2 = 49 + 100 = 149 \neq 17^2 = 289$; (B) $1^2 + 16^2 = 1 + 256 = 257 \neq 17^2 = 289$; (C) $(-8)^2 + 15^2 = 64 + 225 = 289 = 17^2$; (D) $(-8)^2 + (-15)^2 = 64 + 225 = 289 = 17^2$; (E) $(-7)^2 + (-10)^2 = 49 + 100 = 149 \neq 17^2 = 289$.

435. (B), (D) A *function* is a set of ordered pairs for which each first element is paired with *one and only one* second element. In other words, in a function no two ordered pairs have the same first element but different second elements. Only the set of ordered pairs in (B) and (D) satisfy the definition of a function.

436. (A), (B), (C), (F), (G) In a function no two ordered pairs have the same first element but different second elements. Thus, x cannot equal any of the other first elements.

437. (D), (E) Refer to Question 435 for the definition of a *function*. Select (D) because, for instance, the ordered pairs $(3,1)$ and $(3,2)$, which satisfy the equation, $x = 3$, cannot be in a function. Select (E) because, for instance, the ordered pairs $(3,3)$ and $(3,-3)$, which satisfy the equation, $y^2 = 2x + 3$, cannot be in a function.

438. (B), (C) The domain of a function cannot contain a value of x that would result in division by zero. Thus, $x \neq -2$ (B) or 1 (C).

439. (A), (D) $y = \dfrac{(x-3)(x+5)}{(x+2)(x-1)}$ equals zero when $x - 3 = 0$, $x = 3$ (D); or $x + 5 = 0$, $x = -5$ (A).

440. (B), (C), (E) Choice (A) False, a square has four right angles. Not all rhombuses have four right angles. (B) True. (C) True. (D) False, a rectangle has four right angles. Not all parallelograms have four right angles. (E) True.

441. (A), (F) Make a quick sketch and mark on the figure as shown. The perimeter of triangle XYZ is irrational because the length of one of the sides YX is $\sqrt{3^2 + 3^2} = \sqrt{18}$, which is irrational. Select (A) and (F). You could also just eliminate answer choices that are obviously rational. Eliminate (B) because XZ is 7, so the x-coordinate of its midpoint is 3.5. Eliminate (C) because $\overline{YZ}$ is the hypotenuse of a 3-4-5 right triangle. Eliminate (D) because YW is 3. Eliminate (E) because $\dfrac{1}{2}(7)(3)$ is rational.

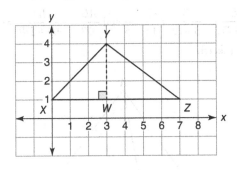

442. (C), (D), (E), (F), (G) In a triangle, the sum of the lengths of any two sides must be greater than the length of the third side (triangle inequality). The lengths given in (C), (D), (E), (F), and (G) satisfy this criterion. The lengths given in (A) and (B) do not.

443. (A), (B), (C), (E) Let $x =$ the length of the third side of the triangle. The perimeter is $10 + 14 + x = 24 + x$. Of the lengths 10, 14, and x, the longest side is either 14 or x. If the longest side is 14, then $10 + x > 14$, $x > 4$. If the longest side is x, then $10 + 14 > x$, $24 > x$. Hence, $4 < x < 24$, which implies that $28 <$ perimeter $(= 24 + x) < 48$. By inspection, Select (B) and (C) and eliminate (D) and (F). Select (A) because $28 < 24 + \sqrt{20} \approx 28.5 < 48$. Select (E) because $24 < 24 + 10\sqrt{3} \approx 41.3 < 48$.

444. (C) Let $x =$ the length of the third side of the triangle. Of the lengths 8, 15, and x, the longest side is either 15 or x. If the longest side is 15, then $8 + x > 15$, $x > 7$. If the longest side is x, then $8 + 15 > x$, $23 > x$. Hence, $7 < x < 23$ (C).

445. (B), (C) Choice (B) $m\angle 1 > m\angle 3$, True (the measure of an exterior angle of a triangle is greater than the measure of either nonadjacent interior angle); (C) $m\angle 4 < m\angle 1$, True (the measure of an exterior angle of a triangle is greater than the measure of either nonadjacent interior angle).

446. (A), (B), (D) Choice (A) can be proved congruent by angle-side-angle (ASA); (B) can be proved congruent by side-side-side (SSS); (D) can be proved congruent by side-angle-side (SAS).

447. (A), (B), (D), (E) Choice (A) $\angle 2 \cong \angle 4$ (equal alternate interior angles); (B) $\angle 3$ and $\angle 4$ are supplementary; (D) $\angle 3$ and $\angle 4$ are right angles; (E) $\angle 1$ and $\angle 5$ are supplementary.

448. (A), (D), (E) Choice (A) It is equilateral; (D) Its diagonals bisect each other; (E) Each pair of consecutive angles is supplementary.

449. (B), (D), (E) If a line intersects two sides of a triangle and cuts off segments proportional to these two sides, then the line is parallel to the third side. Select (B) because $\dfrac{AE}{AC} = \dfrac{6}{14} = \dfrac{3}{7} = \dfrac{AD}{AB}$. Select (D) because $\dfrac{AC - EC}{AC} = \dfrac{12 - 3}{12} = \dfrac{9}{12} = \dfrac{3}{4} = \dfrac{6}{8} = \dfrac{AD}{AB}$. Select (E) because $\dfrac{AE}{AC} = \dfrac{AE}{AE + EC} = \dfrac{3}{3 + 12} = \dfrac{3}{15} = \dfrac{1}{5}$ and $\dfrac{AD}{AB} = \dfrac{AD}{AD + DB} = \dfrac{2}{2 + 8} = \dfrac{2}{10} = \dfrac{1}{5}$.

450. (B), (C) Make a sketch.

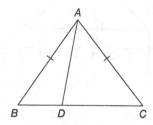

(A) $AD > AB$, False [see explanation for (B)]. (B) $AC > AD$, True. $m\angle ADB > m\angle C$ (the measure of an exterior angle of a triangle is greater than the measure of either nonadjacent interior angle). $m\angle B = m\angle C$ (base angles of an isosceles triangle are congruent). Hence, $m\angle ADB > m\angle B$, which implies $AB > AD$ ($\overline{AB}$ is opposite the greater angle in $\triangle ABD$). $\overline{AB} \cong \overline{AC}$, so $AB = AC > AD$. (C) $m\angle B = m\angle C$, True (base angles of an isosceles triangle are congruent). (D) $m\angle B > m\angle ADB$, False [see explanation for (B)]. (E) $m\angle C > m\angle ADC$, False. $m\angle ADC > m\angle B$ (the measure of an exterior angle of a triangle is greater than the measure of either nonadjacent interior angle). $m\angle B = m\angle C$ (base angles of an isosceles triangle are congruent). Hence, $m\angle ADC > m\angle C$.

451. (A), (C), (E) Select (A) because $\overline{AP} \cong \overline{PC}$, $\overline{BP} \cong \overline{PD}$, and $\angle APB \cong \angle CPD$ (vertical angles are congruent) implies $\triangle APB \cong \triangle CPD$ by SAS. Select (C) because by (A) $\overline{AB} \cong \overline{CD}$ (corresponding parts of congruent triangles are congruent), so $AB = CD$. Select (E) because $\angle A \cong \angle C$ (corresponding parts of congruent triangles are congruent). Thus, $\overleftrightarrow{AB} \parallel \overleftrightarrow{CD}$ (alternate interior angles of parallel lines are congruent).

452. (B), (C) The sum of the measures of the angles of a triangle is $180°$. The angle measures given in (B) and (C) satisfy this criterion. The angle measures given in the other answer choices do not.

453. (A), (B), (D) The sum of the measures of the five interior angles of a pentagon is $(5-2)180° = 3 \cdot 180° = 540°$. Thus, the sum of the measures of the three remaining angles is $540° - 100° - 120° = 320°$. Select (A), (B), and (D).

454. (B) The measure, m, of an interior angle of an n-sided regular polygon is $m = \dfrac{(n-2)180°}{n}$. Solving $m = \dfrac{(n-2)180°}{n}$ for n yields $n = \dfrac{360°}{180° - m}$. Thus, because n is a whole number, $360°$ must be divisible by $(180° - m)$. Eliminate (A) because $360°$ is not divisible by $105°(= 180° - 75°)$. Select (B) because $360°$ divided by $90°(= 180° - 90°)$ is 4. Eliminate (C) because $360°$ is not divisible by $80°(= 180° - 100°)$. Eliminate (D) because $360°$ is not divisible by $52°(= 180° - 128°)$. Eliminate (E) because $240° > 180°$.

455. (A), (B), (D), (E), (F) The possible measures of the exterior angles are $2 \cdot 15° = 30°$, $3 \cdot 15° = 45°$, $4 \cdot 15° = 60°$, $6 \cdot 15° = 90°$, and $8 \cdot 15° = 120°$. The measure, m, of an exterior angle of an n-sided regular polygon is $m = \dfrac{360°}{n}$. Select (A) because $\dfrac{360°}{3} = 120°$. Select (B) because $\dfrac{360°}{4} = 90°$. Eliminate (C) because $\dfrac{360°}{5} = 72°$. Select (D) because $\dfrac{360°}{6} = 60°$. Select (E) because $\dfrac{360°}{8} = 45°$. Select (F) because $\dfrac{360°}{12} = 30°$.

456. (A), (D), (F) Make a sketch. (A) True (a diagonal divides a parallelogram into two congruent triangles). (D) True (alternate interior angles of parallel lines are congruent). (F) True (the diagonals of a parallelogram bisect each other).

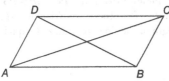

457. (A), (B), (D) All rectangles have the properties given in (A), (B), and (D). Eliminate (C) and (E) because only rectangles that are squares have these properties.

458. (A), (C), (E) The altitude to the hypotenuse of a right triangle is the geometric mean of the segments into which it separates the hypotenuse. That is, if a and b are the lengths of the segments of the hypotenuse formed by the altitude and h is the length of the altitude, then $\dfrac{a}{h}=\dfrac{h}{b}$. Thus for $h=8$, $\dfrac{a}{8}=\dfrac{8}{b}$, which implies $ab=64$. Select (E) by inspection. (A) $2\cdot32=64$; (B) $3\cdot24=72\neq64$; (C) $4\cdot16=64$; (D) $6\cdot12=72\neq64$.

459. (D), (E) Make a sketch.

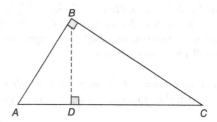

(A) False. The altitude is the geometric mean of the segments into which it separates the hypotenuse (refer to Question 458). Thus, $BD=\sqrt{2\cdot16}=4\sqrt{2}\neq32$. (B) False. Each leg is the geometric mean of the hypotenuse and the segment of the hypotenuse adjacent to the leg. Thus, $\dfrac{AC}{AB}=\dfrac{AB}{AD}$. $\dfrac{18}{AB}=\dfrac{AB}{2}$, $AB^2=18\cdot2=36$, $AB-6$; $\dfrac{AC}{BC}=\dfrac{BC}{AC}$. $\dfrac{18}{BC}=\dfrac{BC}{16}$, $BC^2=18\cdot16=288$, $BC=\sqrt{288}=\sqrt{144\cdot2}=12\sqrt{2}$. (C) False. [see explanation for (A)]. (D) The area of triangle $ABC=\dfrac{1}{2}(18)(4\sqrt{2})=36\sqrt{2}$, True. (E) True [see explanation for (B)].

460. (B), (C), (D), (E), (F) In a right triangle, the square of the length of the longer side equals the sum of the squares of the lengths of the other two sides. The lengths in (B), (C), (D), (E), and (F) satisfy this relationship. The lengths in (A) do not.

461. (A), (C), (D), (E) Choice (B) is the only answer that is false. Only chords that pass through the center of a circle are diameters.

462. (A), (C), (D) The perpendicular from the center of a circle to a chord bisects the chord. $\overline{CE}$, $\overline{CB}$, and $\overline{CD}$ are radii. (A) $AP=PB=12$ and $CB=CD=CE=15$. Triangle CPB is a right triangle. $PB=12$ and $CB=15$. Determine PC, the third side of $\triangle CPB$, using the Pythagorean theorem. Then $PD=CD-PC=15-PC$. You now know the lengths of the two legs of right triangle APD. Use the Pythagorean theorem to determine AD. (C) $AB=2\cdot AP=2\cdot5=10$. (D) In right triangle CPB, $CB=13$ and $CP=5$. Use the Pythagorean theorem to find PB. Multiply the result by 2 to find AB. (E) $CD=CE=16$. $DP=16-CP=16-8=8$. In triangles APD and APC, $AP\cong PB$, $\angle APD\cong\angle BPC$ (vertical angles are congruent), and $DP\cong PC$. Therefore, triangles APD and APC are congruent. In triangle BPC, CP, the length of the side opposite $\angle B$, equals one-half CB, the length of the hypotenuse. Hence, $m\angle B = 30°$. Angles A and B are congruent (corresponding parts of congruent triangles are congruent), so $m\angle A = 30°$.

463. (B), (C), (E) Horizontal lines have slope, m, equal to 0. The slope of the line through points (x_1, y_1) and (x_2, y_2) is $m = \dfrac{y_2 - y_1}{x_2 - x_1}$. This equation is 0 when the y-coordinates are equal and the x-coordinates are unequal. By inspection, the points in (B), (C), and (E) determine horizontal lines.

464. (A), (D) The slope of a vertical line is undefined. When two distinct points determine a vertical line, the x-coordinates are equal and the y-coordinates are unequal. By inspection, the points in (A) and (D) determine vertical lines.

465. (C), (D) $6x° < 180°$ because it is an interior angle of a triangle and $6x° > 90°$ because the measure of an exterior angle of a triangle is greater than the measure of either nonadjacent interior angle. Thus, $90 < 6x < 180$, which implies $15 < x < 30$. By inspection, (C) and (D) satisfy this inequality.

466. (A), (B), (C), (D) Do not assume that the bike rider rode in a straight line. Make a diagram. Show the camp and river as 4 miles apart. Construct a circle centered at the river, with radius 5 miles. From the diagram, $1 \le x \le 9$. Choices (A), (B), (C), and (D) satisfy this inequality.

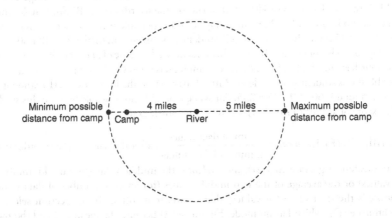

467. (C), (D), (E) The triangle has maximum area when it is a right triangle with 10 and 15 as the legs. Let $15 =$ the base and $10 =$ the height, then maximum area $= \dfrac{1}{2} \cdot 10 \cdot 15 = 75$. Thus, $0 <$ area ≤ 75. Choices (C), (D), and (E) satisfy this inequality.

468. (C), (E) From the question information, $3m\angle B + m\angle B = 120°$, $4m\angle B = 120°$, $m\angle B = 30°$, $m\angle A = 90°$. Thus, $\triangle ABC$ is a 30°-60°-90° right triangle: (A) False, (B) False, (C) True, (D) False, (E) True.

469. (B), (D) The number of ways of selecting r objects from a set of n distinct objects, without regard to order, is $_nC_r = \begin{pmatrix} n \\ r \end{pmatrix} = \left(\dfrac{n!}{(n-r)!r!} \right)$. *Note:* The symbol "!" is read "factorial"; $n!$ is the product of all positive integers less than or equal to n (except $0! = 1$). (A) $\begin{pmatrix} 6 \\ 1 \end{pmatrix} = \left(\dfrac{6!}{5!1!} \right) = 6$; (B) $\begin{pmatrix} 6 \\ 6 \end{pmatrix} = \left(\dfrac{6!}{0!6!} \right) = 1$; (C) $\begin{pmatrix} 5 \\ 1 \end{pmatrix} = \left(\dfrac{5!}{4!1!} \right) = 5$; (D) $\begin{pmatrix} 5 \\ 5 \end{pmatrix} = \left(\dfrac{5!}{0!5!} \right) = 1$.

470. (A), (D), (E) Choice (A) There are 3 multiples of three out of 8 possibilities. The probability is $\dfrac{3}{8}$. (B) There are 3 t's out of 9 letters. (C) The probability is $\dfrac{3}{9} \neq \dfrac{3}{8}$. There are 3 red marbles out of a total of 11 marbles. The probability is $\dfrac{3}{11} \neq \dfrac{3}{8}$. (D) List the possibilities {HHH, HHT, HTH, HTT, THH, THT, TTH, TTT}, where "H" is the coin turns up heads and "T" the coin comes up tails. There are 3 outcomes with exactly two heads out of 8 outcomes. The probability is $\dfrac{3}{8}$. (E) There are 3 prime or even numbers out of 8 numbers. The probability is $\dfrac{3}{8}$.

471. (A), (B), (D) To have an average of 85 on four exams, the total number of points must be $85 \cdot 4 = 340$. (A) Student A's three-exam total is $79 + 80 + 81 = 240$. An average of 85 is possible if this student scores $(340 - 240) = 100$ on the fourth exam. (B) Student B's three-exam total is $65 + 80 + 180 = 245$. An average of 85 is possible if this student scores at least $(340 - 245) = 95$ on the fourth exam. (C) Student C's three-exam total is $75 + 80 + 80 = 235$. An average of 85 is not possible because this student needs a score of at least $(340 - 235) = 105$ on the fourth exam. (D) Student D's three-exam total is $90 + 80 + 76 = 246$. An average of 85 is possible if this student scores at least $(340 - 246) = 94$ on the fourth exam. (E) Student E's three-exam total is $60 + 99 + 75 = 234$. An average of 85 is not possible because this student needs a score of at least $(340 - 234) = 106$ on the fourth exam.

472. (B), (C), (E) The *mean* $= \dfrac{\text{sum of data values}}{\text{number of data values}}$; after the data are put in order (from least to greatest or greatest to least), the *median* is the middle value (for an odd number of data values) or the average of the two middle values (for an even number of data values); the *mode* is the data value (or values) that occurs most often. By inspection select (E) and eliminate (D), which has no mode. Eliminate (A) because the mean is 2 and the mode is 1. (B) mean $= \dfrac{8+5+1+9+2+5}{6} = \dfrac{30}{6} = 5$; median $= \dfrac{5+5}{2} = 5$; mode $= 5$. (C) mean $= \dfrac{-6-9-2-10-3-6}{6} = \dfrac{-36}{6} = -6$; median $= \dfrac{-6-6}{2} = -6$; mode $= -6$.

473. (A), (E) By inspection, select (A) and (E). The standard deviation is 0 for the data in each of these choices. None of the data sets in the other answer choices have 0 standard deviation.

474. (B) Choice (B) has two modes, 1 and 5. The data sets in the other answer choices have only one mode.

475. (A), (B), (F) According to the figure, scores that are more than 2 standard deviations below the mean or scores that are more than 2 standard deviations above the mean will occur less than 2% of the time. Thus, a score that is less than $138-2(5)=128$ or a score that is greater than $138+2(5)=148$ will occur less than 2% of the time. Select (A), (B), (F).

476. (B), (C), (D) One standard deviation above the mean is $100+1(15)=115$. One standard deviation below the mean is $100-1(15)=85$. Thus, scores that satisfy the inequality $85 \leq \text{score} \leq 115$ are within one standard deviation of the mean. Select (B), (C), and (D).

477. (C), (D), (E) The first quartile is the 25th percentile, the score below which lie 25 percent of the data values. Using the figure, estimate that the 25th percentile lies a little to the right of one standard deviation below the mean. One standard deviation below the mean is $118-1(9.5)=108.5$, which (as the figure shows) is the 14th percentile. Select (C), (D), and (E) because these scores are less than 108.5, so they fall below the 14th percentile, and thereby fall below the 25th percentile (the first quartile). Eliminate (A) and (B) because these scores are above the mean. *Tip:* Notice that you can select the correct answers to this question without actually knowing the value of the 25th percentile.

478. (D), (E) The 98th percentile is the score at or below which lie 98 percent of the data values. According to the figure, the 98th percentile is 2 standard deviations above the mean. Two standard deviations above the mean is $160+2(25)=210$. Select (D) and (E).

479. (A), (B), (C) The 90th percentile is the score at or below which lie 90 percent of the data values. Only (D) and (E) must be true. Select (A), (B), and (C).

480. (B), (C), (E) Eliminate (A) and (D) because neither is true in a normal distribution. Only (B), (C), and (E) must be true.

481. (B), (D) Because $\$ = \$20$, weeks with more than six $\$$ symbols ($6 \cdot \$20 = \$120$) have sales over $120. Select (B) and (D).

482. (A) Weeks with less than five $\$$ symbols ($5 \cdot \$20 = \$100$) have sales under $100. Select (A).

483. (A), (B), (E) Choice (A) Life expectancy at birth increased $76-74.1 = 1.9$ years for males. (B) Life expectancy at birth increased $80.9-79.3 = 1.6$ years for females. (C) False. In some years there was no change. (D) False. The gap in 2000 was $79.3-74.1 = 5.2$; in 2009, the gap was $80.9-76.0 = 4.9 < 5.2$. (E) The graph shows women have higher life expectancy at birth than do men for every year from 2000 to 2009.

484. (C), (D), (G), (I) Choice (C) From 2002 to 2003, the gap went from $(79.5-74.3) = 5.2$ to $(79.6-74.5) = 5.1$, a decrease of 0.1. (D) From 2003 to 2004, the gap went from $(79.6-74.5) = 5.1$ to $(79.9-74.9) = 5.0$, a decrease of 0.1. (G) From 2006 to 2007, the gap went from $(80.2-75.1) = 5.1$ to $(80.4-75.4) = 5.0$, a decrease of 0.1. (I) From 2008 to 2009, the gap went from $(80.6-75.6) = 5.0$ to $(80.9-76.0) = 4.9$, a decrease of 0.1.

485. (B), (D), (F) Choice (A) is false. The data for both 1996 and 2006 show that life expectancy for men at age 25 goes up as educational level increases. (B) The data for both 1996 and 2006 show that life expectancy for women at age 25 goes up as educational level increases. (C) is false. The data for both 1996 and 2006 show at age 25, women with bachelor's degrees or higher have greater life expectancy than men with bachelor's degrees or higher. (D) In 1996, at age 25 women with no high school diploma could expect to live 53 years and those with a bachelor's degree or higher 59 years, a difference of 6 years. (E) False. In 2006, at age 25 men with a bachelor's degree or higher could expect to live 56 years and those with no high school diploma 47 years, a difference of 9 years. (F) From 1996 to 2006, the gap in life expectancy for men at age 25 between those with a bachelor's degree or higher and those with no diploma went from $(54-47)=7$ years to $56-47=9$ years, an increase of 2 years. From 1996 to 2006, the gap in life expectancy for women at age 25 between those with a bachelor's degree or higher and those with no diploma went from $(59-53)=6$ years to $60-52=8$ years, an increase of 2 years.

486. (D) Check the answer choices. (A) No change for men; decrease for women. (B) Increase for men; no change for women. (C) Increase for men; no change for women. (D) Increase for men; increase for women.

487. (B), (C)

$$\text{(A) Company } A: \frac{1.50-1.40}{1.40}=\frac{0.1}{1.4}\approx 0.0714=7.14\%$$

$$\text{(B) Company } B: \frac{1.25-1.20}{1.20}=\frac{0.05}{1.2}\approx 0.0417=4.17\%$$

$$\text{(C) Company } C: \frac{1.70-1.60}{1.60}=\frac{0.1}{1.6}=0.0625=6.25\%$$

$$\text{(D) Company } D: \frac{1.20-1.10}{1.10}=\frac{0.1}{1.1}\approx 0.0909=9.09\%$$

488. (A), (C)

$$\text{(A) Company } A: \frac{160-130}{130}=\frac{30}{130}\approx 0.2308=23.08\%$$

$$\text{(B) Company } B: \frac{105-100}{100}=\frac{5}{100}=0.05=5\%$$

$$\text{(C) Company } C: \frac{155-140}{140}=\frac{15}{140}\approx 0.1071=10.71\%$$

$$\text{(D) Company } D: \frac{130-120}{120}=\frac{10}{120}\approx 0.0833=8.33\%$$

489. (B), (D) Eliminate (C) because this company had a decrease in full-time employees. (A) Company A: $12,300-11,700=600$. (B) Company B: $11,400-10,200=1200$. (D) Company D: $13,200-11,900=1300$.

490. (D), (F), (G) By inspection, eliminate (A) January, (B) February, and (C) March. (D) April: $9\%-(-10\%)=9\%+10\%=19\%$. (E) May: $9\%-(-6\%)=9\%+6\%=15\%$. (F) June: $14\%-(-5\%)=14\%+5\%=19\%$. By inspection, select (G) July.

491. (A), (E) Eliminate (B), (C), and (D) because there is insufficient information to make conclusions about the mean. The statement in (A) is true because the median divides the data in half, so $(50\%)(500) = 250$ students receive allowances of $8.55 or less. The statement in (E) is true because $(25\%)(500) = 125$.

492. (A), (E) Check the answer choices. (A) To decide which set of grades has greater variability, compare the ranges of the two sets. The range in the biology class is $93 - 56 = 37$; the range in the history class is $83 - 75 = 8$. Thus, (A) is correct. (B) Incorrect [see explanation for (A)]. (C) The mean in the biology class is $\dfrac{78+88+67+56+93}{5} = \dfrac{382}{5} = 76.4$; the mean in the history class is $\dfrac{75+78+83+83+81+77}{6} = \dfrac{477}{6} = 79.5$. Thus, (C) is incorrect. (D) Incorrect [see explanation for (C)]. (E) The median in the biology class is the median of 56, 67, 78, 88, and 93, which is 78; the median in the history class is the median of 75, 77, 78, 81, 83, and 83, which is 79.5. Thus, (E) is correct. (F) Incorrect [see explanation for (E)].

493. (A), (B), (D) A *scatterplot* is a graph of paired values of data from two variables, plotted on a coordinate grid. The data are paired so that each value from one variable is matched with a corresponding value from the other variable. The pattern of the scatterplot tells you about the relationship (if any) between the two variables. For linear relationships, scatterplots that slant upward from left to right indicate positive linear relationships. In positive linear relationships, whenever one of the variables increases or decreases, the other variable increases or decreases in the same direction. Scatterplots that slant downward from left to right indicate negative linear relationships. In negative linear relationships, whenever one of the two variables increases, the other variable decreases; and conversely. The closer the plotted points cluster together in a linear "cigar" shape, the stronger the linear relationship. Quadratic relationships have a U-shaped appearance. Check the answer choices. (A) The association between variables X and Y is stronger than the association between variables W and U because the plotted points in the X-Y scatterplot cluster together tighter than the plotted points in the W-U scatterplot. (B) The association between variables X and Y is linear because the plotted points cluster together in a linear "cigar" shape. (C) The association between variables W and U is not quadratic because the scatterplot does not have a U-shaped appearance. (D) The X-Y scatterplot slants downward from left to right indicating a negative relationship. (E) The association between variables X and Y is not positive [see explanation for (D)]. (F) The association between variables W and U is not positive because the W-U scatterplot does not slant upward from left to right.

494. (A), (B)

(A) US Stocks: $(45\%)(\$200,000) = \$90,000$

(B) Foreign Stocks: $(30\%)(\$200,000) = \$60,000$

(C) Bonds and Cash: $(20\%)(\$200,000) = \$40,000$

(D) Commodities: $(5\%)(\$200,000) = \$10,000$

495. (A), (B), (E) Choice (A) For male workers, average earnings increase as educational attainment increases. (B) For female workers, average earnings increase as educational attainment increases. (C) For male workers, average earnings do not consistently go up as age increases. (D) For female workers, average earnings do not consistently go up as age increases. (E) Generally, for both male and female workers, average earnings are greater for those who have some college compared to those with no college experience.

496. (C), (D), (E)

$$\text{(A) 18 to 24 years old: } \frac{\$24,117}{\$29,599} \approx 0.8148 = 81.48\%$$

$$\text{(B) 25 to 34 years old: } \frac{\$40,475}{\$49,105} \approx 0.8243 = 82.43\%$$

$$\text{(C) 35 to 44 years old: } \frac{\$47,260}{\$66,788} \approx 0.7076 = 70.76\%$$

$$\text{(D) 45 to 54 years old: } \frac{\$48,929}{\$71,661} \approx 0.6828 = 68.28\%$$

$$\text{(E) 55 to 64 years old: } \frac{\$48,232}{\$67,007} \approx 0.7198 = 71.98\%$$

497. (C), (D), (E) By inspection, eliminate (A) and (B). (C) $\$98,045 - \$43,518 = \$54,527$. (D) $\$109,163 - \$48,224 = \$60,939$. (E) $\$99,572 - \$47,164 = \$52,408$.

498. (C), (D), (E) By inspection, eliminate (A). (B) $\$52,102 - \$27,993 = \$24,109$. (C) $\$65,881 - \$32,947 = \$32,934$. (D) $\$69,698 - \$34,145 = \$35,553$. (E) $\$67,683 - \$34,900 = \$32,783$.

499. (A), (D) Choice (A) True, $100\% - 40\% = 60\%$ yes responses. (D) True, $65\% = 30\% + 35\%$. There is insufficient information to determine whether the other answer choices are true or false.

500. (C), (E) By inspection, eliminate (A) and (D). (B) $30\%(350) = 105$. (C) $60\%(350) = 210$. (E) $65\%(400) = 260$. Eliminate (F) based on the answer to (E).